Creative Philanthropy

Philanthropy is experiencing a crisis due to a lack of awareness about the potential that foundations could have. The ability to overcome this crisis provides the key to reinventing philanthropy as a central institution of modern society. For future growth and legitimacy, achieving greater impact through what we call creative philanthropy is the central issue for foundations today.

That foundations have done much good in the world is beyond doubt. But the key question is not 'do foundations do good?' but rather 'do foundations do the best they possibly could in the current environment?'. To achieve both, a new approach is necessary: creative philanthropy. This book illustrates the creative approach; explores why foundations adopt it; what a creative approach involves in practice; what management tools it requires; the tensions and dilemmas it raises; and the results it achieves.

Foundations are the potential powerhouses of creative thinking and working that modern society needs. The approach proposed here – the creative foundation – could become an important step towards that promise.

Using a collection of vignettes and more detailed case studies of selected foundations in the US, UK and Australia to show real-life examples of theory in practice, the authors have provided us with a unique and inspiring perspective on these exciting and vital organizations.

Helmut K. Anheier is Professor and Director of the Center for Civil Society at UCLA's School of Public Affairs, and Centennial Professor at the London School of Economics.

Diana Leat is a Visiting Professor at CASS Business School, London.

Creative Philanthropy

Towards a New Philanthropy for the
Twenty-First Century

Helmut K. Anheier and Diana Leat

Routledge
Taylor & Francis Group

LONDON AND NEW YORK

First published 2006
by Routledge
2 Park Square, Milton Park, Abingdon, Oxon OX14 4RN

Simultaneously published in the USA and Canada
by Routledge
270 Madison Ave, New York, NY 10016

Routledge is an imprint of the Taylor & Francis Group

© 2006 Helmut K. Anheier and Diana Leat

Typeset in Perpetua by
Taylor & Francis Books

Printed and bound in Great Britain by
Antony Rowe Ltd, Chippenham, Wiltshire

British Library Cataloguing in Publication Data
A catalogue record for this book is available from the British Library

Library of Congress Cataloging in Publication Data
A catalog record for this book has been requested

ISBN10 0–415–37090–6   ISBN13 9–780–415–37090–5 (hbk)
ISBN10 0–415–37091–4   ISBN13 9–780–415–37091–2 (pbk)

Taylor & Francis Group is the Academic Division of T&F Informa plc.

Contents

PART III
Implications   199

Acknowledgments

The thinking that ultimately led us to write this book owes its impetus to a dinner meeting hosted by Lord Smith of Clifton at the Commonwealth Club in London in the Spring of 2001, and to subsequent conversations with Lord Smith, Tony Flowers and Charles Landry that took place in the House of Lords, the London School of Economics, Stepney Green, and Paddington Station among other London locations. As a result of these conversations, the Joseph Rowntree Reform Trust Ltd commissioned a report on the future of organized philanthropy in Britain that would offer both 'diagnosis and cure' and take a critical yet forward-looking approach in examining the state of foundations and charitable trusts. The resulting report was published in 2002 under the title of *From Charity to Creativity* (Bournes Green, Gloucestershire: Comedia).

Since then, and with the support of The Wallace Foundation and the International Network of Strategic Philanthropy (INSP), we have expanded our argument and, in particular, sought to explore what creative philanthropy means in practice. We wish to thank Christine de Vita, Ed Pauly, Lucas Held, and the members of The Wallace Foundation Board for their support and for the opportunity to present our work at their board meeting in New York in January 2005. At INSP, special thanks are due to Volker Then, Dirk Eilinghoff, Karsten Timmer and the members of the international steering committee, in particular Luc Tayart de Borms, Falvio Brugnoli, Craig Kennedy, Ray Murphy, and Christopher Harris.

In the course of this work, we relied heavily on colleagues and friends in the academic and philanthropic communities. We are very grateful to them, and wish to acknowledge their contributions. We thank Perri 6, Ed Pauly, Steven Burkeman, Nicholas Deakin, Elan Garonzik, Margaret Hyde, Richard Fries, David Emerson, Anthony Tomei, Barry Knight, James A. Smith, Danielle Walker, Rupert Strachwitz, Dario Disegni and Clare Thomas, for providing useful comments, suggestions, and feedback.

We are indebted to Myles McGregor-Lowdnes for his hospitality and collegiality, as we are to his entire staff at the Queensland University of Technology in Brisbane, in particular Anita Greene-Kellett and Dot Summerfield, and to the Myer Foundation. As Myer Foundation Fellows, we enjoyed the luxury of time for critical thinking and reflection on the state and future of philanthropy in the beautiful surroundings of Brisbane.

In the same spirit, we thank the staff of all the foundations that agreed to serve as case studies for this book. In particular, we wish to thank: John Naylor, Charlie McConnell, Stephen Pittman, Bud Meyer, Ed Pauly, Sue Urahn, Tom Kern, Kirke Wilson, and Mary Crooks. Jane Kenny of Philanthropy Australia deserves a special mention. We are also grateful to those who shared their thoughts on creative philanthropy with us and provided written reflections for inclusion in this book: Michael Edwards, Urvashi Vaid, Christopher Harris, James A. Smith, Ray Murphy, Margaret Hyde, and Dario Disegni.

At UCLA's Center for Civil Society, Laurie Spivak and Jocelyn Guihama deserve our thanks for managing this project so skilfully and graciously, and we thank Marcus Lam for being a terrific research assistant. We also thank the School of Public Affairs, especially Dean Barbara Nelson and Associate Dean Bill Parent for providing an intellectually welcoming environment for the study of philanthropy, and Wendy Hoppe, Claire Peeps, Joe Lumarda, Fred Ali, Miyoko Oshima and other members of the philanthropic community in Los Angeles.

Finally, we wish to thank the staff of various coffee shops and restaurants for providing flexible 'office space' and comfortable, scenic and inspiring surroundings as we jointly wrote this book while being located on different continents. They truly stimulated our creative thinking, as did extended walks in Brisbane, Santa Monica, New York, and London.

Clearly, not all will agree with our assessment of the current state and the future of philanthropy, and the vision for philanthropic renewal we offer. While we took great care to accommodate different views and the many suggestions we received, final responsibility for this book and its content is ours alone.

Part I

Why philanthropy?

1 The debate about philanthropy

Foundations have enormous potential to add to the problem-solving capacity of modern democratic societies. This potential is currently largely unfulfilled due to a low-key malaise affecting the foundation sector. This malaise is not about money in the sense that limited philanthropic resources keep foundations from achieving greater impact. Nor is it about mandatory pay-out rates and other hotly debated technical issues of how much of their assets foundations should be required to donate to philanthropic causes each year; nor is it about how assets and pay-outs should be valued in financial terms and according to what accounting standard. This low-key malaise is not even fundamentally one of legitimacy and governance, irrespective of more frequent and louder calls for greater accountability and transparency in the world of foundations.

The malaise is less a matter of what *is* or *has been* achieved. It is much more a matter of limited models and approaches. It is about a lack of awareness of what could be possible, and what greater – and largely unrealized – potential foundations could have. In our opinion, the ability to overcome this malaise could provide the key to reinventing philanthropy as a central institution of American society as well as in other parts of the world, in particular Europe, Australia and the developed market economies of the Asian Pacific. For future growth and legitimacy, achieving greater impact through what we call creative philanthropy is the central issue for foundations today.

At their best, foundations are innovative, risk-taking funders of causes that others either neglect or are unable to address. They fit in well with the way American society, and others, is developing in an era of smaller government, higher social diversity, and greater reliance on private action for public benefit (Abramson and Spann 1998; Fleischman, Smith in Clotfelter and Ehrlich 1999; Gronbjerg 1998; Prewitt 1999; Roelofs 2003; see also www.philanthropy-roundtable.org). Nevertheless, we suspect many, and perhaps too many, foundations would be hard pressed to prove the effectiveness of their contributions and the sustainability of the impact achieved. Why?

The answer is not simply the cost of heroic mistakes borne of high-risk philanthropic ventures, nor found in overly cautious foundation boards and staff that fund safe but marginal causes. Foundations' failure to maximize their potential is systemic and rooted in three consecutive approaches that have dominated the world of philanthropy over the last two centuries, and that continue to shape foundation policies and practices. While useful and effective in the respective eras when they emerged, we argue in this book that they have become increasingly inadequate to address the needs and opportunities of the 21st century. In essence, we posit that foundations have to build on these approaches to evolve new models if they wish to maximize their potential in today's world.

We call these three historical approaches or models *charity*, *scientific philanthropy* and *new scientific philanthropy*. Each deserves fuller treatment than we can provide in these introductory paragraphs, but a summary, however simplified, may help to prepare the major thrust of our argument.[1]

The first approach, charity, was the original model that in many ways was well suited to the social and political context of the 19th century and the Gilded Age (Harrison and Andrews 1946; Andrews 1974; Prochaska 1990; Lagemann 1999; Smith 1989, Sealander 1997; Karl and Karl 1999). With inadequate provision by nonprofit organizations and government, foundations provided services to those unable to care for themselves. This largely meant addressing poverty, but also health-care and social services more generally. As governments increasingly began to provide some kinds of services for some groups, and as social security schemes were progressively introduced, foundations began to modify their approach and provide services complementary to those of government.

Until the early 20th century, this approach was probably effective, yet it had, and continues to have, major shortcomings that prevent foundations from exploiting their fullest potential. For one, this approach can be, and is, adopted by other kinds of charities, including religious institutions, and it is not clear where the distinct role of endowed foundations lies relative to that of alternative providers such as nonprofit organizations or government. In terms of sustainability, the charity approach makes a difference to those lucky enough to benefit from the service but, taken alone, has no impact beyond that. Moreover, the approach tends to operate on the now largely false expectation that someone else will take up the job of widening and sustaining the impact. Traditionally, it was assumed that what foundations start, government will, and should, continue (Anheier and Toepler 1999). Finally, the charity model addresses symptoms rather than causes. In an important sense, the charity approach changes very little. This last argument was the key criticism that led to the rise of the philanthropic/science foundation approach.

Scientific philanthropy is different from charity in its emphasis on dealing with underlying causes rather than the symptoms of problems. Instead of feeding the hungry, the real task of scientific philanthropy became to root out the causes of poverty (Bulmer 1995, 1999; Nielsen 1985; Karl 1997; Smith and Borgmann 2001). Again, the rise of the philanthropic foundation was a product of its time. In the early to mid 20th century, belief in the power of a 'scientific approach' was riding high, as was the notion of social engineering. Social, medical, and economic problems could all be solved once their causes were understood and 'scientific' solutions applied. Education and research rather than services to the needy became focal areas of philanthropic activity. For all the achievements of scientific philanthropy, it too suffers from distinct weaknesses when viewed from a 21st-century perspective.

First, like the charity approach, scientific philanthropy fails fully to exploit the unique potential of endowed foundations. For the most part, this approach can be, and is, adopted by other kinds of organizations as well, including governments. Second, it rests on assumptions that may be true in physical science but are questionable when applied to social issues. Even if the causes of something as complex as, say, poverty are identifiable, they may not be susceptible to scientific solutions and simple control measures. Third, while scientific philanthropy has much wider potential impact than the charity approach, it often failed to appreciate how long, slow, complex and expensive the path to effective problem solving could be.

In recent years, and largely in response to criticism of the ineffectiveness of existing philanthropy, new approaches have been added to the foundation lexicon, including strategic philanthropy, venture philanthropy, social investment, the blended value proposition and so on (Breiteneicher and Marble 2001; Carrington 2002; Emerson 2004; Letts *et al.* 1997; Porter and Kramer 1999; Reis and Clohesy 2001). We refer to these approaches collectively as 'new scientific philanthropy' because they are, in many respects, descendants of scientific philanthropy. The new-scientific approaches tend to focus on foundation processes rather than roles – let alone purposes – and do not address the question of the unique value of foundations in a democracy. They apply business models to foundation practices, with the assumption that if only foundations were run like businesses, all would be well.

While new-scientific models have something to offer and have stimulated healthy debate, their fundamental weakness stems, in large part, from their instrumentalist, managerial assumptions. They are inappropriate guides to achieving social change and sustained impact. Social change is a negotiated, contested, political process, not simply a matter of better management. The complexity of social problems is such that their resolution is never in the hands of one actor, particularly so if the actors, like foundations, do not have the resources commensurate with the problem at hand.

Each of the three approaches has its merits. That foundations have done much good in the world is beyond doubt. But the key question is not 'do foundations do good?' but rather 'do foundations do the best they possibly could in the current environment?' Arguably, one of foundations' weaknesses is that the world has changed while they have remained much the same in a variety of ways. We argue that the approaches outlined above are insufficient in today's world, thus preventing foundations from exploiting their distinctive characteristic of freedom from market and political constraints to make a unique contribution to democratic debate and to maximize the scope and sustainability of their impact.

So what do we offer instead? In essence we argue that in order to achieve their true potential and greater impact, a fourth approach is necessary: creative philanthropy. A creative approach builds on some of the elements and practices of the charity, scientific and new-scientific models but is distinctive in adding new and crucial ingredients, increasing the scope and sustainability of foundation impact, and giving endowed foundations a distinctive role in society. Our aim in this book is to illustrate the ways in which foundations can do this by adopting what we call a creative approach; to explore why foundations adopt such an approach; what a creative approach involves in practice; what management tools it requires; the tensions and dilemmas it raises; and the results it achieves.

Foundation Renaissance

After decades of stagnation and then decline, philanthropic foundations are enjoying a renaissance. Countries as different as the United States, the UK, Australia, Japan, Italy, Germany, Sweden, Turkey and Brazil are displaying renewed interest in creating foundations. In 2004, the *Economist* reported 'an explosion' in new private foundations in the United States. According to the Foundation Center, foundation numbers are up from about 22,000 in the early 1980s to 65,000 today (Renz 2004). In Europe there has also been growth (Anheier and Daly 2006). In Germany, for example, formation of philanthropic foundations has risen from around 200 per annum in the 1980s to between 800 and 900 per annum today (Anheier 2003). The inter-generational transfer of wealth looks set to increase the number of philanthropic foundations in Germany yet further from the present count of 12,000. The UK has about 9,000 foundations, which is about the same number as Switzerland (Anheier and Daly 2006), whereas the Netherlands has about 1,000, and Italy 3,000. In these countries, too, further growth is expected.

This significant and prolonged growth notwithstanding, the 'golden age' of philanthropy is usually seen as being the early 20th century when the 'big foundations' were established by Rowntree, Nuffield, Rockefeller, Ford, Carnegie and others. We suggest that the early 21st century, with foundations enjoying unprecedented global growth and increasing policy importance amid heightened expectations, could become a new golden age. For policy makers, and others, the hope is that greater philanthropy will capture greater private wealth for the public good, take some of the pressure off government spending, and both reflect and enhance the renewal of civil society.

But despite the hopes attached to philanthropic foundations there are important questions about the capacity of foundations to make a real, sustainable difference in the 21st century. In many countries foundations have been around for centuries, and have poured huge sums of money into a variety of problems that remain obstinately entrenched, with poverty and social exclusion as perhaps the most obvious examples. Are foundations essentially 19th-century institutions, dispensing charity to relatively small numbers of grantees, or funding to scientists sequestered in ivory towers? More fundamentally, do foundations, spending money as and where they choose with very little accountability, have a place in modern democracies without greater calls for openness and transparency?

As one leading commentator on foundations, Nielsen, remarked in *The Big Foundations* (1972, p. 3), 'foundations, like giraffes, could not possibly exist, but they do'. As quasi-aristocratic institutions, they flourish on the privileges of a formally egalitarian society; they represent the fruits of capitalistic economic activity; and they are organized for the pursuit of public objectives, which is seemingly contrary to the notion of selfish economic interest that originally created their wealth. Seen from this viewpoint, foundations are not only rare, they are also unlikely institutions, 'strange creatures in the great jungle of American democracy', to paraphrase Nielsen (1972, p.3).

The Case Against Foundations

In most countries, renewed interest in philanthropy in general, including foundations, has gone hand in hand with greater scrutiny of the freedoms and privileges enjoyed by both public and private foundations (Ilchman and Burlingame 1998; Nielsen 1979; Frumkin 1998; Fleishman 1999; Van der Ploeg 1999; Anheier and Toepler 1999; Brilliant 2000; Schlüter *et al.* 2001). The media have stepped up their interest in foundations, and in the United States in particular have found sufficient salacious stories to whet their appetites for more (Gaul and Borowski 1993; Fleishman 1999, 2005). It may be merely a matter of time before journalists in other countries develop similar interests.

Foundations, especially in the United States, are under attack from across the political spectrum – from various House and Senate committees, government agencies, advocates for the nonprofit sector, and from within their own ranks (Dowie 2001; Eisenberg 2002; Fleishman 2005; Williams 1998; Panel on the Nonprofit Sector, 2005). The debates over pay-out and estate duties and taxes, as well as actual and proposed restrictions on foundations' freedom to give grants where they see fit, have all served to bring foundations into the limelight. At the same time, from within their own ranks, foundations are suffering the effects of abuse and mismanagement by a minority, as well as criticisms that they have become 'flabby' and 'complacent' (Eisenberg 2002).

The charges against foundations in the United States are varied. Issues of contention include insider relationships between foundations and outside vendors, corporate abuses including use of charitable gifts as bribes to overlook financial improprieties (as in the Enron case), conflicts of interest with grantees, issues around Donor Advised Funds, trustee self-dealing, salaries and severance packages, trustee compensation, and so on (National Committee for Responsive Philanthropy 2004).

In 2004 and 2005, the US Senate Finance Committee responded with a series of recommendations, including a requirement that nonprofit organizations file detailed information every five years showing that they continue to operate for tax-exempt purposes, tougher conflict-of-interest standards, a requirement for detailed descriptions of performance goals and measures for meeting them, controls on donor-advised funds, and tougher controls on administrative costs and pay-out.[2]

Foundations in other countries, such as the UK (Leat 2005) and Australia (Crimm 2002), are facing similar and growing demands for greater oversight and accountability, even though the particular issues may be different. The European Union, too, is taking a more pronounced interest in foundations, and some philanthropic leaders in Europe are calling for the establishment of a new legal instrument, the European Foundation, to overcome the complexities and inefficiencies of national laws and the weaknesses of oversight regimes in many member states (Anheier and Daly 2006; see www.efc.be).

At the same time, foundations as far apart as the United States, the UK and Australia faced dramatically reduced income between 2000 and 2003. A report by the Foundation Center (2003) suggests that two-fifths of foundations surveyed expected giving to decline in 2003, and this was greater among larger foundations. Foundation giving rebounded somewhat in 2004 (Foundation Center 2005).

Foundation Responses

Foundations have mounted a number of responses to these threats. The dominant response to increased demand and expectations in the face of declining income is to emphasize their limited resources: 'To bolster civil society, philanthropy must do all it can – but it cannot do it all' (Cohen 2003).

Various responses have been made to accusations of abuse and mismanagement (see National Committee for Responsive Philanthropy 2004). Some foundations have attempted to blame all that is wrong on smaller foundations, and there have been calls for minimum levels of capitalization for foundations (National Committee for Responsive Philanthropy 2004). The reality is undoubtedly more complex: not all small foundations are badly managed, and not all large foundations are well managed.

Responses to calls for greater regulation and accountability have also been varied. Some have seen this as a good idea, protecting the sound majority from the few bad apples in the barrel (National Committee for Responsive Philanthropy 2004). Some have accepted the broad principle of greater scrutiny but have quibbled with the detail, arguing that foundations are too varied in size to permit simple rules and formulae. Others raised questions about the dangers and inappropriateness of over-regulating what are essentially private institutions, albeit for the public good (see www.cof.org).

Reframing the Question

Current debates concerning foundations, we suggest, start from the wrong angle. Underlying all of the responses above – 'limited resources', 'too small to be capable', 'the devil in the detail', 'private institutions' – is a more fundamental question: what are foundations for, and what is it they do that they alone can do? *This is the key question*: If foundations 'cannot do it all' what is it that they *can* do? Where should they concentrate their resources? If there can be no simple formulae, why is that? If it is dangerous to (over-)regulate private foundations, how is the balance between public and private to be reconciled?

These, we argue, are the fundamental questions. By contrast, focusing on pay-out rates, accountability, or declining income is putting the cart before the horse. Process issues should follow consideration of roles, not vice versa. Until foundations make a clear, well-reasoned case for their unique role and value in a democracy they will be forced to respond to debates framed in terms that miss the fundamental questions.

Rather than responding to a debate the terms of which have been set by others, foundations urgently need to redefine those terms and vigorously defend, define and illustrate their unique strengths and the roles that they, and only they, can play in strengthening and defending democracy. In this way they can turn a low-key crisis into an opportunity.

To make this happen, foundations need to move the debate away from concerns with processes to the more fundamental question of what value they add in society. They need to illustrate their unique roles with success stories, and consider ways in which these success stories can be replicated. What is more, foundations must do more in promoting these messages to policy makers, the media, the nonprofit sector and the public. These are some of the challenges we address in this book – challenges that foundations must face if they wish to seize the opportunities of renewal presented to them.

The Unique Value of Foundations in a Democracy

Foundations' value does not lie in their assets or expenditure per se. Their unique value lies in what they uniquely can do. Endowed foundations need to stop playing to their weaknesses and start playing to their strengths. Lack of both resources (relative to the costs of provision) and democratic mandate are foundations' key weaknesses, but they are also among their key potential strengths. The key is that foundation resources are 'free' relative to both governments and markets. Foundations enjoy the luxury of freedom from market and political constraints and constituencies. Many also enjoy the luxury of perpetuity.

Foundations have sufficient resources and 'space' to allow them to think, to be truly innovative, to take risks, to fail, and to take the longer-term view. Furthermore, in an important sense, foundations exist in a world of their own.

They do not fully belong to any one sector but have, or could have, a foot in all. They are not, yet, dominated by any one professional group and thus have the freedom and space to think and work across conventional wisdoms, and disciplinary, organizational and sectoral boundaries.

These characteristics of endowed foundations give them the potential to make a contribution to society way beyond that which their limited resources might suggest. Furthermore, building on these characteristics enables foundations to build a robust role that harnesses their 'privateness' for the public good. Susan Berresford, president of the Ford Foundation, has called for a revisiting of the implications of the 'public' definition of foundations, calling attention to the intersection of philanthropy, democracy and freedom (Public Obligations of Foundations, April, 2004, www.fordfound.org / news). We argue that the characteristics of foundations outlined above should be recognized as a cause for celebration rather than apology, providing one of the keys to unlocking the 'private/public' conundrum.

At a time when many commentators see democracy in the United States and elsewhere as under threat from a combination of the demands of global capitalism and overly powerful political parties, we argue along with other experts that foundations have never been more important (Prewitt 1999; Porter and Kramer 1999; Letts *et al* 1997; Schlüter *et al* 2001). The role of the wider nonprofit sector, dependent for resources on contracting, corporate fundraising and popular sympathies moulded by the media, is constrained in what it can offer.

Foundations have to acknowledge that they have neither the resources nor the democratic mandate to fill all the gaps, provide everything the state does not provide, and support unpopular causes in the long term. What is more, foundations should no longer use resource limitations as an excuse to turn down grant-seekers, but to make it very clear that they are not in the business of stepping in for what governments, or market firms might be better at.

Endowed foundations are uniquely placed to bring genuinely creative, innovative ideas to the intransigent problems of our age. Free of market and political constraints, they are uniquely able, if they choose, to think the unthinkable, ignoring disciplinary and professional boundaries. They can take risks, consider approaches others say can't possibly work – and they can fail with no terminal consequences. Equally important, foundations can take a longer-term view. Foundations are free to be imaginative and creative, working across sectoral, organizational, professional and disciplinary boundaries, without the stifling constraints of short-term, ill-conceived performance measurement criteria. They can change the way in which we think about things, our priorities and our ways of creating a truly civil society characterized by respect and dignity for all. As Carson (2003b) has noted, foundations need to spend more time and money on 'projects that have the promise of changing how an issue is viewed or handled'. We refer to this as 'creative grant-making' (Anheier and Leat 2002).

Re-Thinking Foundations

The creation of the early 20th-century philanthropic foundations was related to the perceived social responsibilities and moral obligations attached to the large fortunes made during the industrial revolution at a time when the powers of the state to tax and regulate were comparatively underdeveloped (see Smith and Borgmann 2001). Today's renaissance of philanthropic foundations, however, has some obvious links with the general re-appraisal of the role of the state in modern society (Anheier and Salamon 2006), and a refocus on private and corporate responsibility. Long-term economic growth and prosperity, the growing divide between rich and poor, the 'new money' of the 1990s linked to information technologies, the globalization of financial and other markets and less demanding tax policies have further encouraged the renaissance of interest in philanthropy. These changes raise the question of whether foundations are best suited in mission, structure, strategy and process to fulfil the expectations of this renaissance.

At worst, foundations are little more than tax shelters that allow the privileged to pursue some 'favoured' cause or charity. There are foundations that serve the privileged few, with no apparent net benefit added to society as a whole – this is the charge sometimes made against the wealthy endowed 'public' (fee-paying) schools in the UK. Others use their endowments less to support some specified cause, however beneficial, esoteric or necessary it might be, than to safeguard and add to the fortune already in place (Arnove 1980; Nielsen 1996). Yet others do very little at all, hold ritualistic board meetings and resemble rather passive, even docile institutions seemingly at odds with the faster pace of the 21st century.

Many foundations do a huge amount, busily making grants to 'good causes', helping numerous organizations to start up, develop and survive. These foundations work across a wide range of areas, from the environment to the arts and welfare and, without question, contribute enormous public and individual benefit.

Generalizations about foundations are dangerous, to be sure, and as students of philanthropy we are well aware of this danger and cognizant of the often highly individualistic nature of foundations in terms of their founder and deed. Foundations come in many shapes, sizes and guises, and one of the fundamental problems is that so little is known about them beyond their numbers and size (and in some countries even those basic data do not exist). But despite their differences there are some common threads in the foundation world.

Pots of Money

First, foundations are seen, and to a large extent see themselves, in terms of their financial assets. Foundations have been described as 'warehouses of wealth' or as pots of money with, or in search of, a purpose. Dwight Macdonald described the Ford Foundation as 'a large body of money completely surrounded by people who want some' (quoted in Hammack 1999). Significantly, foundations rank themselves not by what they do or how effective they are, but by the size of their assets and income. Thus the 'top' foundations are not the ones that have achieved the most but the ones that have the most money.

Nevertheless, foundations' financial resources pale into insignificance when compared with government spending or even the nonprofit sector as a whole. Anheier and Salamon (2005) offer evidence that foundations' share has declined in the 1990s in favour of earned income. Thus, judged solely in terms of their financial resources, foundations have little scope for making a widespread and sustainable impact.

We will argue that foundations are about much more than money. Money is a necessary condition for achieving impact, but it is not a sufficient means. We will also argue that the focus on financial resources has diverted public and political thinking about foundations down numerous side alleys, away from the more fundamental question of foundations' unique roles in modern democracies.

Endowed Grant-makers

Second, the term 'foundation' is increasingly reserved for endowed grant-making bodies. Bodies that operate their own programmes themselves, rather than make grants, are referred to as operating foundations and are, to a large extent, set apart from pure grant-makers. The endowed grant-making foundation as established in the United States is taken to be the foundation 'gold standard' by which foundations in other countries increasingly measure themselves. In fact, endowed grant-making foundations are a product of a particular period of US history and are not the dominant model in many other countries, including large parts of Europe (Toepler 1999).

We will argue that the distinction between grant-making and operating foundations is not as clear as it seems, and it is time to move beyond this separation. Indeed, some foundations that previously were predominantly grant-making are now exploring operating styles in order to increase their impact.

Relay Races and Marathons

The dominant style of much foundation giving is that of the relay race. Many foundations give short-term grants and then expect the baton to be picked up by others. Some develop creative ideas and programmes, but expect the baton of implementation and sustainability either to run its own race or to be carried by others. Foundations are sometimes great sprinters but poor marathon runners. Typically, their weaknesses include thinking and working short-term, giving up too soon, not fully understanding the resources needed to finish the course, not systematically building their strength over the long term and not equipping themselves for the rigours of ensuring sustainability. And, if they measure their performance at all, they often use measures and timing better suited to the speed and style of a relay race than the pace of the marathon.

We will argue that if foundations wish effectively to fulfil their unique roles in a democracy they need to adopt the habits and practices of marathon runners rather than relay sprinters.

Opening up Debate

We are supporters of foundations and philanthropy, and we defend the right of independent private action for common benefit, and would like to see such actions encouraged by public policy. We believe that foundations ultimately add to the problem-solving capacity of modern societies in dealing with the challenges they face, be it in the field of education, health, culture, or policy development, among others. The freedom that foundations have from both ballot box and shareholder expectations affords them great latitude in pursuing private objectives and agendas while serving a public purpose. Some foundations take full advantage of this freedom; others are not achieving their full potential and the great promise they hold for modern societies.

This book seeks to open up debate regarding the proper roles of philanthropic foundations in modern, democratic society. We believe that foundations are especially relevant in the current political climate that puts less emphasis on governmental responsibilities and actions, and allocates more 'space' to private institutions serving the public benefit. We illustrate the potential of foundations with a series of case studies and vignettes of foundations in three countries: the United States, the UK and Australia.

Philanthropy underwent its last real modernization in the early part of the 20th century with the introduction of the large-scale US foundations (such as Carnegie and Ford), on which foundations in other countries were often modelled. Since then philanthropy has become largely synonymous with grant-making foundations and charitable trusts, and being a philanthropist is synonymous with the individual largesse of rich donors. Innovations in the world of organized philanthropy have been rare, and only in recent years have new forms such as venture philanthropy begun to emerge (Breiteneicher and Marble 2001; Letts *et al.* 1997; Porter and Kramer 1999; Reis and Clohesy 2001).

There is, then, an urgent need for a vigorous debate about the roles of endowed foundations in a changed and changing world in which the meaning and processes of democracy have been transformed. We have to re-assess philanthropy not so much because of the easy promise it might entail, but much more so because other mechanisms (taxation, state action, private markets) are increasingly becoming, or are believed to be, inefficient and ineffective in a variety of fields ranging from social services and health to education and culture.

Part of the problem is a need to be frank and open about institutions that appear inherently good, at least at first glance. Yet it is now of paramount importance for policy-makers, and not only a matter of academic discourse, to ask: what in the institution of philanthropy is worth preserving, developing, even nurturing? By implication, are there other elements that are best left by the wayside, or actively discontinued? What is the true potential of philanthropy for the future of developed societies – societies that are likely to be less egalitarian, less state-oriented and less stable, but more mobile and individualistic, and with greater institutional uncertainties and higher risks? What are the distinctive, unique roles of endowed foundations in a modern democracy?

These questions are particularly timely in the current policy environment. In many countries, changing ideas about the role of the state in meeting the social, educational, cultural and environmental challenges of modern societies have brought private voluntary action and philanthropy closer to the centre stage of current policy debates. Meanwhile current debates around foundations centre on how they are organized rather than on their roles. Structures and processes need to flow from roles, not vice versa.

Perhaps as little as twenty years ago, foundations' roles were relatively clear and generally agreed. Holcombe (2000) argues that at the beginning of the 20th century, foundations, then few in number, had clearer roles than at the close of the century, when, grown in numbers and in resources, they nevertheless seem less clear and focused. Now the environment in which they work has changed and the old roles are less easy to defend. Foundations need a new philosophy adapted to the changes in the world around them. Without a new, clearly articulated vision the danger is that foundations will have inappropriate roles and expectations thrust upon them. Without such a modern vision, it seems unlikely that foundations will be able to inspire the next generation of philanthropists. Without a clear sense of the distinctive roles of endowed foundations in democracy, policy makers, and foundations, will continue to struggle with identifying the proper balance between the 'privateness' and the 'publicness' of foundations.

Foundations have been criticized for being too large or too small, too conservative or too liberal, and so on (Brilliant 2000). Most often, they have been criticized for how they behave – their processes (Arnove 1980; Allen 1987; Holcombe 2000; Dowie 2001; Roelofs 2003). But, we suggest, part of the real problem lies in the fact that the world around philanthropy has changed, while philanthropy itself, with some exceptions, has both held onto the roles, models, practices and culture of the past and, at the same time, forgotten its best role models. The time has come to reinvent philanthropy, taking the best of its past and applying it to new circumstances and needs.

Defining Foundations

What kind of foundations will be the subject of this book? Even a cursory look at the United States, the UK, other European countries and Australia reveals a variety of philanthropic institutions and a great variety of forms. Thus, one of our first tasks is to bring some conceptual clarity and focus to the subject, and to state what types of foundation we have in mind, and which ones are outside our primary interest. For the purposes of this report, we follow the structural-operational definition of nonprofit organizations proposed by Salamon and Anheier (1997) and define a foundation as an asset, financial or otherwise, with the following characteristics (Anheier 2001):

Non-Membership-Based Organization

The foundation must rest on an original deed, typically signified in a charter of incorporation or establishment that gives the entity both intent of purpose and relative permanence. Other aspects include some degree of internal organizational structure, relative consistency through time of goals, structure and activities, and meaningful organizational boundaries. Thus, a foundation is not only a financial or other type of asset, but also an identifiable organization.

Private Entity

Foundations are institutionally separate from government, and are 'non-governmental' in the sense of not being an instrumentality of government. Therefore, foundations do not exercise governmental authority and are outside direct majoritarian control.

Self-Governing Entity

Foundations are equipped to control their own activities, have their own internal governance procedures, enjoy a meaningful degree of autonomy, and have a separate set of accounts in the sense that assets, expenditures, and other disbursements must not be part of either governmental or corporate balance sheets.

Nonprofit-Distributing Entity.

Foundations do not return profits generated by either use of assets or the conduct of commercial activities to their trustees or directors. A foundation may accumulate surplus in a given year, but the surplus must be applied to its basic mission, and not be distributed to owners or their equivalents.

Serving a Public Purpose

Foundations should do more than serve the needs of a narrowly defined social group or category, such as members of a family, or a closed circle of beneficiaries. Foundations are private assets that serve a public purpose. The public purpose may or may not be charitable, and therefore tax-exempt in the letter or spirit of charity law. What is important is that the purpose be part of the public domain.

The term foundation or trust is usually used to refer to organizations that have an endowment from which they derive income. However, some foundations do not have a permanent endowment. Some may, for example, derive their income from a regular covenant (e.g. some company foundations), while other types such as community foundations may have an endowment but also raise money for current expenditure and for building up their asset base. Other foundations may have little or no endowment, and instead raise money annually, but behave in many important respects much like endowed foundations. In this book, we are primarily concerned with endowed foundations, though we make reference to other types. We focus primarily on endowed foundations, rather than foundations or charities in general, because endowed foundations are freer than charities that have no independent, secure income to fulfil the creative roles we believe are urgently needed in modern society.

Overview

This introductory chapter is followed by a chapter that looks at strengths and weaknesses in the approaches of mainstream philanthropic foundations. In the third chapter we look more closely at creativity and innovation: what the terms mean, how they are related and under what conditions they occur. This chapter concludes with a discussion of potential constraints on creativity and innovation in and by foundations.

In the following chapters (four and five), we present a series of short vignettes and then more detailed case studies of foundations adopting a creative approach – who they are, their financial resources, missions, activities, the drivers behind their approaches, their processes and strategies, and the issues and dilemmas with which they grapple.

Chapter six considers what makes for a creative approach – how and why foundations adopt a creative approach and how the approaches of creative foundations differ from mainstream practice. In chapters seven and eight we discuss the implications for management and practice, including the tensions and obstacles experienced by creative foundations. Finally, we consider ways forward.

2   Models of philanthropy in
context

What can we say about the role and functions of foundations in modern society? Already back in the 1950s analysts suggested that foundations are uniquely qualified to enable innovation, take social risks, and serve, in today's parlance, as philanthropic venture capital: foundations 'have a special mandate to enter fields of controversy, where the explosive nature of the issues would make suspect the findings of less independent organizations and where needed financing from other sources might prove difficult' (Andrews 1956:19; see also Nielsen 1985, 1996; Smith 1999).

The argument that foundations have these special competencies rests on the assumption that foundations, unlike other institutions, are largely free from direct external control, as they are not accountable to voters, members, consumers, shareholders or other stakeholders. Classically self-supported by endowment income, foundations and their trustees are usually only bound by the donor's will, as laid down in the charter, – though naturally within the constraints of the overall legal and regulatory framework of the country in which they are established. This potential of endowed grant-making foundations has long been recognized: the 1949 report of a programme and policy study committee of the Ford Foundation, for instance, noted that the 'freedom from entanglements, pressures, restrictive legislation, and private interest endows a foundation with an inherent freedom of action possessed by few other organizations' (quoted in Andrews 1956: 21).

However, the foundation literature also testifies to the difficulty of using private funds to the greatest public benefit possible. The absence of market and political correctives also implies that no stakeholders are present to monitor whether foundations are meeting these functions to the fullest, or have been proven to divert from the will of the donor, leading to goal displacement (Holcombe 2000).

Foundations have been subject to a wide range of criticism about their behaviour in terms of governance and management and their actual contributions and impact (e.g. Anheier and Leat 2002; Frumkin 1998; Letts *et al.* 1997; Porter and Kramer 1999; Dowie 2001). Yet what are foundations to do? As a first step towards making a case for creative philanthropy, it is useful to diagnose what is wrong with current approaches so as to obtain a better understanding of the reasons underlying the foundation critique. We will, therefore, take a closer look at the prevailing approaches or models for foundations, and the various roles that have been ascribed to them.

Foundation Approaches

As suggested in the previous chapter, three major models or approaches have developed that in broad terms ascribe certain functions and activities to foundations. These are the charity/service approach, the scientific/philanthropy approach, and the new-scientific approach. We will discuss each in turn.

The Charity/Service Approach

The charity/service approach is the original model, developed throughout the world in different guises and going by different names. Originally the charity approach (for short) was rooted in ancient religious beliefs such as alms giving and tithing on the one hand, and moral codes such as *noblesse oblige* on the other. Its late-19th and early-20th-century application by charitable foundations was linked in some countries to the secularization of giving and the growing role of the industrial elite and urban middle class in philanthropy (Smith and Borgmann 2001).

The charity approach was in many ways well suited to its social and political context. In the absence of adequate provision by church or state, foundations provided services to those unable to care for themselves. As, through the early parts of the 20th century, governments increasingly began to provide some services for some groups, foundations adapted the service approach to provide services complementary to those of government or to fill gaps in statutory provision. Foundations began to stress their roles as innovators, risk-takers and funders of unpopular causes. At certain periods in many societies, foundations added a 'demonstration' or 'pump-priming' element to the charity approach. Foundations innovated or spotted as yet unacknowledged needs, in effect doing the initial 'R and D', in the expectation that over time some other funder would pick up the project, method or need, and make it more widely known and available. In the mid-20th century in particular, this service demonstration effect was probably very effective.

In many countries the charity approach remains the dominant model today, despite the challenges of the other approaches introduced in the early and late 20th century. Acknowledging that the charity approach has done much good over the centuries, what are its weaknesses in the current social and political environment? We list several such weaknesses:

Failure to Exploit the Unique Potential of Endowed Foundations

For the most part, this approach can be, and is, adopted by other non-endowed fund-raising charitable, as well as non-charitable, organizations.

Limited Impact

The charity approach makes a difference to those individuals lucky enough to benefit from the service but, taken alone, has no impact beyond that. When a demonstration aim is added, the service approach may have, or at least intend to have, wider impact extending beyond direct-grant recipients. But, as discussed below, this wider impact is often restricted because of failure to analyse and act upon the conditions for effective dissemination and replication.

False Expectations

As noted above, the charity approach tends to operate on the now largely false expectation that someone else will take up the job of widening and sustaining impact. Although many foundations act as though they believe that 'big' government is bad, they have also traditionally assumed that what foundations start, government will, and should, continue (see, for example, Douglas and Wildavsky 1980–81; Karl and Karl 1999).

Another danger of the charity approach is that it may create a hope or expectation on the part of others that foundations can be relied upon to provide. Whereas in the past government and other funders may have stepped forward to pick up the baton from foundations, today, in an era of neo-liberalism, many governments are more likely to step back from involvement in issues and areas taken up by foundations, because the foundation is seen to be filling the need instead.

What governments seem to fail to realize is that most of even the very richest foundations have resources that could not keep one major service running nationally for more than a few days. More disturbingly, few governments and institutions seem to realize that over-dependence on foundations may be dangerous. If, for example, the Gates Foundation suddenly decided to stop funding HIV/AIDS research and treatment, how many governments could or would step in to fill the gap?

Lack of Sustainability / A Short-Term Difference

Another aspect of the limited impact of the charity model is that although it makes a difference to direct beneficiaries, it addresses symptoms rather than causes. In an important sense, the charity approach changes very little. This was the key criticism of the charity approach that led to the rise of the philanthropic/ science foundation approach we will discuss next.

The Philanthropic / Science Approach

The criticism that fundamentally nothing changes as a result of the charity approach was the driving force for the development of philanthropic/

science-oriented foundations. Although the distinction between charity and philanthropy is somewhat eroded today, originally 'philanthropic' foundations distinguished themselves from charitable foundations in their emphasis on addressing the causes rather than the symptoms of problems.

This was the approach adopted by the Rockefeller, Carnegie, or Russell Sage foundations, among others, in the United States in the early 20th century, and by, for example, the three Joseph Rowntree trusts in the UK. Rowntree captured the new philosophy of these foundations when he wrote in his original trust deed that the foundations should distinguish themselves from then current philanthropic efforts by searching out underlying causes rather than 'remedying the more superficial manifestations of weakness or evil'.[1]

Again, the rise of the philanthropic foundation was a product of its time. Belief in the power of a 'scientific approach' was riding high, as was the notion of social engineering. Social, medical, and economic problems, it was thought, could all be solved once their causes were understood and 'scientific' solutions applied (Bulmer 1999). Foundations adopting a philanthropic approach (for short) undoubtedly did, and continue to do, hugely important work, with the establishment of the research university and other higher-education institutions as cases in point. But for all the achievements of the philanthropic approach, it too suffers from some weaknesses when viewed from a 21st-century perspective. As with the charity approach, we list several:

Failure to Exploit the Unique Potential of Endowed Foundations

Like the charity approach, the philanthropic approach fails fully to exploit the unique potential of endowed foundations. For the most part, this approach can be, and is, adopted by non-endowed foundations and other charitable and non-charitable organizations. In addition, today this approach sometimes leads to some delicate balancing acts regarding the ownership and commercial value of intellectual property.

Questionable Assumptions

The science approach is based on assumptions that may be true in physical science but are questionable when applied to social issues. Even if the causes of something as complex as, say, poverty are identifiable, they are not susceptible to scientific solutions and simple control measures.

Stunted Impact

In theory, the philanthropic approach has much wider potential impact than the charity approach. Understanding the causes of poverty, disease, climate change and so on should benefit the whole society. But the problem is that the philanthropic approach often fails to take into account the further steps necessary for the understanding of causes to have a real effect on people, organizations, practice and policy.

Foundations adopting the philanthropic approach often fail to appreciate the long, slow, complex and expensive path to effective dissemination. They often fail to understand the social, cultural, professional and political obstacles that may lie in the path of adoption and implementation. They often fail to take into account the complexity of policy processes and overestimate the importance of research alone (Bothwell 2003). In theory, the impact of a philanthropic approach goes way beyond grantees, but in practice, it may get lost in a small number of specialist professional journals read by a small number of other professionals.

'New' Scientific Philanthropy

'Venture philanthropy', the 'new philanthropy', and 'entrepreneurial philanthropists' are terms that refer to the way funds are distributed. The rapid accumulation of new wealth by entrepreneurs and the run-up of the stock market in the 1990s enabled many individuals to increase their philanthropy or to engage in formal philanthropy for the first time. Many were young, confident, aggressive venture capitalists for social change, who viewed existing charitable organizations as lacking management capacity and capitalization and who saw charitable actions as investments that demanded a demonstrable 'return on investment' (see Breiteneicher and Marble 2001; Carrington 2002; Emerson 2004; Letts *et al.* 1997; Porter and Kramer 1999; Reis and Clohesy 2001).

For many of these 'new philanthropists', philanthropy is an investment, not charity, and its aim is to create social wealth. The new philanthropists are generally results-oriented; they want to see the impact and the results of their giving relatively quickly. This is often in direct conflict with the realities of the nonprofit sector and the systemic problems that exist in cultures and communities, as well as historical information about the development of social movements. None of these were created overnight, and therefore they cannot be changed overnight. Few were the creation of a single author or organization and few can be changed by working on a single author or organization. In spite of this, there seems to be some indication that aspects of the new 'bottom-line thinking' are proving to be a valuable addition to the nonprofit sector's operations because it creates a new way of thinking and operating that, in the long term, could be a value-added commodity.

Strategic philanthropy refers both to the working philosophy and the programme strategies of a foundation. It originates from an entrepreneurial view of foundation activities that focuses on strategy, key competencies and striving for effective contributions to social change (see Prager 2003; Emerson 2004;

www.blendedvalue.org; www.effectivephilanthropy.org; Nicholls 2005; Hopkins 2005).

These new kids on the block are, in many respects, modern descendants of the scientific philanthropy approach. While they have stimulated healthy debate, they share some weaknesses that stem, in part, from their fundamentally instrumentalist assumptions. First, they tend to focus on foundation processes rather than roles. They do not address the question of the unique value of foundations in a democracy. Second, they apply managerialist business models to foundation practices. The assumption on which they operate is that if only foundations, and their grantees, were run more like businesses, all would be well. As Sievers (1997) has remarked, their emphasis is on technical interventions in systems to improve performance, and as such it reflects the pragmatic, fix-it character of American social policymaking.

Strengths and Weaknesses of Current Approaches

In addition to the specific weaknesses of both the charity service and philanthropic science approaches, there are some general weaknesses of current foundation cultures and practices.

Elitist and Out of Touch?

One frequent criticism of foundations is that they are elitist and out of touch with real social issues. So, for example, Odendahl (1990: 27) charges that 'the rich do not give to the poor but to institutions they use and cherish – the charity of the wealthy doesn't just begin at home, it stays there.'

The criticism that foundations do not question or probe the system – but rather, they *are* the system – gains some support from analyses of patterns of foundation grant distribution. For example, one study of foundation giving in the UK found that three-quarters of religious grants go to Christian causes, and 24 per cent to Jewish causes. Muslims are specifically mentioned in only 1 per cent of grants examined by Vincent and Pharoah (2000). Three per cent of all grants specifically mention black and ethnic minority needs (it is, of course, possible that other grants addressed these needs).

In the United States the vast majority of funding (in share of dollars and numbers of grants) goes to education (26 per cent/21 per cent), health (18 per cent/12 per cent) and human services (15 per cent/26 per cent). Grants for public affairs or the benefit of society receive 11 per cent of grant dollars, and 12 per cent of grants. Three per cent of grant dollars goes to international affairs. Ethnic or racial minorities receive around 8 per cent of grant dollars. While programme support consumes over 40 per cent of grant dollars, general operating support receives less than 20 per cent (Foundation Center 2004). It seems that foundations are still more focused on projects rather than supporting core costs despite the constant pleas of more for the latter from nonprofit grantees.

Followers of Fashion

McIlnay (1998) argues that foundations follow rather than start things. For example, the US civil rights movement began in 1955 with the Montgomery bus boycott, but foundation grants were not significant until 1962. 'Foundation grants to organisations directly serving women and minorities have been minuscule, dispelling the myth that foundations are crusaders for social change and contradicting the descriptions that foundations have given of themselves' (McIlnay 1998: 11). Similarly, Vincent and Pharoah (2000) in the UK suggest that grant-makers as a whole tend to approach problems similarly, indicating a considerable degree of conformity in the way foundations address needs. Grant-making reveals strong patterns of 'fashion' across foundations.

Funding Rules not Project Needs

Another criticism of foundations is that grant size tends to be determined by general principles within foundations, rather than the needs of the project or proposal. In other words, grant size is related not to what is needed to achieve the goals of the grant but to foundations' own organizational needs (for risk control or for spread of grant distribution, and so on).

Too Little for Too Little Time

Various commentators have criticized mainstream foundation practices for their focus on small, short-term grants. Skloot makes the point most colourfully when he criticizes foundations for behaving 'like gamblers playing the two-dollar slots in Vegas. We sit straight ahead, holding our little bucket of metal coins. Repeatedly, we drop in small change, hoping for a big pay-off . . . We put large dreams on small coins . . . we almost always feed the slots more than we win' (Skloot 2001).

Let a Thousand Flowers Bloom – and Die

The complaint that foundations are ineffective because they spread their money too widely and too thinly is closely related to the criticism that they are ineffective because they fail to make choices and lack focus. For example, Covington (1997) typifies thinking in foundations as 'small, non-strategic, and non-visionary'; and Schumann (1998) concludes that the basic problem is that too much money is spent 'foolishly'.

Mainstream foundations have typically seen their lack of pre-defined focus as a virtue, demonstrating their democracy and responsiveness. But, 'whilst some might argue that this 'let 1,000 flowers bloom' approach is inherently democratic, normal and typically American, I suggest it is autocratic, ineffective and willful – and typically American' (Skloot 2001: 3).

Overly Narrow/Overly Prescriptive

While mainstream foundations have been criticized for their lack of focus in the areas of activity and numbers of organizations they fund, they have also been criticized for the opposite vice – an overly narrow or premature focus in project plans and grant agreements. There is a view that foundations fail to be fully effective because they are overly prescriptive about the work they fund, closing down debate over the definition and nature of problems too early. Tomei, for example, argues that the defining characteristic of foundations is to support the unexpected and unorthodox and to fill gaps. Foundations are not equipped directly to make change happen. 'Their role rather is to identify creative and talented individuals in their fields of interest and to support their work.' Tomei draws a comparison with publishing. The publisher's job is to bring a range of skills and expertise to the business of bringing the written word to the public. Publishing skills include editing, marketing, design and, above all, the ability to recognize and encourage talented writers. But publishers do not write novels themselves (Tomei 1998).

Over-Emphasis on Project Funding

Ask any nonprofit organization what they most need and want and the reply will be 'more core funding and operational support'. But what mainstream foundations most often give is (short-term) project funding. Again, this is said to be one reason why mainstream foundations are less effective than they might be. Both Bothwell (2001) and Burkeman (1999) relate the apparent preference for project funding to mainstream foundations' lack of trust in grantees and thus their reluctance to engage in the level of loss of control entailed in core funding.

Silo Funding

Criticism of mainstream foundations' over-emphasis on project funding is related to the claim that they have been ineffective in building sustainable change because their funding has adopted a traditional policy and programme 'silo' approach (that is, seeing social problems as discrete and unrelated to each other). This may not only hamper the emergence of new, creative ideas and solutions to old problems, but also create, or perpetuate, 'barriers to permeation and cross-issue connections' among nonprofits. 'Organizations operating in isolation failed to work with stakeholders outside their traditional networks, thereby failing to advance broader changes' (Bothwell 2002, quoting Drabble and Abrenilla 2000).

Romantic Notions of Nonprofit Organizations

Most foundations appear to operate on the assumption that (i) what nonprofit organizations choose to do is an adequate index of social needs and the problems of society, and (ii) nonprofit organizations are the major locus of new thinking and innovation generally. These assumptions persist despite numerous studies that demonstrate that the existence of nonprofit organizations is very imperfectly related to social need (see Anheier and Kendall 2001; Flynn and Hodgkinson 2002; Perrow 2001), and that nonprofit organizations are not particularly innovative (Kramer 1990). The important point, however, is that foundations seem somehow locked into funding nonprofit organizations and find it more difficult to fund individuals or groups other than tax-exempt entities. Of course, a major reason behind this convention is the tax law, particularly in the United States, and one could question the overall utility of this approach.

Lack of Collaboration and Learning

The criticism that foundations are overly individualistic, poor at collaboration, sharing and learning is often voiced. Skloot, continuing his gambling analogy, suggests: 'We sit straight ahead, rarely pulling our eyes away from the spinning icons. We don't interact with the other players on our left or right. If we did, we wouldn't learn much anyhow – they're behaving in just the same way' (2001: 3). Much of philanthropy, 'especially at the largest 100 foundations', 'works in isolation, rarely sharing the task or the results. We make grants based on inadequate due diligence, partially relevant information, or simple intuition. After a grant is made we rarely share what we really know – the good, the bad and the ugly – with grantees or with our own colleagues. We are novices at cross-program collaboration and rarely buddy-up for mutual gain . . . there are no incentives in philanthropy to do that. Finally, we don't measure our successes, course-correct and learn intentionally' (Skloot 2001: 3–4). One recent poll at a TPI conference suggested that lack of collaboration was seen as one of the biggest problems in philanthropy (reported in Aspen Institute: July/August 2004).

Apologetic Attitude to Overhead Costs

Some so-called overhead costs may indeed be wasteful and inefficient. Others are simply the costs of making good grants and of achieving sustainable change, and are more like investments and R&D expenditure than overhead costs proper. Nonetheless, too many foundations are overly apologetic about overhead costs instead of robustly defending these as essential for knowledge management and effectiveness. The cost of penny-pinching on overhead is often the cost of a less than fully effective grant.

Over-Emphasis on Planning

While some foundations abhor planning, for others making and sticking to a plan has become a sort of Holy Grail that will make everything right. Planning is based on a set of managerialist or rationalist assumptions that may or may not work in business but are generally somewhat ill-suited to the real-world complexity of social change where qualities such as flexibility, serendipity, opportunism and compromise all play a part.

Foundations work with an array of rationalist assumptions that implicitly or explicitly underlie their grant-making policies and practices. Most obviously these theories include the assumption that 'good and successful' projects are a function of good ideas, well-thought-through plans, and good organization. Organizational structures and processes, management, and financial resources are seen as major determinants and predictors of the likely success of the project: clear objectives, planning, and control processes are particularly important indicators of the 'good' or capable organization.

More fundamentally, dominant rationalist approaches to grant-making assume that it is possible to predict and create a knowable future (Fowler 1995). In this view, problems all have causes that are singular, knowable, and uncontested; there is a known solution that money can produce. 'The future of nonprofit organizations and the environments in which they work will be a continuation of present trends' (Leat 1999). These are just some of the assumptions underlying the rational model of planning and change implicitly adopted by many mainstream foundations and expressed in their grant-making processes.

A less rationalist, perhaps more realistic, view would be that organizations exist in complex and constantly changing social, political, economic, legal and organizational environments that impinge on, constrain, subvert, and support courses of action. Certainty is in short supply and workable social plans are usually those that provide a basis for departure rather than a blueprint for action. Knowledge, authority, compliance, resources and so on are often limited and, for that reason as well as others, linkages and networks are often crucial in getting things done. Organizations and structures may give the comfort of the mappable, but people – individuals – may matter more than structures, not least in their capacity to constantly adapt to new demands and obstacles and to make relationships (Hogwood and Gunn 1984; Leat 1999).

Inadequate – or Any – Theory of Change

Underlying many of the limitations above is lack of an adequate – or indeed any – theory of social change. Foundations say that they want to make a difference but often fail to think through what or who would have to change in order for that to happen, or how those people or institutions might be reached. For example, many foundations have aimed to address child poverty without making the link to either low wages in many predominantly female occupations or inadequacies of child-support payment systems.

Social change is complex and involves working on several fronts to build constituencies and pressures for change. Social change is also not entirely 'rational', and developing a theory or model for it should not be confused with the philanthropic version of conventional business plans. Achieving a theory of change involves pragmatism and opportunism, as our case studies demonstrate.

Failure to Follow Through

Foundations' lack of a theory of change has two other consequences. One is that many foundations are less effective than they might be because they fail to build on creativity to achieve innovation. They fail to understand the importance of dissemination and 'marketing' in getting new approaches adopted and embedded. The other is that they fail fully to appreciate the importance of relating to policy and policy-shapers and makers. An example of a foundation successfully doing this is the Joseph Rowntree Foundation's publication of widely disseminated but carefully targeted short Findings for each of its key projects. As part of a wider communication strategy to stimulate government and media debate, these significantly increased the level of attention to its work.

Failure to Relate to Policy

Although foundations sometimes (wrongly, in our opinion) cite legal restrictions as the reason for avoidance of involvement in policy issues, another reason may be lack of any realistic theory of social change. As a result of this, foundations often fail to realize that sustainable change happens only rarely without government involvement of some sort and at some level – whether as policy innovator, funder, implementer or champion. Our case studies provide various examples of the ways in which government involvement significantly increases the scope and sustainability of change.

Overly Focused on Money

The foundation world tends to rank its members by the size of their assets and income; money is also the currency that foundations give and by which they account for their activities (e.g., the size and number of grants given). Underlying this focus on money there are some complex assumptions about the power of money.

'The traditional dependence solely on grant-making in achieving foundation goals may be the single biggest liability in the field of philanthropy' (Prager 1999). The emphasis on grant-making affects everything a foundation does, perpetuating the imbalance of power and making it impossible to form meaningful partnerships, which are key to addressing complex social problems. To make a difference, foundations should act systematically to strategically deploy all available resources.

Grant-making – the transfer of financial resources from the foundation to other organizations – implicitly assumes that social problems can be solved directly or indirectly by money. Money is the root of all solutions, goes the thinking, and more money to make more grants makes foundations more effective. The assumption is that we know what needs to be done; money is all that is missing.

In reality, lack of solutions to problems is often related to lack of knowledge, ideas, or political will, rather than lack of money. Over-emphasis on the power of money may distract foundations from the difficult task of analysing what really is needed to achieve a sustainable difference. Lack of an articulated theory of social change, combined with a focus on money, is a potentially soporific combination lulling foundations into a happy acceptance of existing ways of working. Ironically, foundations possess, or potentially possess, important resources other than money.

Finding a Distinctive Role

Very different claims have been put forth about foundations, their very existence (Box 2.1, p. 29) and continued rationale (Box 2.2, p. 30). Analysts such as Odendahl (1990) have suggested that foundations may exist not only as a solution to a variety of social problems, but also as an option for the well-to-do rather than necessarily for all members of society. Foundations may not serve merely as socially legitimate tax shelters, but also as a means of averting criticism of and resentment towards unequal wealth in a democratic society; salving consciences (about being overly rich and about how the founder's wealth was made or acquired); achieving personal goals and interests; avoiding state intervention in problems in which the donor has an interest; and, crucially, doing all of this with the possibility of donor control. Arguably, what differentiates foundation formation from other charitable giving is that in practice (though not necessarily in law) the donor and his/her family and chosen associates retain control over what is done with the gift (Burkeman 1999; Odendahl 1990; 1979; Whitaker 1974). Similar points might be made about some corporate foundations.

Porter and Kramer (1999: 121–30) argue that foundations have a responsibility to achieve a social impact disproportionate to their spending, not least because some of the money they give away belongs to the taxpayer. They reach two conclusions: too few foundations work strategically 'to do better' to achieve this disproportionate

Box 2.1 Why Foundations?

Irrespective of their historical development as charitable institutions, what theoretical and empirical arguments can be made for and against their existence in the 21st century?

Claim: Foundations exist because they bring private money into play for public benefit and thereby provide additional options to state or market provisions. Specifically:

- *For founders*: as an institution, foundations respond to existing demand, and provide (actual and potential) philanthropists with a legal instrument for expressing and pursuing their philanthropic interests.

- *For government*: foundations provide additional resources (funds, expertise, direct services, and so on) that supplement government action, thereby achieving a more optimal use of both public and private funds.

- *For civil society*: foundations are an independent source of funding that helps civil society counterbalance the forces of markets and state, helping to prevent either from dominating and atomizing the rest of society.

Counterclaim: Foundations may have some useful features, but they are ultimately elitist, undemocratic, and basically irrelevant to modern society. The privileges they receive and reinforce may well surpass the wider benefits they create.

- *For founders*: foundations exist to provide a solution to the problems of the rich rather than the poor.

- *For government*: foundations interfere with democratic processes and suck wealth out of the nation's tax base; they represent a misallocation of public funds.

- *For civil society*: foundations continue to exist not because there is evidence that they do anything valuable or that they command widespread support, but because of ignorance, lack of political will and interest, and belief in foundations' myths about themselves.

Box 2.2. A World Without Foundations?

What would we lose if foundations were abolished? Would we reinvent them?

Claim: Foundations provide social benefits that outweigh their costs, and this value added would be lost if foundations were abolished or not encouraged through tax legislation.

- *For founders*: among the forms of philanthropic activity, the foundation has proved more beneficial and reliable for donors, trustees and beneficiaries than alternative forms, in particular 'unorganized', individual philanthropy.

- *For government*: foundations are doubly useful: they add to government activities where needed and politically expedient, and they can be used as tools of government policy.

- *For civil society*: foundations are the banks of civil society; they help fund innovative, risky projects that neither market nor state would support. A functioning civil society needs independent financial institutions.

Counterclaim: Foundations are an expensive way to allocate private funds for public benefit; rather than generating added value, they are a net cost to the taxpayer. Public policy should not encourage the creation of foundations, and existing foundations should be phased out.

- *For founders*: while foundations may have been useful instruments in the past, there are now more efficient and flexible options available for philanthropic activities.

- *For government*: foundations fall into the class of tax-inefficient means of achieving public benefits; their tax-exempt status seems difficult to justify unless they meet clearly specified public needs and conform to government programmes.

- *For civil society*: foundations are cultural leftovers of the industrial era, are continued expressions of old class systems, and are yet to become part of a modern society that is more mobile, open, and diverse.

impact; and foundations are a costly way of creating social benefit relative to taxation or direct individual giving. The delayed social benefit that results from
foundation endowments, when compared to the benefit arising from taxation and
direct giving, has to be put in the context of two additional sets of costs: administrative costs incurred by the foundations and costs to grantees in complying with
application and reporting processes. Taking all these factors into account, Porter and
Kramer (1999) conclude that foundations may be socially expensive and hence
inequitable ways of allocating private funds to public purposes.

The literature on foundations has identified a number of roles for foundations
(see Anheier and Toepler 1999; Prewitt 1999; Anheier and Daly 2006). 'Roles' are
understood as the normative expectations stakeholders have as to the purpose and
performance of foundations. As we will see, the roles cluster around certain
approaches. Before we address this issue, we introduce what these roles are, and
consider the evidence to suggest that foundations fulfil the expectations these
roles entail.

The Role of Foundations is to Redistribute Resources from Rich to Poor

The idea that the major role of foundations is to engage in the redistribution of
resources fits with the popular and historical image of helping the poor and needy.
This role also fits with many, especially 19th-century, philanthropists' descriptions of
the charity approach, and their motives of giving back and paying dues, and perhaps
betrays a moral uneasiness about the size of the divide between rich and poor.

Certainly, today many foundations deliberately adopt a policy of funding work
in especially disadvantaged communities, hoping in some way to equalize the
distribution of resources. Redistribution of resources is obviously an attractive
goal, for several reasons. One is that it helps to create a fairer society without
radical, social and economic upheaval. Another is that it is essential to the longer-
term sustainability of existing social and economic arrangements. In other words,
redistribution is a way of dealing with the damaging side-effects of a market
system.

But there are various problems with redistribution as a primary or sole justification for the existence of foundations. Perhaps the two most important
weaknesses in this approach are that:

- It is not clear that foundation giving overall is actually redistributive. Indeed,
  a large proportion of total foundation giving undoubtedly goes to support
  areas of interest and geographical areas that are very far from the needs and
  interests of most disadvantaged groups in society.

- Even if foundations did actually spend the bulk of their money in redistributive ways, it is not clear that the outcome would be as redistributive as, or

any more redistributive than, it would have been had foundation funds been taxed and spent by the state (Prewitt 1999). In other words, foundations would have to be highly redistributive relative to forgone tax revenue in order for this justification to be effective.

The Role of Foundations is to Promote Innovation

Promoting innovation in social perceptions, values, relationships, and ways of doing things has long been a role ascribed to foundations. Innovation is a goal pursued by foundations working in a wide range of areas in science, research, the arts, health, social welfare, and the environment.

The role of promoting innovation is attractive to foundations for several reasons. One is that it provides an apparently simple demarcation line between the role of government and that of foundations. Another is that, in the past, it has served as a way of restricting foundation involvement to manageable proportions. If foundations exist to support innovation, this enables them legitimately to engage only in short-term funding. Once something is no longer innovative, foundations may pull out with a clear conscience and move on to another piece of short-term support. The foundation has done its job. Picking up the ongoing longer-term bill is someone else's concern.

Another reason why supporting innovation is said to be especially suited to foundations is that their lack of accountability to constituents and customers means that they can run ahead of public opinion. They can take the risk of buying art or putting on performances the public may not initially like, they can fund research and experiments that may turn out to be a dead end, they can support work with drug users, paedophiles, asylum seekers, and other groups commanding less than total public sympathy. This ability to take risks has led recently to a currently fashionable view of foundations as social venture capitalists. This view has subsequently been developed by various writers, but it has also been challenged as a dangerous model, encouraging over-involvement, even interference, by grant-makers (see, for example, Letts *et al.* 1997; Sievers 1997).

But whether foundations succeed in promoting innovation is open to question. First, because foundations are reluctant to spend money building up and maintaining a sound knowledge base, it is not clear that foundations are actually capable of distinguishing truly innovative work from what is merely new or even 'repackaged' work. The failure of foundations to spend money on dissemination, and if necessary replication, means that money spent on innovation is sometimes just an expensive candle snuffed out too quickly. There is nothing efficient or socially effective about funding innovation unless processes are in place to learn and communicate positive and negative lessons to the wider society. Innovations are ultimately sustainable and valuable only if resources are available for development and maintenance, as we will discuss below. Foundations generally do not see this as their responsibility, and governments are increasingly unwilling to take on the funding of innovations initiated by foundations.

The Role of Foundations is to Promote Social, Policy and Practice Change

Closely related to innovation is the role of creating or promoting social change, which is frequently ascribed to foundations, not least by the foundations themselves (Prewitt 1999). Several somewhat different versions of the social-change role are ascribed to foundations. These include:

- promoting radical structural change (most commonly attributed to some US foundations at certain periods in history by their conservative critics);

- fostering recognition of new needs and 'giving voice';

- 'oak trees from acorns' – that is, funding small-scale, often local, projects from which it is hoped that larger, wider-scale activities will grow;

- changing the way in which we think about social issues and their solutions, and adding to the cultural and political menu of possible solutions;

- increasing participation and empowerment of people excluded from policy and practice solutions;

- demonstrating the feasibility of new ways of working;

- encouraging the exploration of new ideas and cultural forms.

The notion that foundations can or do promote social change has always had its critics. As one leading American practitioner and commentator wrote at the time of the congressional inquiry into US foundations:

> The great myth about foundations today is that they are firmly ensconced on the leading edge of social change, managed by far-sighted trustees and staff who make brilliantly daring decisions about the disposition of the funds over which they have stewardship. In this myth the funds are known as seed corn and venture capital thereby associating the foundation vicariously with two of the noblest traditions in American life, the agrarian and the entrepreneurial. But foundations in fact have a highly restricted capacity to influence social change. This is so because in most cases the funds at their disposal are too small to have sufficient leverage and because the very nature of fiduciary management and spending of trust funds makes for caution. Furthermore,

foundations may sense that the public is uneasy about having them play too influential a role in determining where the society is headed, and this awareness is inhibiting to them.

(Pifer 1984: 11)

Curiously, examples of foundations creating major social change, despite in some cases huge aggregate expenditure over many years, are hard to find. For example, despite the hundreds of thousands of pounds spent in recent years on racial justice by (mostly Quaker) foundations in the UK, elements of the institutional racism first identified as such by the Stephen Lawrence Inquiry remain. Clearly positive examples include Cadbury's funding of the Runnymede Trust, the Joseph Rowntree Charitable Trust's contribution to the signing of the Amsterdam Treaty, and, much further back, Carnegie's support for public libraries, or the success of the conservative political foundations in the United States as well as recipients of the Robert W. Scrivener Award for Creative Philanthropy, which we will review in Chapter 5.9.

Of course, one has to acknowledge the difficulty of pointing to the precise contributions that foundations have made to social change, and a greater research effort is clearly called for to examine the issue more fully. At the same time, a few swallows do not make a summer. Had foundations' roles been more than marginal in bringing about social change, specific examples would be easier to identify, the rule rather than the exception.

Related to the social change role is policy and practice change. Again, there are different versions or elements in this role:

- examining public policy (see, for example, Reeves 1969);

- shaping public opinion (see, for example, Arnove 1980; Roelofs 1984/5);

- developing social and other research regarding social ills and government policy (see, for example, Bulmer 1999);

- coping with government failure and adopting a longer view beyond the time frame of electoral cycles;

- promoting integrated planning and service provision that is related to real people;

- experiences and problems in overcoming departmental and professional divisions;

- providing a space for discussion and expression of values which fit neither government nor market logic (see, for example, Nielsen 1985).

US studies of foundation roles, especially in health-care reform, have shown how effective they may be in providing a basis for policy discussion. Foundations were viewed as credible actors, non-partisan in their approaches, and concerned with the public interest. They also got good marks for adequate levels of investment and timeliness of intervention in the policy process (Abramson and Spann 1998). But, as Abramson and Spann (1998, p. 10) point out, US foundations frequently failed fully to exploit these opportunities, and policymakers viewed foundation timidity and lack of adequate communications strategies and products as major constraints on their effectiveness in the policy arena.

The Role of Foundations is to Preserve Traditions and Cultures

At the same time, some foundations specifically play the role of preserving traditions, ideas, cultural artefacts (for example, the UK's National Trust or the Getty Trust's Preservation Institute in Los Angeles) and, more generally, the existing social order (see, for example, Fischer 1983). The social-change and preserving-tradition approaches to the role of foundations are obviously subject to the criticism above that in real life David rarely beats Goliath. Both roles – promoting change and preserving tradition – require recognition of three important factors.

First, the more effective foundations are in achieving or opposing change, the more likely they are to encounter strong public opposition from interests not served by those changes. Second, there is a view that foundations cannot operate on a scale that is transformative if they work alone. Without assistance from government and the market, foundation interventions are likely to be swamped by larger social, cultural, and economic forces. Third, how powerful foundations can be in promoting or resisting social change depends in part on the theory of social change in which one believes: do ideas 'drive' history, or are technological development, the power of social movements, market incentives, government interventions, or indeed moral exhortation the key factors?

The Role of Foundations is to Promote Pluralism

Promoting pluralism is the role many foundations ascribe to themselves, particularly in the United States, and commentators such as Prewitt (1999) see the promotion of pluralism as the most persuasive argument for the existence and legitimacy of foundations.[2] The promoting pluralism role takes various forms:

- promoting social experimentation and diversity in general;

- curbing the dominance of government in modern society (see Karl and Katz 1981), and serving as an antidote to state control of social, economic, cultural, and environmental policy (see, for example, Alchon 1985); and

- protecting dissent and civil liberties (Dowie 2001; McIlnay 1998; 1984; Ostrander 1993).

For example, Prewitt, in a speech at the Second International Foundation Symposium in Germany in 1999, suggested that foundations could fund the unusual or the unexpected because

> they are not beholden to the consensus-forcing demands placed on the public sector. In short, foundations can intensify the natural diversity of the nonprofit sector, and thereby contribute to pluralism. Here, then, is a justification for the foundation sector. Not redistribution, not efficiency, not even social change, though some amount of all those occur, but an ongoing and lasting contribution to the pluralism of practice and thought, and via that contribution a deep commitment to the principles of tolerance and openness that flow from pluralism (Prewitt 1999).

Note that this requires an acceptance of a lack of 'consensus-forcing demands', and the assumptions that foundations are pluralist in their funding (which evidence suggests they are not; see Vincent and Pharoah 2000) and that those they fund are likewise 'pluralist' (and, of course, that pluralism per se, rather than pluralism promoting the ends of which the speaker approves, is desirable).

Quoi faire?

What is behind the critique of foundations? Without foundations the world would undoubtedly be a different place: they have been responsible, at least in part, for a range of products and services ranging from art galleries to libraries to vaccines; and they have brought about policy changes of many kinds. Interestingly, many of the most enduring institutions pioneered by foundations came from the programmes of foundations that adopted something very close to what we call a creative approach. For example, the Peabody Education Fund, created in 1867, sought not merely to provide education but to launch a movement for public education in the US South. To achieve this it recruited a politically astute and well-networked board of trustees, mounted carefully targeted publicity campaigns 'always seeking to popularize a single animating idea: universal education for whites', used demonstration sites and matching grants to convince local school district leaders, and engaged in direct lobbying (Smith 2002).

Yet, as we suggested in the previous chapter, we find that current foundation models and roles are increasingly at odds with the world around philanthropy. Society's needs have changed, and new and different tools for addressing them

Table 2.1 Role Emphasis in Different Foundation Approaches

Role / Approaches	Charity and Service	Scientific Philanthropy	'New' Scientific Philanthropy
Redistribution	High	Low	Low
Innovation	Medium	High	High
Change Agent	Low	High	Medium
Pluralism	Low	Medium	Low
Preservation	Medium	Low	Low

have been developed, be they nonprofit organizations, private–public partnerships, corporate social responsibility, or devolved governments. The result of these changes has been that the conventional models of foundations no longer fit their purpose as well as they did in the past. The true potential of foundations remains unexploited, inviting criticism from across the political spectrum.

Table 2.1 presents the combination between approaches and roles for foundations. For the charity approach, the emphasis on redistribution combined with innovation and preservation fits less well the demands of fast-changing societies in which redistribution is less of a political issue, and in which taxation regimes are in place that have long made public-sector solutions to social needs possible. Their role as innovator and complement to governments, too, has been challenged on many grounds, as we have seen.

The scientific philanthropy approach, with an emphasis on change and innovation roles, faces a widening gap between potential and reality, with the planning ethos and mechanistic practice of grant-making often an obstacle to renewal and innovative ways of using philanthropic resources. In other words, the inertia that has built up in the philanthropic model over recent decades stands in the way of the very innovations and changes that foundations seek to achieve. Furthermore, without attention to dissemination and implementation (often a matter of political priorities and resource allocation) even the most innovative ideas may fail to have much impact.

Likewise, the new-scientific philanthropy approach suffers from its underlying business and managerial ethos, similar to the way in which the original scientific philanthropy suffers from misapplication of the scientific-planning method. Innovation and social change as goals do not easily fit the short-term managerialism of much of new-scientific philanthropy, when knowledge, long-term engagements, partnerships, working from different angles and communication are called for, demanding stamina as well as flexibility.

In sum, we suggest that current approaches do increasingly less justice to the way in which foundations can achieve their potential. To remedy this situation, we propose a new model, creative philanthropy, to reinvigorate the roles that we and others such as Prewitt (1999) see as key to modern foundations: innovator, change-agent and contributor to pluralism. The next chapter will take a closer look at two of the key concepts involved: creativity and innovation.

3 Creative philanthropy

A key element of our argument for a renewal of philanthropy so far has been that much of what foundations do could be done, and perhaps done equally well, by other nonprofit organizations, and even public agencies and businesses. We also suggest that other foundation-like forms such as donor-advised funds and community foundations could take on roles more conventional foundations play. Foundations should therefore concentrate on doing those things only they have the potential to do better than other institutions.

Foundations have, in an important sense, had it right all along. The only justification for independence from government and market accountability (as distinct from transparency) is their potential to be a source of innovation – and, we would add, creativity – that is unconstrained by short-term market forces and political–electoral considerations, and that in the aggregate contributes to greater pluralism. In so doing, creative philanthropy provides a space for alternative thinking, voices and practices. In encouraging constructive conversations about new approaches to old and new issues, creative foundations increase the problem-solving capacity of society and reinvigorate civic engagement and democracy.

Understanding Innovation and Creativity

Clearly, innovation and creativity become central elements of the renewal of foundations that we propose. Therefore, it is important to have a good understanding of what these terms involve, and how they are related, both conceptually and in practice. Generically, the term 'innovation' refers to a change process that rests on some idea, either new or perceived as new, that is applied to existing ways and means of doing things. 'Innovation is the generation, acceptance, and implementation of new ideas, processes, products or services' (Kanter 1983: 20). As we will see, this definition of innovation encompasses the rather different processes of generation, acceptance, implementation and diffusion of new approaches.

As a first step to a better understanding of innovation, we want to separate out the initial generation of an idea – creativity – from subsequent acceptance, implementation, and diffusion. The relationships between these stages are shown in Figure 3.1, which according to Rogers (2003), involve four main elements, to which we add creativity as the initial step. Specifically:

Creativity is the act of finding an approach to a solution of a perceived problem or need, and for generating or making possible some kind of innovation in response. An innovation is 'an idea, practice, or object that is perceived as new by an individual or other unit of adoption' (Rogers 2003: 12). Diffusion is a particular type of communication about a new idea, and the process in which an innovation is communicated through certain channels over time among the members of a social system (Rogers 2003). *Our argument is that foundations are uniquely situated to become major agents and sources of creativity and innovation, enhancing diffusion processes towards desired outcomes or objectives.*

Figure 3.1 summarizes our argument, which we will explore more in the balance of this chapter. The innovation process entails three consecutive components: initiation, implementation and diffusion. Initiation begins with agenda-setting and the recognition that a problem or issue is in need of innovation. Creativity implies finding both approaches to problem-solving and, ultimately, solutions to the perceived problem or issue. The implementation process contains refinement and further developments, and the diffusion process involves the rollout and routinization of the innovation.

Critical for innovation and diffusion patterns is the degree of similarity among communicators, i.e., between the actor in possession of a creative idea and the actor accepting, rejecting or modifying the implied innovation. Homophily is the degree to which two or more individuals who interact are similar in certain attributes, such as beliefs, education, socio-economic status etc. Sociological studies have shown that in free-choice situations, when individuals can interact with any one of a number of other individuals, the tendency is to select those who are similar. By contrast, heterophily is defined as the degree to which two or more individuals who interact are different in certain attributes.[1]

Clearly, homophilous communication processes yield diffusion patterns different from heterophilous ones. In the former, an innovation is more likely to remain within certain fields, groups or social systems, whereas in the latter, it is more likely to spread widely but also more 'thinly'. *We argue that foundations are uniquely situated to make possible both homophilous and heterophilous diffusion patterns by spanning boundaries, linking actors and convening constituencies that would otherwise be unconnected.*

Time is another element of diffusion, and involves (1) the innovation–decision process by which an individual passes from knowledge of an innovation through its adoption, modification or rejection; (2) the innovativeness of an individual or other units of adoption in terms of the relative earliness or lateness with which an innovation is considered; and (3) an innovation's rate of adoption in a system, usually measured as the number of members who adopt the innovation in a given time period. *We argue that foundations are uniquely situated to manage the time element of the*

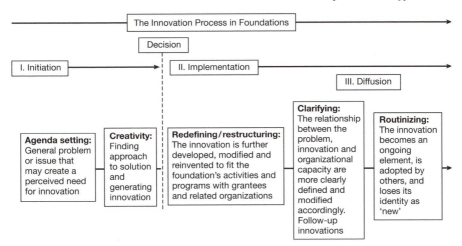

Figure 3.1 The Innovation Process
Source: adapted from Rogers 2003: 421

diffusion process; they can mobilize and target resources in the short term to help bring about innovations and their diffusion; and they can support and maintain diffusion processes, including modification and further adaptation of innovations, in the long term.

Finally, innovations take place and unfold in a wider social system, defined as a set of interrelated units that are engaged in joint problem-solving to accomplish a common goal. The units of social systems include individuals, informal groups, and formal organizations, and subsystems. Members co-operate at least to the extent of seeking to solve a common problem in order to reach a mutual goal, but they typically seek to maximize their own well-being in economic, political or social terms, and may even compete on many levels. *We argue that foundations are uniquely situated to take a systemic view with the overall public benefit in mind, and may ensure that innovations reach optimal entry and diffusion points, help otherwise neglected or disadvantaged constituencies, and affect wider policy change addressing issues of equity and social justice.*

Successful innovations typically show a distinctive combination of characteristics (see Kanter 1983). First, innovation involves a significant degree of *uncertainty* in the sense that both process and outcome may be difficult to predict. This means that foundations wanting to innovate would have to embrace uncertainty, be open about it, and not hide behind demands for short-term performance and output indicators or 'safe' funding practices to justify their legitimacy. Supporting innovation has to take the risk of failure into account. The important point is that foundations, unlike other institutions, can afford to take such risks.

Second, innovations are *knowledge-intensive*, since those close to the locus of innovation tend to possess most knowledge about the definition of the situation, the process involved, and the possible outcomes, at least at the initial stage.

Foundations wanting to be innovative would therefore have to build up, and build on, their existing knowledge, engage in active knowledge management, involve grants officers with first-hand knowledge more fully in executive decision-making, and seek more diverse board compositions to draw in different experiences and knowledge sets.

Third, innovations are typically *controversial*, as they tend to confront established interests and may take resources away from alternative uses. Thus, foundations wanting to innovate would not shy away from controversy and the public eye, but be open about what they fund and for what reasons. Innovation is not just a matter of new ideas and practices; innovation is also a political process in the sense that change requires challenging existing accepted policies and practices, whether at the level of government or of organizations.

Fourth, and finally, innovations tend to *reach across established boundaries* in organizations, fields or sectors. Again, foundations have a potential advantage here in that they are, in theory at least, critical boundary-spanners in modern society, sitting on the edge of an array of institutions, disciplines and professions. Foundations' independent resources mean that they can develop relationships with the powerful and the powerless, the rich and poor, and are free to mix disciplines and professions. Foundations can converse with everyone and be dependent on none.

Two additional results of research on innovation are worth mentioning. First, ever since Coleman's study of innovation in the late 1950s (Coleman *et al.* 1957), a persistent finding of innovation research has been that innovation and adaptation of innovative ideas and practices happens at the margins, not at the centre of the system under consideration. The centres of power and wealth in society are rarely the locus of innovation – be it in the field of technology, finance, culture or politics. More likely, innovations spring from individuals, groups, and organizations outside the mainstream, or at the crossroads of different systems. Thus to be innovative a foundation needs to remain outside the centre, rather than being too deeply embedded in one 'inner system'.

The second major finding of innovation research is that innovators are encouraged in situations or networks that involve significant overlaps among groups, cultures, and perspectives. Innovations happen not in isolation but at cultural, political, and social crossroads, and in situations that bring different and frequently contradictory elements together – in other words, the combination of homophilous and heterophilous network patterns mentioned above. For foundations to become innovators, therefore, they must actively seek out dissenting voices and create opportunities for bringing them together.

Against these somewhat abstract considerations, and the significant potential we see in foundations as agents of innovation, what are some of the challenges in common philanthropic practices? First, generating new ideas, services and so on involves very different tasks, and often different environmental conditions, from getting those ideas accepted and implemented. Indeed, foundations appear to be generally more comfortable with the notion of generating new ideas than with that of getting them implemented and accepted on any scale, with all that that entails. As we have suggested above, and will elaborate on later, foundations seem to prefer to run relay races, handing over the baton to someone else (who may or may not be in place and ready).

The distinction between creativity and innovation is useful because it enables us to ask questions about creative ideas that fail to become accepted and implemented, that is, they fail to become innovations. Yet the potential gap between creativity and innovation is often not fully understood in the world of foundations, the assumption being that creativity automatically leads to innovation: 'if you build a better mousetrap the world will beat a path to your door'. This has been the assumption on which many foundations appear to have worked: a 'pilot' or 'demonstration' project will, by some mysterious process of osmosis, be accepted, implemented, spread and sustained by others. In reality, as experience in a number of fields demonstrates, there is a vast gap between creativity and innovation in terms of time, resources, talents and so on. The people we often think of as having created something, are often not its creators but its innovators. Clearly, for example, Ray Kroc did not create the original McDonald's hamburger, but he was the architect of its establishment and spread.

Creativity

Creativity is making new combinations, seeing new links between existing elements, making up new mixes, and so on. According to Landry (2000), creativity requires resourcefulness and problem-solving capability based on thinking in an open-minded way. Creativity is a frame of mind that questions rather than criticizes, which asks 'why is this so?' and is not content to accept the answer: 'it has always been like this'. Creativity challenges not only things seen as a problem but also things currently thought of as adequate. 'Creative people and institutions are willing to rewrite procedures or principles and so to imagine future scenarios, conditions, inventions, applications, adaptations and processes. They look for threads among the seemingly disparate, bringing together unthought-of combinations that solve a problem. Most important, perhaps, is the capacity to look at situations in an integrated, holistic way, laterally and flexibly' (Landry 2000: 13).

Creativity (and thus innovations) may involve radical breakthroughs, significant procedural modifications, minor improvement, or 'architectural' changes. For example, the development and marketing of small personal computers has transformed the home as well as the way we work. Not all creativity is technical in nature; some is primarily about new ways of seeing issues, conceptualizing phenomena, and framing problems. These paradigmatic shifts may occur less frequently than procedural and programmatic creativity and innovations, but they tend to lead to some of the most profound changes. For example, the realization in the 19th century that many diseases were spread by poor living conditions led to the rise of public-health programmes. Similarly, Freud, Einstein, Picasso and Stravinsky all radically changed the thinking of their respective domains (Gardner 1993).

In most cases, however, creativity and innovation are not 'pure'; it is frequently the importation and modification of ideas from different circumstances, or the pursuit of analogous problem-solving techniques from quite different fields and contexts, that lead to creativity, and may then lead ultimately to innovations. This quality is related to heterophily and to being at the crossroads rather than inside an homophilous centre. For example, venture philanthropy imports the idea, and its analogous investment approach, from the field of finance into the field of philanthropy; similarly, the routine processing of large numbers of grant applications according to set and standardized assessment criteria reflects the procurement process of government contracting.

Sources of Creativity

Landry (2000: Ch. 1) identifies seven characteristics of a creative milieu:

- a level of original and deep knowledge coupled with a ready supply of skills, competence, and people who have the need and the capacity to communicate with each other;

- a sound financial basis, adequate room to allow for experimentation without tight regulation;

- an imbalance between the perceived needs of decision-makers, business people, artists, scientists, and social critics, and the actual opportunities available to them;

- the capacity to deal with complexity and uncertainty about future changes in cultural, scientific, and technological fields;

- good possibilities for informal and spontaneous communication internally and externally; an environment catering for diversity and variety;

- a multi-disciplinary and dynamically synergistic environment that especially links developments in the sciences and in the arts, and

- structural instability.

We suggest that some of these milieu characteristics can be identified in creative foundations, as the case studies in Chapter 5 will illustrate. First, however, we need to look at the relationship between creativity and innovation.

From Creativity to Innovation

Not all creative 'products' become innovations, in the sense that they fail to be accepted and implemented on any scale. Kao (1991) uses the term 'entrepreneurship' to refer to the process of making things happen and pushing for their implementation (what we are calling innovation-diffusion processes, following Rogers 2003), and distinguishes this from creativity as such. The two do not necessarily go together: an organization may be high on creative capacity but low on entrepreneurial capacity, and vice versa. As shown in Table 3.1, Kao identifies four types of organization.

Table 3:2 adapts Kao's typology to foundations. We suggest that many foundations adopting a conventional approach might fit into Type IV – low on both creative and entrepreneurial capacity; some such foundations might fit Type II – high on creative capacity but low on entrepreneurial capacity, generating new approaches but then leaving to (unspecified) others the responsibility for doing something with those approaches.

Yet other foundations may be of Type III – good at getting their approaches implemented but basically producing more of the same. We are interested in those foundations of Type I – organizations that are high on creative capacity and the capacity to get those creative approaches implemented and out into the mainstream, changing the way people and organizations think and work in addressing deep-rooted problems. These are the foundations that seek to cope with uncertainty and controversy; that promote, gather, disseminate, and develop knowledge; that reach across established disciplinary, organizational, and sectoral boundaries; and that allow room for experimentation. These foundations address both the how and the what.

Table 3.1 Entrepreneurial capacity and creative capacity

	Entrepreneurial Capacity	
	High	*Low*
Creative Capacity		
High	**Type I** Creative industries	**Type II** Think-tanks
Low	**Type III** Fast-food franchiser	**Type IV** Mature bureaucracy

Source: Adapted from Kao 1991, p. 18

Table 3.2 Foundation types

	Entrepreneurial Capacity	
	High	*Low*
Creative Capacity		
High	**Type I** Creative foundation	**Type II** Relay philanthropy
Low	**Type III** Ad hoc new -scientific philanthropy	**Type IV** Traditional service philanthropy

Obstacles to Creativity and Innovation in Foundations

Yet to what extent do foundations currently display such qualities of creativity? Do they possess 'original and deep knowledge' in Landry's sense, and do they communicate to both homophilous and heterophilous audiences, or are they content to talk only to the converted, or perhaps to assume that speaking, being heard and being listened to are one and the same? Are they multi-disciplinary organizations?

Creativity requires not just a creative milieu but also the triggers that can kickstart creative processes. One problem is that many of the triggers of creativity in other types of organizations do not apply to endowed, resource-independent foundations. Crucially, the pressures of necessity and scarcity, inescapable for many organizations, are pretty much escapable for foundations. As resource-independent organizations existing in perpetuity, foundations are immune to obsolescence, further compounded by the fact that their 'customers' (grant applicants) are very unlikely to tell them that their purposes are obsolescent.

Similarly, creative triggers of ambition, aspiration, and competition do not apply to foundations in any obvious way. Foundations rarely openly compete with each other (except perhaps in size of assets), and without competition the motives of ambition and aspiration are less pressing. Again, political change, criticism, crisis, and structural instability – important triggers for creativity in other organizations – are often seen as 'ills' that foundations rarely suffer. Interestingly, however, when foundations do experience either significant reduction or increase in income, this sometimes provides one trigger for creative thinking about programmes.

Other triggers of creativity, such as discovery, luck, participation, idea gathering, and learning from others, are not fully exploited by many foundations because learning and networking are not part of their culture. We have argued elsewhere (Anheier and Leat 2002) that there are some more fundamental structural characteristics of foundations that may present obstacles to creativity in them.

The first challenge is the tension between the will of the donor, as specified in the original deed, and the need for change, to adjust the vision and operation of the foundation to changing circumstances. Clearly, the more precise the stipulations of the deed and the more finely objectives, modes of operation, and recipients are specified, the more difficult it is to be creative and innovative over time. Conversely, a deed that leaves the mission and objectives of a foundation wide open and with little guidance can easily lead to 'lost' institutions over time.

Some foundations are, or were, restricted in purpose. Other foundations have restricted purposes but considerable freedom of interpretation. The various foundations created by Joseph Rowntree are good examples here. The foundations are restricted to addressing the causes of social problems, but Joseph Rowntree had the foresight explicitly to give his future trustees the freedom to interpret this in ways relevant to contemporary perceptions.

The very decision to establish a foundation as charitable can be highly restrictive. Band Aid, and more recently the allocation of charitable funds raised after 11 September 2001, are good examples here. But in some cases successful innovation may be restricted less by what the law says and more by what boards think the restrictions of the law are.

Second, in most organizations it is external economic or political pressures that act as the driving forces behind creativity and innovation. Yet foundations are largely shielded from such corrective and creative influences. They have no owners or electorates with clear incentives to monitor performance or, more fundamentally, the fit between mission and programme activities. Staff may try to address these issues, but they are, legally, merely agents of the board. As a result, the creative character of a foundation will largely depend of the board of trustees. The board, however, is bound by the deed and the rules of the regulatory framework, and cannot act with the same flexibility and managerial repertoire as corporate boards. In fact, foundation boards have typically much less flexibility than the trustees of other nonprofit organizations. But it is also the case that some foundations do achieve significant innovation. Why and how do they do so? This is one of the questions explored in the case studies that follow.

But whatever the incentives and obstacles to creativity in foundations, there is another issue: when foundations are creative, do they take the next step to innovation?

Building on Creativity

Some foundations are creative, but relatively few build on creativity to produce effective innovation. In other words, few engage in Rogers's (2003) innovation-diffusion process outlined above. Perhaps the major reason why foundations fail to build on creativity to produce innovation is their assumption that innovation is no more than a 'good idea' that will be taken up by others. But grant-making for new ideas or new ways of doing things is the first step, not the last. In reality, creative projects have to be deliberately, slowly, strategically and opportunistically – often painfully – embedded in wider structures and processes. In the past, others may indeed have taken forward creative ideas; in the current political environment and the crowded market of competing communication and resource allocation, this cannot be assumed.

Moving from creativity to innovation may be especially challenging for foundations. Much of the literature on moving from creativity to innovation is based on the example of business organizations. Some of this literature focuses on the processes and the challenges of managing change across divisions or departments within business firms. Without underplaying the complexity and difficulty of this in many cases, it is also true that managers within an organization have the power, and a variety of sticks and carrots, to encourage acceptance of change. Foundations are, in this respect, in a different position.

Because foundations do not have the financial resources or the democratic mandate to innovate on any scale, they are always dependent on their ability to influence others: to 'sell' their wares in the marketplace of ideas and, often, in the public policy marketplace. Indeed, Orosz (2000: 211) writes of the 'make or break potential of public policy to leverage or deflate project impact'. While acceptance in the public-policy arena is not the only way of being innovative, it can be crucially important in ensuring the sustainability of innovations.

In selling their wares in the policy marketplace foundations are in a similar position to corporate managers attempting to innovate outside the organization in the market – and, as illustrated below, foundations have something to learn from such managers. But again there is a difference. Businesses arguably have a wider range of culturally legitimate tools at their disposal than do foundations. For example, businesses may buy television advertising and other means of influence; such tools are only rarely seen as acceptable by foundations.

So there are a range of factors, including the will of the donor, the lack of economic and political pressures, the narrowness of the deed, the regulatory framework, and foundations' self-imposed limitations, that may act as constraints on foundations' flexibility to change, and to be creative and innovative. But there are at least two problems with this argument. First, some foundations (perhaps a minority) have a proud history of creativity and innovation. Second, our research demonstrates, and the following vignettes and case studies illustrate, that creative foundations exist today. What is different about these foundations? We will explore this question in the next chapters.

Part II

In Search of Creative Philanthropy

4   Vignettes of creative philanthropy

Our initial approach to studying creative philanthropy in action was necessarily exploratory, not least because there was no readily identifiable population of creative foundations, programmes and similar sets of activities from which to select some form of a representative sample. What is more, before selecting samples of creative philanthropy, it seemed necessary to explore a wider range of examples in order to sharpen our understanding of what constitutes creative philanthropy; how it differs from more conventional forms; and by what characteristics and indicators it can be identified in action.

In our selection of foundations and programmes for further exploration in the United States, the UK and Australia, we began by conducting a review of annual reports and other printed information as well as material available on foundation websites. We supplemented this trawl with information derived from consultation with experts and observers of the foundation field (such as the National Center for Responsive Philanthropy), relevant publications (such as *Foundation News* and the *Chronicle of Philanthropy*), announcements (such as the Robert W. Scrivener Award for Creative Grantmaking), and from our own knowledge of the field (Anheier and Daly 2006; Anheier and Leat 2002).

In many of the cases we explored, a foundation displayed only some of the characteristics of creativity and the creative milieu that we were looking for. For example, in some instances, philanthropic activities, while being very knowledge-intensive and reaching across boundaries, involved no or little risk and were largely uncontroversial. In other cases, the programmes displaying the characteristics of creative philanthropy constituted only a small proportion of the foundation's overall work. For the aim at hand – to explore creative philanthropy more fully – we decided to select only those foundations that displayed most of the characteristics of creative philanthropy, and did so in a significant proportion of their programme activities. By the same token, we by no means intended to dismiss those many foundations and programmes we did not select; rather, we were primarily interested in a full expression of creative philanthropy, and less so in its less-developed forms and facets.

In the UK and Australia, where foundations are less numerous, this approach provided us with a relatively manageable short-list of foundations and programmes for further study. In the much larger foundation world of the United States, we had a longer list, which would have been beyond our resources to include in the current study. Given our purpose of exploring the characteristics of creative philanthropy, it was important to ensure some variety in the foundations and programmes studied. For example, while we obviously sought to examine the larger foundations – the famous 'brand names' of philanthropy – we also wanted to include those with smaller endowments in order to illustrate and explore the creative opportunities open to foundations with limited resources.

Moreover, we also wanted to cover 'well-established' as well as 'newer' foundations to explore the impacts of organizational age, the period of creation (for instance, foundations established during the Depression, in the 1950s, after the 1990s and so on), organizational development, learning and experiences on creative philanthropy. Lastly, we intended to include a variety of fields in which foundations operate, such as education, public affairs, arts and culture, and human services. Thus, in all three countries, we narrowed our short-list by selecting a variety of foundations in terms of endowment size and revenue, age, and fields of primary interest.

We should stress that such a sample frame is based on purposive rather than statistical sampling, and our approach was guided by what qualitative methodologists call 'analytic generalization', based on in-depth case studies and multiple data sources (Yin 1989) rather than 'empirical generalizations' based on random sampling. Nonetheless, and despite the care we have taken in identifying creative foundations and programmes, the sampling method used here has a distinct disadvantage: in the final analysis, it is impossible to guard against sampling bias, and no statistical estimation procedures are of assistance in making a case for the representativeness and generalizability of our findings.

Having identified foundations and programmes fitting most of our criteria for creative philanthropy in a significant range of their activities, we began by constructing a series of vignettes. These vignettes are short portraits that explore different facets of creative philanthropy. Constructed from published material, annual reports, articles by or about the foundations as well as published interviews and speeches, our primary aim in the vignettes was to illustrate the range, rationales and work of creative philanthropy. The vignettes also provided a useful source for the formulation of hypotheses that we could then explore further in the more detailed case studies presented in the following chapters.

The Vignettes

Ms. Foundation for Women

Given that only 6.4 per cent of all foundation funding is specifically reserved for women and girls, the very existence of the Ms. Foundation for Women illustrates the potential role of foundations in changing agendas.[1] The foundation was started in 1972, and its annual budget has increased over the last 17 years from $400,000 to $8.6 million, with a $16 million endowment. This foundation illustrates a creative approach to changing public perceptions and cultural patterns – for instance, in regard to young women and the workplace – as well as addressing issues and needs that other institutions neglect, such as women and HIV/AIDS.

The Ms. Foundation for Women created *Take Our Daughters to Work Day*, which has become a US institution. The programme arose out of research showing that girls' early success and confidence diminishes in their teens as their bodies develop and come to be seen by the girls themselves as a source of weakness and unwanted attention. The aims of the programme were to highlight the issues, to give girls attention for their potential rather than their bodies, and to connect girls with adults in the workplace. The Ms. Foundation established the Collaborative Fund for Women's Economic Development, which won the 1999 Presidential Award for Excellence in Micro Enterprise Development. It also created the Reproductive Rights Coalition Fund, and the Women and AIDS Fund, the only US programme then identifying and supporting community-based organizations run by and for women living with HIV/AIDS. In 2002 the Foundation won the Robert W. Scrivener Award for Creative Grantmaking.

New York Foundation

The New York Foundation, established in 1909, provides a somewhat different illustration of the role of foundations in changing agendas: the use of litigation by philanthropy to challenge the status quo.[2] The New York Foundation had for many years supported civil legal-aid programmes. From the late 1990s, and in the aftermath of the Clinton Welfare Reforms, such programmes increased within the overall grants portfolio, with a growing number of grants related to changes in welfare policy in New York City. But the Foundation realized that grants for organization and advocacy were not going to be enough to protect the rights of New York's most disenfranchised. This led to a cluster of project grants to legal-aid organizations that offered representation, class-action suits and challenges to welfare policies and programmes. From June 2002 onward, these grant opportunities were specifically mentioned in the Foundation's funding guidelines.

In 2001 the New York City administration refused to allow welfare advocates to enter city-run welfare centres. The foundation made a grant to the Brennan Center for Justice at NYU School of Law for a civil lawsuit attempting to gain access. This was followed by a grant to South Brooklyn Legal Services (SBLS), which had discovered that the city was routinely underpaying family day-care workers by calculating payments on a monthly rather than daily basis. SBLS could not take this matter up because it receives Legal Services Corporation (LSC) funds, one of the conditions of which is that it cannot initiate advocacy on any issue, or advertise, or represent many categories of immigrants, or bring class-action suits, even if the organization is doing so with private money. The foundation saw these LSC requirements as interfering with foundations' right to allocate money as they see fit. The board of the New York Foundation agreed to become a plaintiff in Dobbins *vs*. Legal Services Corporation to challenge the LSC restrictions.[3]

Fannie Mae Foundation

In the United States, few issues are as politicized as housing, and few issues are as relevant to people's economic and social well-being.[4] For a long time, the Fannie Mae Foundation has been devoted to building healthy communities and creating affordable housing opportunities throughout the country. Among other programmes, it has focused on the problems generated by predatory lending, to address which it has funded a consumer guide (*Borrowing Basics: What You Don't Know Can Hurt You*) and a personal finance curriculum tailored to Native American communities.

Yet at its 20th anniversary celebration in 2000, the foundation announced a new strategic plan for the next five years building on the recognition that 'one of the Fannie Mae Foundation's most valuable assets is the extensive store of information we have to share'. This led to the development of KnowledgePlex. The goal of KnowledgePlex is to promote innovation, enhance best practice and strengthen the analysis and implementation of projects that have an impact in the field of housing. The KnowledgePlex website for policy makers, practitioners, scholars, non-profits and researchers provides a one-stop forum for gathering and sharing information and practice news on current housing issues, national housing policy debates, and the latest in housing research. Seeking information from other knowledge leaders, the aim is to make Knowledge Plex a truly collaborative partnership and comprehensive resource. KnowledgePlex hosts online communities of interest and practice with live, moderated chats and threaded discussions on various housing topics. Community-of-interest members can retrieve items from the KnowledgePlex library and submit items for discussion.

The foundation works closely with university research centres, and emphasizes the importance of dissemination and debate by publishing newsletters, scholarly journals, research reports and other publications. It has sponsored or co-sponsored numerous conferences of leaders, academics, policy-makers and practitioners, in the hope that the 'synergistic effect of these exchanges will add to the overall knowledge and inspire the continuing efforts' to ensure affordable housing for all citizens. In short, the Fanny Mae Foundation is a good illustration of philanthropy working in a knowledge-intensive field by trying to provide access, involving and linking diverse networks, and identifying good and bad lending practices and housing policies.

Paul Robeson Fund for Independent Media

The Paul Robeson Fund for Independent Media illustrates that it does not take millions of dollars to engage in creative philanthropy: in 2001, the fund gave away a total of $246,000.[5] The Fund aims to cultivate a new wave of media activism by encouraging established as well as emerging media producers to use their talents and creativity to support social issues. It funds pre-production, production and distribution of films, videos and radio programmes on social issues. Local, state, national or international organizations, as well as individual media producers, may submit projects. The aim is to support projects that address critical social and political issues, and combine intellectual clarity with a creative use of the medium for progressive social change.

Tides Foundation

The Tides Foundation is a collaborative group of donors who offer a full range of programme services, similar to those of a community foundation.[6] Its mission is to work towards a more just, peaceful and sustainable world. Donor testimonies suggest that they are drawn to Tides by both its emphasis on social change, and its democratic reputation in the field. The case of the Tides Foundation illustrates creative philanthropy as a multi-tiered and long-term investment in moving social issues forward, and in ways that involve coalition-building among otherwise unconnected actors and constituencies. It also shows that creative philanthropy is not limited to the actions of individual donors but can also be achieved through collective action, including community foundations. Examples of creative philanthropy at the Tides Foundation include:

Bridging the Economic Divide

Recognizing the widening economic disparity of the 1990s amid growing prosperity, the Tides Foundation launched a programme on 'Bridging the Economic Divide' in 2000, focusing funding on living-wage campaigns and economic-justice coalitions. The programme involves long-term donor investment, supporting organizing campaigns, strengthening leadership among and involvement of those affected by poverty, and building strategic alliances among community, labour and faith-based groups.

One specific grant to Direct Action for Rights and Equality, DARE Rhode Island, illustrates the objectives and operations of the programme. Founded in 1986, with a membership of 700 families, DARE led a successful campaign to make Rhode Island the first state to provide health insurance to family home day-care providers. In Providence, RI, DARE's Jobs with Dignity campaign aimed to improve wages and working conditions of low-income jobs either based on, or linked to, municipal finance and contracts. DARE fought successfully to achieve an ordinance requiring such jobs to provide living wages with benefits: the ordinance applies to all employers receiving city contracts of more than $25,000, or receiving city subsidies over $100,000, or to non-profits who contract with the city of Providence and employ a chief executive officer with a salary over five times that of the lowest-paid worker.

Native Communities Initiatives

The Tides Foundation has a history of working with Native-American communities for social, economic and environmental justice. It partnered with Honor the Earth, a national Native-American-led grant-making and policy advocacy organization, to develop the Native Communities Initiative, focusing on grassroots responses to the nation's dependence on fossil fuels and nuclear energy and proposing alternatives for sustainable development.

Tides Death Penalty Mobilization Fund

To support the anti-death penalty movement the Tides Foundation launched the Tides Death Penalty Mobilization Fund. The fund has two grant-making programmes: monthly 'rapid response grants', which provide short-term funding for concrete projects and usually involve coalition-building and collaboration at local, regional and national levels; and larger 'State Strategy' grants to support growth of state-wide activist organizations that work towards a moratorium on the death penalty and, ultimately, its abolition.

The California Community Clinics Initiative

This initiative provides up-to-date techniques for strengthening the internal operations and information systems of community clinics. It also tries to link community clinics with other health-care and social-service providers and associations to promote integration, sharing of resources and information, and to create opportunities for innovation to impact health-care policy.

The George Williams Fund

This fund at the Tides Foundation, and the Funding Collaborative on Drug Policy Reform, have supported, among others, the Harm Reduction Coalition to provide an alternative model for dealing with the drug crisis. Aiming to reduce the negative consequences of drug use, including promoting safer use, managed use and abstinence. Via workshops aimed at service providers and the general public, the coalition provides an alternative to the conventional approaches of criminal law enforcement and incarceration.

Michigan Partnership to Prevent Gun Violence

Another example of Tides Foundation support is the Michigan Partnership to Prevent Gun Violence. This is a collaboration of law, medical and public health personnel in a concerted inter-professional effort to plan and implement public policies aimed at preventing gun violence.

Ford Foundation

The Ford Foundation, one of the largest foundations in the world, works in three major programme areas: 'Asset-building and community development', 'Peace and social justice', and 'Education, media, arts and culture', now redesignated as 'Knowledge, creativity and freedom'.[7] The following vignettes and the statement about the role of social justice in Ford's grant-making in chapter 6 (Box 6.1) illustrate that creative philanthropy can well flourish within large, professional foundations that otherwise, encouraged by bureaucratic inertia, might too easily shy away from acting quickly and taking risks.

As part of the programme 'Education, media, arts and culture', the Ford Foundation funded *Rethinking Schools*, a newspaper based in Milwaukee, WI, focusing on education reform. In the wake of 11 September 2001, *Rethinking Schools* produced a report titled *War, Terrorism and America's Classroom*, which offered views, reflections and expert analyses from scholars, journalists, poets, activists and representatives of policy groups not often found in the mainstream press. The project was based on the view that 'education must be about developing the skills and disposition to question the official story, to view with scepticism the stark us-against-them (or us good, them bad) portrait of the world' (*Rethinking Schools* 2001, p. 2). The report offered educators teaching suggestions, writing activities and role-playing exercises to help them lead their students in addressing the emotionally and politically complex issues surrounding 11 September. Articles ask readers to face hard questions about all of the events leading up to 11 September. 'In doing so the report reminds us that democracy depends on the free exchange of ideas' (*Rethinking Schools* 2001, p. 2). Thirty thousand copies were distributed to middle- and high-school teachers.

Emphasis on creating democracy underlies much of the foundation's work in this and other fields. Janice Petrovich, director of the Ford Foundation's Education, Knowledge and Religion Unit, writes of 'the Ford Foundation's ultimate goal in the field of education and scholarship, namely to create conditions for vibrant and equitable democratic societies. To advance this broad objective, the foundation seeks to foster a well-educated citizenry capable of holding public institutions accountable for the common good.'

'One strategy for making education more equitable and effective entails building constituencies for reforms. To that end, the foundation seeks to strengthen the relationship between schools and the communities they serve and to promote public dialogue about the options at hand' (*Rethinking Schools* 2001, p. 8). One example of this approach is its funding of the movement to revitalize the Oyster Elementary school in Washington, DC. In 1971 the foundation started funding the school's innovative approach to bilingual education; beginning in 1995, it supported a group of parents who had found a novel way to finance a new school building from collaborative sources. This group later contributed plans to renovate all of the district's public schools and became a national resource for civic leaders working to generate public will and capacity to improve urban school facilities.

The Minneapolis Foundation

Founded in 1915, the Minneapolis Foundation is one of the oldest community foundations in the United States. With assets of $543 million in 2001, the foundation awarded $5.4 million in unrestricted grants to organizations in key priority areas: well-being of children, youth and families; educational achievement; affordable housing and accessibility; and regional economic growth.[8] The case of the Minneapolis Foundation illustrates that community foundations are potentially well situated to engage in creative philanthropy.

The foundation describes its mission as 'addressing underlying issues and effecting long-term change to improve the lives of people in our community' (Minneapolis Foundation 2002: 12). Its core business is seen as 'becoming a comprehensive center of giving that would be a central source of philanthropic knowledge and a catalyst for community change'. 'To be effective in addressing these issues, the Foundation has increasingly partnered with businesses, nonprofits and government to support innovative nonprofit programs as well as efforts to inform the public and influence public policy decision making' (p. 2).

The foundation's funding guidelines state: 'We prefer to award grants that:

- Pursue public policy change to solve critical needs and increase opportunities

- Address structural causes behind key issues

- Lead to long term sustainable solutions

- Build on community strengths, including cultural, racial and ethnic diversity

- Use broad-based, cooperative and collaborative approaches

- Involve key constituents in the development and implementation of activities

- Incorporate clear methods to measure and report impact' (Minneapolis Foundation 2002: 12).

In the 1990s, after many years of grant-making to local communities, the foundation realized two trends: first, the population in the Minneapolis metropolitan region was becoming more ethnically diverse; second, lack of affordable housing was coming to a crisis point and affected broad segments of diverse communities. The foundation saw in affordable housing the basis for long-term social and economic stability for the city and the region. At the same time, while many agencies were addressing the housing problem, they failed to achieve the momentum necessary to influence public awareness, let alone policy-making. In response, in 1999 the foundation issued a request for proposals (RFP) for co-ordinated efforts to build state-wide awareness and support for affordable housing. This led to a $250,000 grant for the creation of Housing Minnesota, a coalition of 75 groups that decided to work together on educating the public and to spur legislative change.

A public information campaign was mounted to change public perceptions and highlight the fact that in a booming economy thousands of working Minnesotans were unable to afford basic housing. A 'Let's Fix This' information campaign launched in 2001 included prime-time television slots, newspaper and magazine advertisements and articles, appearances on radio and television public-affairs programmes, plus thousands of educational brochures (the latter with the Target Corporation). The public responded and volunteer agencies were enlisted to help direct people to ways in which they could contribute time and resources. Citizens were encouraged to call and write to elected officials to promote changes in public policy, and were directed to the website to learn more about the issues. Donor advisors and funders were invited to meet with housing experts and advocacy and service organizations to explain ways to help. Moreover, the foundation hosted an annual exhibition of paintings, photographs and sculptures, entitled 'Home Beckons Us'.

Through community action grants and participation of funding partners, the foundation has granted more than $1.1 million towards affordable housing. In 2001 it brought politicians together with a diverse group of community and civic leaders to examine the problems and explore solutions at a conference titled 'Troubled Waters: Growing Up Homeless in Minnesota'. The 550 people attending also included Minnesota's state governor, who spoke on the topic of homelessness and encouraged legislation.

McKnight Foundation

Winner of the 2002 Paul Ylvisaker Award for Public Policy Engagement, the McKnight Foundation believes that public policy change is built on direct service.[9] Since 1997, it has spent $27 million on the Welfare to Work Initiative with the goal of helping welfare reform succeed in Minnesota by expanding job placement to skill training and career laddering, helping families obtain and maintain employment. The McKnight Foundation shows creative philanthropy in action as a bridge and coalition builder in addressing pressing, complex social issues.

Federal and state reforms require welfare recipients to find jobs in five years. Rather than adopting the individualistic government approach, McKnight saw the problem in more systemic ways as a collective community issue. Via 22 cross-sector partnerships, McKnight's financial support persuaded public and private agencies to assume collective responsibility for making welfare-to-work transitions successful. The result of the initiative was a $53 million grant by the state of Minnesota for work modelled on the McKnight programme, and apparently lasting change in the way policy-makers and practitioners think and organize the welfare-to-work transition.

McKnight's key strategies to link partnerships to public policy include:

- Convening state-wide conferences and gatherings with national experts and state policy-makers

- Establishing websites as clearing houses of information about welfare reform and issuing newsletters regarding partnership activities

- Building capacity of community leaders to affect policy, and encouraging partnerships to leverage resources to sustain activities beyond McKnight Foundation support

- Recognizing the human dimension of policy work via, for example, awards to individual welfare recipients who exemplify qualities for successful welfare-to-work transition; mounting extensive press coverage to remind policy-makers of the human dimension

- Shaping an informed voice to educate policy-makers by enlisting independent evaluations of partnership work, conducting site visits, and briefing state legislators individually to share preliminary findings about best options for welfare reform. (*Foundation News and Commentary*, May/June 2002, p. 19)

BBC World Service Trust

While the Minnesota Foundation and the McKnight Foundation address local and regional problems, the BBC World Service Trust operates internationally with the aim of 'promot[ing] development through the innovative use of the media'.[10] The vignette shows the use of creative philanthropy in a developing-country context, and illustrates the skilful transfer of knowledge to build local media infrastructures.

The trust was set up in October 1999 as an independent charity within the BBC World Service, which broadcasts all over the world. In 2002, it had income of £5.1 million from a variety of sources, including other foundations and UN agencies, UK government departments and the general public. It aims 'to reduce poverty through the innovative use of the media in developing countries and countries in transition and to help build media expertise within those countries' (www.bbc.co.uk/world-service/trust). The Trust is a UK-registered charity with a board of trustees comprising experts with backgrounds in business, international development and the media, and representatives of a number of divisions within the BBC itself.

The trust has produced a series of groundbreaking and thought-provoking projects in many of the world's poorest countries: it has helped develop the capacity of local and national media, supported building civil society, provided training in media skills, and assisted in developing health and educational campaigns. The trust sees its key resources as follows: 'Through the World Service, the Trust has access to an unparalleled resource to provide trusted information to millions of people around the world'. Its work 'focuses on four areas in which our unique attributes can be used to the greatest effect' (www.bbc.co.uk/worldservice/trust). Specifically:

Social Development – Democratizing Debate

The trust makes wide-ranging programmes for audiences in developing societies, which help people discuss change and rebuild their lives. The projects open up debate on development issues, help closed societies make sense of the wider world, and empower citizens at grassroots level by providing them with informed choices. These projects specialize in developing sustainable projects that in the medium to long term can be run and financed locally. The trust also helps professionals working in the broadcast media to rebuild and strengthen media infrastructures in post-conflict societies. These projects aim to empower regulators, media managers, editors, journalists, engineers and support staff to adapt to new conditions and to serve the public interest.

Educational Broadcasting

Educational projects aim to provide audiences with accurate information, explorations of the choices available to them, and examples of where change and progress are being made. The trust works in partnership with BBC language services and departments, NGOs, educational institutions and broadcasters across the globe.

Multimedia Health Campaigns

Multimedia health campaigns work in partnership with local broadcasters throughout the developing world to organize broad-based multimedia campaigns to raise awareness about health issues and encourage the adoption of good practices. Campaigns are structured to address the specific conditions of each project area and the circumstances of the target populations – a combination of television, radio, print and community media materials may be used. Programmes are produced locally and based on qualitative and quantitative background research.

For example, the trust used the medium of a detective series in its campaign to reinforce key messages about HIV/AIDS in India. *Jasoos Vijay* (Detective Vijay), India's first interactive detective drama, was screened three times per week and was consistently in the top ten of Indian TV shows. In Russia, *House 7, Entrance 4* is a radio soap opera with 13.4 million listeners. The storylines offer practical advice on topics from infertility and sex trafficking to water filtration, passport applications and Downs Syndrome through the experiences of the characters.

Journalism Training

The trust delivers journalism and technical training around the world. These projects are funded by international development agencies and charitable foundations, and are delivered mainly to countries in transition or in crisis. The trust works with local organizations in these countries to design strategies that create sustainable outcomes. This enables local broadcasters to continue best practice training after the trust's involvement has ended. In 2003 the trust won a major UK award for its work in helping post-war Afghanistan to rebuild its media.

Bridge House Estates Trust

Originating in 1097 (as a tax for the maintenance of London Bridge) and adopting its current form in 1957, Bridge House is remarkable not least for the fact that it holds its grant allocation meetings in public.[11] The trust gave grants of £16.1 million in 2001–02. Constrained by its deed to give only in London, the trust's priority areas in 2001–02 were: transport and access for older and disabled people, environmental conservation, children and young people, technical assistance, and older people in the community.

One of its creative programmes is the London Sustainability Exchange (LSx). The Trust had been funding in the area of environmental protection, but received few good applications. It realized that there was no hub of knowledge about what was going on in relation to sustainable development across natural, human, social, and other capital. To address this gap the trust commissioned the Urban Economic Development Group (URBED) to research the need for a centre promoting sustainable development and turning it into a reality for the public, private and voluntary sectors. The research established that London organizations needed quality information and guidance on how to apply sustainability principles in their own operations. The research also emphasized the value of a cross sectoral partnership.

A cross-sector consortium led by Forum for the Future developed LSx to promote sustainable development in the public, private and voluntary sectors. Sustainability is defined as including: natural capital, human capital, social capital, manufactured capital and financial capital. LSx acts as an information centre communicating best practice in all three sectors, drawing on ideas and examples from urban sustainability resources and talents. LSx aims to help set London on course to become the world's most sustainable city (see Bridge House Trust 2001).

In 2002 the trust launched a one-off £2 million grants scheme to commemorate Queen Elizabeth II's Golden Jubilee. The scheme had two key themes: Safer London and Linking London's Communities. Linked to the scheme the Trust set up the Jubilee Learning Network for peer support, to share good practice and to learn from mistakes. This network was one expression of the trust's aim 'to do more than just distribute money. We know that the groups we fund have vast collective knowledge but also can have common problems. We have a responsibility to recycle learning and broker mutually beneficial relationships among grant holders' (Bridge House Trust 2004: p. 28).

More recently, the trust has become involved in a major project entitled Fear and Fashion, addressing the growing problem of young people in London carrying and using knives and other weapons. Having received few applications for the programme, the trust commissioned research to pull together the facts and figures to provoke informed debate. The research report was actively communicated to the media and others and was taken up by *Panorama* (one of the BBC's flagship current affairs programmes). The Home Office then announced a package of proposals to address the issue; although the proposals are not fully in line with the trust's analysis, the trust welcomes them as the beginning of a conversation. The trust is now (2005) committed to five-year funding of two exemplar projects, developing a collaboration with five partners, inviting multi-agency partnerships to bid, creating a steering group of funders, practitioners and a strategic advisory group, and ensuring independent evaluation, dissemination and replication of successful projects.

Nuffield Foundation

The Nuffield Foundation was established in 1943 by William Morris (Lord Nuffield), the founder of Morris Motors. The foundation's mission is to 'advance social well being', particularly through research and practical experiment. The foundation's income is around £9 million a year. 'The Foundation's financial independence and lack of vested interests helps to ensure an impartial and even-handed approach to problems in the projects it funds' (www.nuffieldfoundation.org).

The majority of the foundation's income is spent on research, practical innovation and development; 'the preference is for work that has wide significance, beyond the local or routine. The Foundation looks to support projects that are imaginative and innovative, take a thoughtful and rigorous approach to problems, and have the potential to influence policy or practice' (www.nuffield foundation.org). The foundation also runs a number of grant programmes for specific purposes, including support for scientists and social scientists at the early stages of their careers. The foundation also sets up and runs projects of its own. Currently the two largest are related to bioethics and to educational curricula.

The foundation's grants supporting research and innovation in 2004–05 include:

- Child protection, family law and justice – helping to ensure that the legal and institutional framework best meet the needs of children and families.

- Access to justice – promoting access to, and understanding of, the civil justice system.

- Older people and their families – promoting the autonomy and well-being of older people by developing policy and practice.

- Open door – supporting projects of exceptional merit straddling or lying outside the above three areas.

One of the foundation's best-known achievements was in the 1980s, when it supported the development of integrated (mixed Catholic and Protestant) schools in Northern Ireland, later adopted by government. Among its more recent areas of influence are new approaches to education for circus, fairground and gypsy children; public misconceptions of youth crime; coordination of policing methods; and new developments in science education and the curriculum.

The Diana, Princess of Wales Memorial Fund

Established following the death of Diana, Princess of Wales, on the basis of spontaneous public subscriptions, and subsequently the sale of endorsed products, the fund gave total annual grants of around £7 million in 2001 and 2002.[12] The fund has made grants under nine headings: advocacy, campaigning and awareness raising; young people and learning disabilities; young people and mental health; young people with a parent or prime carer in prison; young refugees and asylum seekers; communities affected by landmines; children and young people post conflict; rebuilding communities; and palliative care.

The fund describes its mission as ensuring that its grant-making and other initiatives 'leave the best possible lasting legacy, measured in opportunities for the most disadvantaged to change their lives' (Diana Princess of Wales Memorial Fund 2001: p. 2). For the fund this means 'continuing to work strategically on issues such as palliative care and explosive remnants of war when we believe we have a distinctive contribution to make and, working with partners, we can achieve cumulative impact. It means evaluation and learning from funded work, sharing insights and lessons as well as seizing opportunities to press for changes in policy and professional practice. It means encouraging users of the projects we support to insist that their voices be heard, helping where we can to break down the barriers which exclude so many young people from full participation in their communities' (Diana Princess of Wales Memorial Fund 2001: p. 13).

The fund is governed by 12 trustees, some of whom are relatives or close friends and associates of the princess. The fund conducts regular assessments of its work by independent evaluation, and reviews its practices accordingly. It has developed model practices in application procedures and is committed to evaluation, sharing of knowledge and learning for practice.

What the fund refers to as 'championing causes' is one part of its work. The thinking underlying this category is: 'The fund believes there are issues where it can add the value of its name and profile to important causes over and above the money it gives in its grant programme. Through championing of issues, it seeks to play a part in promoting change – change in public attitudes, law or policy and a different way of delivering services' (Diana Princess of Wales Memorial Fund 2001: p. 7).

Innocent Victims of War

In 2001 the fund, together with Landmine Action, began a strategic campaign to draw international attention to the little publicized dangers of unexploded cluster bombs and other explosive remnants of war (ERW). Building on research and a published report, the fund and Landmine Action promoted a joint media programme during the war in Afghanistan to raise global awareness of the dangers of cluster bombs. In addition, the fund and its partner developed an advocacy plan aimed at bringing cluster bombs and other ERW within humanitarian law via a new protocol of the UN Convention on Conventional Weapons.

Other projects with Landmine Action include Crosslines, a meeting of representatives from parties in the Sudan conflict to discuss shared concerns around landmine action. This led to, among other things, major support from the EU for emergency mine and UXO clearance. The fund and Landmine Action also produce an education pack on landmines and ERW for use in school curricula. In 2004 the fund sponsored a book to examine achievements on mine action since the Ottawa Treaty, what could be done better, and the issues that needed to be addressed during the formal review of the treaty in Nairobi in late 2004.

Dying People in Africa

The fund has embarked on a major advocacy campaign and grant-making initiative in developing countries to promote the inclusion of palliative care in government health policies, medical and nurse training, and for it to be an accepted part of care for all with life-limiting diseases. This programme includes work to effect policy change, as well as grants for good-practice demonstrations and for training of health professionals.

People Living with HIV/AIDS

The fund was the main founding funder of the Stop AIDS Campaign – a group of 22 UK-based development and HIV/AIDS charities. This programme includes funding for the Diana, Princess of Wales Lecture on AIDS, which was given by President Bill Clinton in 2001. The aim of the lecture series is to attract high profile speakers, and media attention, to keep the issues of HIV/AIDS at home and abroad on the public agenda, and to highlight creative action.

Prisoners' Families in the UK

In the UK the fund supports young people in prisoners' families – 'a group who are hidden from society yet affected in complex ways by imprisonment as they live their everyday lives on the outside'. As well as giving grants, the fund supports the Federation of Prisoners' Families Support Groups to make sure the needs of prisoners' families are heard and acted upon. A report based on the first comprehensive research into how young people are affected when a parent or sibling is in prison set out 24 recommendations to official agencies, and encourages action at different levels by prisoners' families support groups to address the needs of these young people.

Doing a Lot with Very Little

In 2003 the fund was legally obliged to freeze its grants, resulting from the lawsuit brought against it by the US Franklin Mint Corporation. The full story of how the fund worked under these difficult circumstances is too long to recount here. However, some points are worth highlighting.

The fund's passion for its work and its relationship with its grantees was such that freezing grants was not an option. The fund launched a Dunkirk-style initiative, inviting other grant-giving organizations, large and small, to provide replacement funding to the fund's 127 grantees. The fund's reputation and relationships were such that it was able to raise £8.5 million from 25 different sources. The success of this operation was remarkable for at least two reasons. First, although the fund undertook to repay the money when its grants were unfrozen, this could not be a certainty. Second, the fund was, in effect, asking other grant-makers to help support charities and causes that some of them would not otherwise have supported. One outcome of this has been that some funders are now interested in continuing to make grants in these areas.

Although it could no longer make grants, the fund continued to work with its partners on landmines, cluster bombs and innocent victims of war. With Landmine Action it spent time in the run-up to the war in Iraq lobbying against the use of cluster bombs. After the war it worked to draw public attention to the civilian casualties caused by the use of cluster bombs and the continuing death and injury caused by unexploded cluster-bomb bomblets. Similarly, the fund continued its behind-the-scenes lobbying in the period leading up to the UN Convention on Conventional Weapons annual meeting of states parties in The Hague in 2003, at which a legally binding protocol relating to the clearing up of unexploded cluster bomblets was adopted.

In association with the UK's All-Party Parliamentary Group on AIDS, and Help the Hospices, the fund organized a dialogue between practitioners of palliative care in Africa and other organizations working in HIV/AIDS prevention and care. The aim was to bring together two groups of professionals working to the same end but with little previous collaboration. One of the speakers at the resulting 2003 meeting, Dr Joseph F. O'Neill, deputy global AIDS coordinator at the US Department of State, has paid tribute to the work of the fund: 'The vision and models of care that sprang from [the fund's] effort formed a cornerstone of the US Government's President's Emergency Plan for Aids Relief – a $15 billion program that will spend over $2 billion on palliative care in Africa, the Caribbean and Asia. In my view, we are standing on the shoulders of the Diana Fund's efforts in regard to palliative care and should recognize their work as an example of the ways that private philanthropic initiatives can positively influence government policy' (interview).

In other fields the fund continued to use its name and media profile to support its chosen causes. This included an award for the most promising young journalist who had written or produced a programme for broadcast on mental health issues for a young audience, and another to recognize schools that are particularly good at welcoming and working with young refugees and asylum-seeking children.

Esmée Fairbairn Foundation

Formed in 1961, the Esmée Fairbairn Foundation's mission is to improve the quality of life for people and communities in the UK, both now and in the future.[13] In 2002, the foundation made grants of £25.7 million in five key programme areas: arts and heritage, education, environment, social development, and re-thinking crime and punishment.

The foundation describes its underlying philosophy as follows: 'The Foundation has always believed in the need to support and maintain a free, stable and socially cohesive society, where enterprise is encouraged and people are able to realise their potential, take advantage of opportunities and play their part in democratic life' (Esmée Fairbairn Foundation 2002: p. 13). It also believes that 'one of the roles of charitable foundations should be to highlight issues that are not benefiting from mainstream statutory funding. This could be because emerging issues have yet to enter public awareness, or because old issues have slipped off the agenda and become neglected' (Esmée Fairbairn Foundation 2002: p. 13). For example, in the early 1990s the foundation commissioned research on the case for greater political independence for the Bank of England. The study was published in 1994 and was influential in making the case for an independent Bank of England, implemented soon after the Labour Party came to power in 1997.

The foundation has recently made significant organizational changes, and has held a strategy review. This review suggested that key players in the nonprofit sector perceived that the foundation '[has] the capacity and respect to move forward new ideas and issues, is large enough to try new things, can emphasise experimentation and risk-taking and can keep room for the speculative and inspirational' (Esmée Fairbairn Foundation 2002: p. 5). But the foundation decided to look for further improvements 'to expand the services we offer and to improve learning from our grantmaking' (Esmée Fairbairn Foundation 2002: p. 5), 'learning from our grantmaking and enabling others to do so is important to us'.

The strategy review also recommended a programme called 'Grants Plus' to 'express ways in which we can add value over and above the grants we make in appropriate cases' (Esmée Fairbairn Foundation 2002: p. 6). This might include: additional funding to help with a grantee's training or planning needs, organizing networking opportunities between grantees, sharing learning from grant-making through seminars, and offering grantees the use of meeting rooms. Whereas most grants are responsive, in recent years – as the foundation has become better known and more experienced – it is becoming more strategic as well as proactive in devising its own initiatives. Since 1999 the foundation has set up eight strategic initiatives with total funding of £5.8 million. 'All address a gap, need or opportunity at a strategic or system level which an ordinary "responsive" grant would not normally be able to do' (Esmée Fairbairn Foundation 2002: p. 6). One of these is Rethinking Crime and Punishment, a £3 million programme discussed in more detail below.

Environmental Programme

The foundation is now one of the largest, perhaps the largest, trust funder of environmental organizations in the UK. Some grants are designed to solve problems at source, rather than remedying problems once they arise. This is the thinking behind grants to the Forum for the Future and the Soil Association to help them work constructively with business; similarly, grants to the Council for National Parks, the Green Alliance, and the Institute of Economic Affairs are for work to influence policy-makers. At the same time, the foundation is aware of the need to exit from programme areas when the funding environment changes. For example, it is currently looking at whether recycling, which has benefited from EU directives and increased government support, still needs charitable funding.

Social Development

The Social Development programme aims to tackle poverty and social disadvantage. The foundation believes that people need support, skills and other resources to take advantage of opportunities available, but that 'some problems are more entrenched and organizations, policy makers and institutional practices need to become more open and responsive to the needs of disadvantaged people' (Esmée Fairbairn Foundation 2002: p. 16). Grant-making reflects this philosophy: some grants, for example, are for stimulating social and community enterprise, while others are aimed at influencing policy and practice 'potentially benefiting a larger number of people than funding direct services' (Esmée Fairbairn Foundation 2002: p. 17). Grants designed to influence policy and practice include: Women's Aid Federation England to press for improvements to law and practice on domestic violence, Race on the Agenda for research and information, and Democratic Dialogue to support their work on dispute resolution in Northern Ireland.

Rethinking Crime and Punishment

This is one of the foundation's flagship, strategic initiatives. It is designed to raise the level of debate about responses to crime and to identify credible alternatives to prison in the UK. Its three aims are to improve public understanding about criminal justice, to inject fresh thinking into the debate, and to increase public involvement in prisons and alternatives to custody. The programme has so far identified types of offenders for whom prison is particularly counterproductive, and targeted grants at projects that address these issues; it has also funded various projects exploring the role of restorative justice. The foundation submitted evidence to the Home Office Correctional Service Review, as well as contributing to more than 20 conferences and seminars and House of Lords debates. As the programme has progressed, the issue of alternatives to prison has become of central importance. Consequently, the programme has decided to fund an independent inquiry into the adequacy of existing alternatives.

The Myer Foundation and the Sidney Myer Fund

The Myer Foundation, and its older sister the Sidney Myer Fund, represent one of Australia's largest and highest-profile philanthropic institutions.[14] Sidney Myer, a refugee from Russia, arrived in Australia in 1899 and founded the Myer retailing business. On his death in 1934, he left one-tenth of his estate for the benefit of the community in which he made his fortune. The fund was initially known as the Sidney Myer Charitable Trust, later renamed the Sidney Myer Fund. In 1959 the Myer Foundation was established and initially endowed by Sidney Myer's sons, Baillieu Myer and the late Kenneth Myer. It is now supported and governed by three generations of Myer family members. Although the two foundations continue to have separate legal identities, in the last two years they have come under the single management of the Myer Foundation.

In 2002–03 the Myer Foundation had total assets of around $AU39 million (data not available for the Sidney Myer Fund). The two foundations together spent $AU7.7 million in grants, special projects and administration.

The Myer Foundation's mission is to work 'to build a fair, just, creative and caring society by supporting initiatives that promote positive change in Australia, and in relation to its regional setting' (Myer Foundation 2002–03: p. 2). Grant-making comes under five main headings: the arts and humanities, beyond Australia, social justice, water and the environment, and the G4 fund. This last is administered by a committee made up solely of members of the fourth generation of the Myer family, working with the CEO in making grants of their own choosing; in the last year G4 have identified Environmental Education and Youth Health as their priorities. In addition to these grants programmes, there are a number of special 'projects', some of them closely linked to the Sidney Myer Fund.

One foundation special project is the Asialink Centre, initiated by the foundation at a time when looking to develop cultural and trade links with its nearest neighbours (as historically close relations with Britain became looser) was a contentious issue in Australia. The centre, located at and co-funded by Melbourne University, works with government, business, media, education, NGOs and cultural organizations to promote knowledge of and relationships with Asia. The centre receives its core funding from the foundation, with which it has a very close ongoing relationship.

Another special project is the Cranlana Programme, modelled on the Aspen Institute in the United States. This runs a regular series of colloquia, symposia, policy seminars and fora. The programme 'brings a new level of thoughtfulness, breadth and wisdom to leadership and decision-making in Australia' at a time when 'the ever-growing amount of information available to those in positions of responsibility is accompanied by escalating uncertainty and confusion about the challenges and opportunities that we face in the world' (Myer Foundation 2001–02: p. 28). Having previously been run as a special project of the foundation, in 2003 the programme formally became an independent foundation in its own right.

In the last year, at the time of writing, one of the Myer Foundation's major concerns has been the treatment of asylum seekers and refugees under current Australian federal government policy. The foundation more than tripled its funding in this area, making grants for case workers, project-staff salaries, and advocacy and research, including one project investigating the impact on asylum seekers when they are forced to return to their countries of origin.

Another major, related concern has been the effects on Australia's multicultural society created by adverse media coverage of Muslim peoples and issues (which was exacerbated by the 2002 Bali bombing in which many Australians were killed or injured). As a first step, the foundation undertook discussions with state and national Muslim leaders to identify ways of increasing understanding of Islam in Australia.

One project already funded is Sharing Insights on Reporting Islam, organized by the Asia Pacific Journalism Centre with assistance from the Jakarta Editors' Club and the Jakarta-based Freedom Institute. Australian and Indonesian journalists travelled together by bus through Java, exploring contemporary Islam in the nation with the largest Muslim population in the world. After a briefing in Bali, the journalists travelled to Jakarta, visited Islamic organizations, Islamic leaders, informed observers, civic leaders and members of the community along the way. 'The program will give Australian journalists an opportunity to learn how Islam is practised within Indonesia and allow participants from both countries to gain insights into how political and cultural issues to do with Islam, including the reporting of it, are seen from within Indonesia and from outside' (Myer Foundation 2002–03: p. 14).

Millfield House Foundation

The Millfield House Foundation (MHF) was established in 1976 with shares from a food-retailing firm sold in 1985 to generate income for the foundation.[15] Its income in 2004 was £140,000 per annum. The foundation 'works to tackle poverty, disadvantage and exclusion and to promote social change in the North East of England, particularly Tyne and Wear'.

In its early years the foundation gave grants to local projects to improve the lives of the most deprived people in Tyne and Wear. In 1996, MHF decided to change its approach radically, moving from service delivery to policy influence. It did so on the grounds that public policy disposes of vastly greater resources than a small charitable trust, and can tackle the causes of deprivation, not just alleviate their effects. The foundation now funds projects that inform discussion and influence public policy and attitudes, with the aim of diminishing social exclusion and empowering communities. This includes giving voice to excluded groups, bringing first-hand experience of poverty to the attention of policy-makers, promoting debate on social-policy issues and campaigning on local social issues.

The foundation attaches particular significance to effective dissemination and communication. A one-day consultation with grant-holders revealed that bodies that can research and report on social issues often feel that their work is finished when the project is written up, and have little knowledge of how to get their findings into places where they can be used to make a difference. The foundation now gives supplementary grants for public relations assistance to enable research findings to be communicated to the media, the public, politicians and others.

One example of the foundation's work is support to a group (BAN Waste) bringing together local residents, city council officers and others concerned about an incinerator at Byker. BAN sought a consensus on issues affecting people in the neighbourhood of the incinerator and beyond. Local politicians were ambivalent about the effects of the incinerator, so BAN organized three series of 'Select Committee' hearings at which visiting experts and local representatives were cross-examined. It also produced reports that attracted local and national media coverage, and community events. Despite some tensions, the group remained broadly based, and achieved its goal of ending incineration in the area and a review of the city's targets for recycling.

Conclusion

The foundation vignettes presented in this chapter do indeed reveal some of the characteristics we associate with creative philanthropy. Their activities showed significant degrees of uncertainty and risk of failure; were based on knowledge intensity; took up controversy; reached across established boundaries; took place at the margins by involving individuals, groups and organizations outside the mainstream; and built and enlisted rich networks that brought together diverse interests, perspectives and skills.

What is more, creative foundations appear to be open to change, and have processes to encourage this: they are reflective, they take stock, review the efficacy of their existing patterns of grant-making and, as a result, change strategy and develop new approaches. Creative foundations attach significance to building legitimacy and authority via development of a sound knowledge base. Creative foundations work with sophisticated theories of how social change happens, whether explicitly expressed or implicitly understood. Closely related to that, they attach importance to public and political understanding and opinion, and they work on building constituencies for change in order to change the way people think. Creative foundations are prepared to work long term, often for 10 years or more on one project.

The vignettes also suggested that foundations adopting a creative approach are diverse in terms of age, income and mission. Size of income appears to be no barrier to working creatively. Age, too, seems to bear little relationship to adopting a creative approach. Some of these foundations have always worked in this way; others adopted a creative approach as a result of a review of old practices. Yet the vignettes also bring up new questions and point to further areas for exploration, which we will take up in a series of more detailed case studies in the next chapter.

5 Case studies of creative philanthropy

The aims of the case studies presented in this chapter are twofold. First, they are meant to further illustrate the range, rationales and work of creative philanthropy; and second, they are meant to help explore the policies, organizational structures and practices that underlie such work, in order to develop hypotheses about the conditions under which creative approaches are most likely to develop and be sustained. We wanted to understand how foundations become creative; their governance, management and organizational characteristics; the obstacles and tensions they experience, and how these are managed; and how a creative approach is sustained over time.

The first task was relatively simple in that it mainly required a largely descriptive account of what the foundation or a particular programme does, why it does it, and how. The second task, however, was more challenging in that it implied some tentative hypotheses to identify areas for further enquiry. In identifying such areas for detailed exploration we were, as suggested in Chapter 3, influenced by the sociology of innovation and diffusion, in particular Landry's (2000) notion of the creative milieu and Rogers's (2003) systemic organizational approach in drawing out some of the preconditions for creativity and innovation. These include:

- personal qualities – imagination, people working together, thinking openly and flexibly, constantly learning, and showing a willingness to take risks;

- will and leadership;

- human diversity and access to varied talent – a mix of perspectives, cultures and disciplines, outsider and insider knowledge;

- an organizational culture that encourages learning, risk-taking, and 'outside-the-box' thinking;

- organizational capacity; and

- rich networks to generate new ideas and, crucially, to facilitate effective implementation.

These preconditions are, in some respects, a re-statement of the conditions for innovation, and thus of our defining characteristics of creative foundations. However, they also provided us with some key areas for exploration in the case studies. These included:

- How do creative foundations encourage 'imagination', outsider knowledge and outside-the-box thinking? And what, if any, tensions does this create?

- What is the role and impact of board composition and selection, e.g. are boards of creative foundations drawn from wide social strata?

- What about staff composition and selection policies? Do creative foundations deliberately seek to recruit staff from across or outside established disciplinary and professional boundaries?

- Where does the 'will and leadership' in creative foundations come from?

- If creative foundations value knowledge as highly as their financial assets, how is this managed in practice?

- How do creative foundations encourage constant learning?

- If creative foundations spend more time looking outside rather than inside the foundation, how is this manifested in structures, policies and practices, job descriptions and so on?

- How do creative foundations establish 'rich networks', and what do these look like?

- How do creative foundations/programmes manage working in partnerships, and what are the obstacles and tensions involved?

- How do creative foundations perceive and manage the pressure for performance measurement and square this with the need for 'space', flexibility and risk-taking associated with creativity?

Regrouping these issues, we identified a list of key areas for exploration in the case studies. These are triggers for creativity; rationales and perceptions; key players and actors; obstacles and tensions; organizational approaches; and ongoing issues and dilemmas.

A   Triggers for Creativity

- What are the essential building blocks of a creative approach?

- When and why do foundations adopt a creative approach?

- What role is played by tradition and values, in particular in terms of organizational vision and mission?

B   Rationales and Perceptions

- What are the key rationales in adopting a creative approach?

- Do creative foundations work with an articulated theory of what makes social change happen? If so, what is it?

- Are the rationales seen as one of a menu of options, or as experiments for potential wider adoption in future?

C   Key Players

- Who is driving creative approaches within the foundation?

- Which individuals and groups, inside and outside the foundation, are important in making creative approaches effective?

D   Organizational Implications

- What are the implications of adopting a creative approach for governance, management, staffing and structure?

- What are the implications for grant-making policies, processes and practices?

- What are the implications for relationships with grantees, and others?

E Obstacles, Dilemmas and Tensions

- What are the obstacles and dilemmas encountered within the foundation in adopting a creative approach?

- What are the on-going tensions in maintaining a creative approach, and how are these managed?

F Mixing Creative and Other Approaches

- Why do some foundations adopt a creative approach in some programmes but not in others?

- Are there other synergies between charity and creative programmes in the same field?

With the help of these questions, we looked at a wide range of foundations, and after initial exploration, selected eight for more detailed examination on the grounds that they revealed the characteristics of creative philanthropy in illustrative and instructive ways. These eight case studies are from the United States, Britain and Australia, and cover foundations that differ in age, size and field of activity. Each case study draws on published reports, internal documents, other published and unpublished material, and interviews with key staff and stakeholders. The face-to-face interviews were semi-structured, exploring the key topics outlined above. The numbers of interviews varied depending on the size of the foundation and the number as well as the complexity of its programmes.

1   The Wallace Foundation[1]

> 'Developing and sharing effective ideas and practices in our chosen fields [is] our most important stock in trade – far more than just giving away money.'

The Wallace Foundation is an example of what for many years was a sizeable yet rather conventional foundation that had to reinvent itself through a prolonged process of rethinking and reorganization to become the creative philanthropic institution it is today. While The Wallace Foundation – like the others presented here – shares the major characteristics of what we define as signature elements of creative philanthropy, it represents a case that is particularly instructive for two reasons: its dual emphasis on innovation that involves an explicit theory of change on the one hand, and on the other, a belief that knowledge, not money, is the real currency of social change. Both combine with a preference for collaboration with key stake-holders to produce significant impact beyond immediate grantees in the fields in which the foundation operates. However, as the case study will show, getting there has not been easy, and involved trial and error. The foundation's ability to remain creative presents old and new challenges to the board and the programme staff.

History and Background

The Wallace Foundation is an independent private foundation established by DeWitt and Lila Acheson Wallace, founders of the Readers' Digest Association. During the 1950s The Wallaces created a collection of small family foundations, which after their deaths in the 1980s became known respectively as the DeWitt Wallace-Readers' Digest Fund and the Lila Wallace-Readers' Digest Fund. The latter was concerned primarily with promotion of the arts (Lila's passion) and the former primarily with educational and youth development (DeWitt's interest). Over the next 50 years the two foundations operated separately, providing nearly $2 billion to support their chosen causes. In the 1990s alone $1 billion was spent on over 100 different programmes. In 1999 the two foundations made a decision to reorganize in order to better meet the challenge of 'transforming the systems and institutions that affect everyday life', and broaden the reach of the funds' impact far beyond its limited financial resources. In 2003 the two foundations legally merged to form The Wallace Foundation.

In December 2004 the foundation had $1.3 billion in assets, and made grants in 2004 totalling $61.2 million.

Governance and Staffing

The foundation currently has 10 board members, including the president. Board members are drawn from a variety of backgrounds with experience in, among other areas, publishing, banking, education and government. The foundation employs 48 staff.

Current Mission

The foundation's 2003 mission is to 'support and share effective ideas and prac-tices that enable institutions to expand learning and enrichment opportunities for all people . . . In everything we do, we want to be a resource dedicated to helping create, support and share insights, tools and effective practices, that can have a transformative effect on major public systems and, ultimately, on people's lives' (President's message, Wallace Foundation 2003: 4). More specifically, The Wallace Foundation incorporates the original interests of its two founders and the two foundations from which it was formed. Today The Wallace Foundation has three objectives:

- Strengthening education leadership to improve student achievement

- Improving after-school learning opportunities; and

- Expanding participation in arts and culture

> A single goal unites our work in each area: to foster fundamental improvements not only in places where we make grants but also in places where we do not. We have a single way of working: we invest in both the development of innovative ideas in specific sites, and in the development and spread of knowledge to inform policy and practice, not only in the sites we fund but also in many others beyond our direct reach. And in each, the real test of our success is whether practitioners and policy makers are persuaded by the evidence of our work to use it without our financial support.
>
> (President's message, Wallace Foundation 2003)

The foundation's strategy puts emphasis on what are called 'innovation sites'. The innovation sites are where new approaches are developed by grantees, and are tested and closely monitored. Implementation and results are analysed, and changes made where necessary. Innovation sites provide the data on what works, under what conditions, and what helps or impedes success. Taking the lessons beyond the innovation sites involves investing in developing and sharing knowledge. While much of this knowledge comes from the actual innovation sites themselves, the foundation also sponsors research to fill in any gaps that might exist or emerge. Sharing the knowledge nation-wide requires investment in a variety of communication techniques and strategies.

Current Programmes

Education Leadership Initiative: State Action for Education Leadership Project (SAELP)

SAELP, combined with the Leadership for Educational Achievement in Districts (LEAD), which includes 12 districts located within the SAELP states, is one of the cornerstones of the foundation's education leadership initiative. Launched in 2000, its aim is to strengthen the ability of principals and superintendents to improve student learning, including a major effort to support innovation in the states' laws and practices. By 2004 changes included: a shift from efforts to expand the labour pool of new school principals to a focus on strengthening the ways principals work (based on three labour market studies that firmly contradicted the widespread assumption of a nationwide principal shortage); all 15 SAELP states had established ways of bringing together key constituencies to promote the importance of school leadership and evaluate possible policy options; five states had changed certification requirements; three had revised alternative licensure rules; and three enacted new leadership preparation standards. These changes are one example of the way in which foundation-supported learning has had a significant impact both on grantees and more widely.

The programme is also now producing policy briefings, research results and lessons for the wider field beyond the original district sites. A foundation-authored policy briefing, *Beyond the Pipeline: Getting the Principals We Need Where They Are Needed Most,* re-framed the debate on the so-called principal shortage as a problem of poor working conditions. A synthesis publication, *Leading for Learning,* based on interviews with practitioners, describes a number of action pathways school leaders can take to advance student learning. To expand awareness of the challenges and opportunities of education leadership the foundation has provided multi-year support to leading, trade, general and broadcast media, including the New York *Times* News in Education Foundation and Channel Thirteen/WNET New York.

After-School Programmes

This programme builds on the foundation's long-standing support for out-of-school learning in libraries, parks and other community institutions. It aims to provide new knowledge and practical guidance on how to start and maintain high-quality programmes that make a real difference to the lives and learning of children. Two major policy-relevant studies commissioned by the foundation, *Making Out of School Time Matter: Evidence for an Action Agenda* and *All Work and No Play? Listening to What KIDS and PARENTS Really Want from Out-of-School Time,* analysed evidence on the demand for and quality of after-school activities for children. Published evaluation of 60 programmes funded by Wallace over the past five years has led to a clearer picture of what 'quality' looks like – a development of great relevance to policy-makers allocating scarce resources in the hope of making a difference in the lives of children. As of 2004, the foundation has begun to undertake an ambitious experiment in two innovation sites – New York and Providence, RI – where top political leaders have committed to redesigning their highly fragmented out-of-school learning systems so that more low- and moderate-income children can benefit from participation in high-quality programmes. The mayors of both cities have taken up leadership of the Learning in Communities initiative.

Arts Programmes

The foundation has a long history of supporting arts organizations. In 2000 it sharpened its focus to one goal: 'help create and promote new norms of practice for cultural organizations and funders that increase arts participation on a scale, and with a sustainability, beyond the reach of our direct support' (Wallace Foundation 2003–04: p. 22). The Leadership and Excellence in Arts Participation (LEAP) programme supports a variety of innovative arts organizations to develop and test a variety of practices for building arts participation. The State Arts Partnerships for Cultural Participation (START) supports 13 leading state arts agencies and challenges them to change their missions and practices better to encourage arts participation.

The work of Wallace's partner cultural organizations and state arts agencies has begun to inform policies and practices of cultural institutions and funders interested in building public participation and making art part of people's everyday lives. For example, RAND's publication in 2001 of the foundation-funded analysis *A New Framework for Building Participation in the Arts* has stimulated considerable interest in improving the design and targeting of efforts to expand arts participation. The foundation believes this is a result of synergy between Wallace's investments in practice-based innovations of leading arts organizations and the research by RAND, the Urban Institute and others that it has sponsored and shared with the field through convenings, a growing library of publications and its website. Wallace is currently supporting an extensive study by RAND of the full range of benefits of the arts (*Gifts of the Muse: Reframing the Debate About the Benefits of the Arts*), from student learning to community development, so that policy-makers and practitioners can make more informed decisions at a time of deep budget cutbacks.

Developing Strategy: The Move to a Creative Approach

After Lila and DeWitt's deaths it was decided that the foundation(s) would focus on a small number of issues related to the founders' interests. Education and arts were chosen and, in the light of a desire to benefit ordinary people, this was further refined to an emphasis on public education and participation in the arts. In the first 5–10 years of the foundation's life it behaved as a traditional grant-maker, and always hired staff from the field.

Reviewing its work on the Library Power project, the foundation found that for its $45 million, invested in 700 schools in 19 communities, it had achieved clear benefits for curriculum, instruction and professional development, and its work had become the American Libraries' Association (ALA) standard for school libraries. But there was no significant adoption or use beyond grantees, and nothing in school libraries across the country had fundamentally changed. The foundation concluded that having successful projects and good evaluation information is necessary but not sufficient to reach non-grantees. If you want to reach non-grantees, you need to build that goal into the strategy from the beginning; engaging key decision-makers is imperative; and it is essential to pay close attention to the context and field in which the work is being done.

As a result of this learning, in the late 1990s the foundation engaged in a major programme of 're-invention'. Board and staff adopted the goal of making fundamental improvements that last, and reach beyond grantees and across the country. The foundation recognized that it lacked democratic authority and legitimacy for political action, and that its financial contributions were minuscule on the national scale. But it saw opportunities in contributing new and useful ideas backed by innovative example, the experience of the lessons it had learned, and evidence.

The foundation embarked on an 'integration strategy'. The aim was to recreate the foundation as a knowledge hub based on objective, credible information, and responsive to sectoral needs. The first question in this approach is always: 'What exactly do we want to change, and what has to happen to bring about that change?' Desired results come first; means and methods follow and are more flexible. The approach required significant change in the foundation. Instead of relying solely on conventional programme officers, the foundation integrated the knowledge and skills of programme, evaluation and communications staff in coordinated action plans. The story of the foundation's adoption of a creative approach to its work is one of change driven by self-criticism and constant learning.

Drivers of a Creative Approach

The Board and CEO

For some time after the deaths of the founders the board of the foundation and of the Readers' Digest Association overlapped. It took 15 years (finishing in 2003) to complete the sale of all RDA shares and the full merger of the foundations. The nine board members and the CEO were recruited primarily to manage this lengthy process. One of the distinguishing characteristics of the RDA was its emphasis on market research and marketing, its emphasis on valid predictive knowledge, and its awareness of the wider public and political environment. There was also considerable diversity in board membership, partly related to the sorts of people the Wallaces drew around them. Because the transition was taken at such a gradual pace, board membership was very stable. One effect of these various characteristics was that board members began to question the effectiveness of the foundation's way of working.

By the mid-1990s the board began asking 'What's changed, and how do we know?' It concluded that it didn't know, and didn't have the capacity to find out. It also became clear that there were too many programmes; that board members were becoming less and less engaged; and that staff were losing enthusiasm. The CEO requested a thorough review of the foundation's work and the then five-member board enthusiastically agreed.

Radical Review of Resources

Five internal cross-disciplinary strategic planning teams were created, and a decision was taken to involve no outside consultants in order to ensure full ownership of decisions within the foundation. At the end of the process, board and staff held a retreat, at which they considered 15 proposals or ideas. All had come from the staff, so whatever ideas or proposals were chosen would have in-house ownership. Two ideas were selected (with a third added a year later), and the necessary staff reorganization undertaken. Fundamentally, this reduced the foundation's specialized programme fields from more than 100 to three, and the foundation began to redefine its role, resources and strategies, with a new in-depth focus on results. Perhaps most important of all, the foundation came to see its key resource as knowledge rather than dollars. 'Developing and sharing effective ideas and practices in our chosen fields [is] our most important stock in trade – far more than just giving away money' (Chairman's Letter, The Wallace Foundation 2003–04).

Elements of a Creative Approach

The Role of the Foundation: Beyond Money

Whereas most people equate foundations with money and grant-making, The Wallace Foundation believes that funding good programmes is not enough: 'National foundations need to find ways to extend their reach beyond their direct grant investments' (www.wallacefoundation.org). The foundation aims to change public systems that affect everyday lives. It accepts the argument that its resources are minuscule in comparison to the budgets of public institutions, but does not see this as a reason for despair – not least because money is often not the key issue. The foundation believes that the greatest contributions made by foundations come about through a combination of innovation, knowledge and public engagement. Lack of funding, contrary to popular belief, is rarely the most important reason for lack of progress.

Knowledge for Change

Progress, the foundation argues, is as likely to be hampered by lack of knowledge about what works, inadequate strategies for mobilizing change, and bureaucratic resistance, as it is by lack of funds. The foundation sees knowledge as the real currency for creating social change, and its role as being co-generator and disseminator of knowledge for change. Achieving large-scale benefit, beyond the direct effects of its grants, is central to the foundation's philosophy. It describes its goal as 'to help others use what we learn to leverage change, and to leave as our legacy a public record upon which others can build' (www.wallacefoundation.org). The Wallace Foundation's strapline is: 'Supporting Ideas, Sharing Solutions, Expanding Opportunities'.

Evaluation for Learning

The foundation's emphasis on knowledge to inform policy and practice has led to a distinctive approach to evaluation. Evaluation is not about checking up on the performance of foundation staff and grantees. Rather it is about creating learning opportunities that help leaders in a field – grantees and non-grantees alike – make the changes that will enable them to meet the major challenges they face. For example, the focus of the LEAD districts was on improving the preparation and training of school leaders, based on analysis of what currently works and learning what could be improved by listening to those involved.

The Enlightenment Effect

Like many other US foundations, The Wallace Foundation does not wish to be perceived as partisan. The first time the foundation presented results of its work in a briefing for lawmakers, the board required considerable reassurance that the foundation was not becoming too 'political'. In the event it emerged that both Republican and Democratic legislative staff members saw something useful in the work, albeit for different reasons. It also emerged that the Republican and Democratic Congressional committee staff members had had little contact in the year preceding the foundation briefing. The board were delighted to play this informing and brokering role and when the findings from the foundation's work ended up in legislation six months later, they were equally pleased. (The foundation had known of the Congressional review, but was also aware that many ideas feed into such reviews, and few are taken up).

Despite its success in contributing information and analysis that were subsequently used in legislation, the foundation's model is not focused on developing programmes that will then be taken up by federal government. It believes that research studies rarely trigger policy change in a direct cause–effect way. It sees its research as having an 'enlightenment effect', creating a different quality of discussion. The foundation looks for issues that get little attention and asks 'what would it take to inform people to possibly open a policy window for new practices and policies to enter?' This in turn involves a push-and-pull model. Getting journalists asking questions, raising public attention, achieving learning and coverage. 'We want to get more eyes and ears around a problem.' Media and broadcast investments are seen as being most powerful in bringing attention to an issue. 'Building a more informed dialogue leads to better results than just pushing a particular policy.'

Knowledge Is Not Enough

The foundation attaches considerable significance to the power of knowledge. But it also believes that knowledge alone is not enough to drive change. People have to be able, and want, to use that knowledge. This 'beyond knowledge' approach has led the foundation to adopt a highly integrated, 'value-added' approach with clear goals, multiple strategies, objective data and targeted communications techniques. The foundation works through multi-disciplinary teams, working with partners across institutions and sectors to generate credible, usable knowledge that responds to needs and realities on the ground; this credible, usable, relevant knowledge then has to be disseminated 'smartly' to practitioners and policy-makers.

The foundation sees the ultimate test of its effectiveness as whether its products – ideas and solutions – prove to be compelling enough to influence the thousands of organizations in its chosen spheres that do not receive its direct financial support. 'How well we compete in the marketplace of ideas will determine how effectively we are meeting our mission and, thereby, serving the public' (Chairman's letter, Wallace Foundation 2003–04: p. 2).

In each of the main programme areas – education, arts and communities – teams include staff with expertise in relation to:

- Programmes – providing in-depth knowledge of the field, identifying effective organizations and assessing readiness and capability in specific institutions and the field in general.

- Evaluation – assessing learning opportunities from programmes and activities and planning new research that can provide useful lessons with the potential for advancing knowledge and practice in the field.

- Communications – raising public awareness of needed changes, sharing new knowledge and ideas with people and institutions whose work is at the centre of desired changes, and translating knowledge gained from the foundation's work into clear, useful forms for policy-makers, practitioners and the public.

Foundations: Non-ideological Connectors

For Wallace, foundations have at least two important advantages in generating and disseminating knowledge for social change. Because they are independent of market and state, foundations are well positioned to act as non-ideological honest brokers of solutions. Second, and closely related, foundations are well positioned to make connections between seemingly unrelated ideas and people – 'change requires not just finding the connections among ideas, but between ideas and those who can bring them to life', developing 'effective solutions to pressing problems with partners and in places that appear to be poised for change, with people who are committed to driving that change' (Wallace Foundation 2002). For example, both the SAELP and LEAD programmes work closely with states committed to making change.

Communications: From Headline Chasing to Change

Working on a genuine communications strategy is seen as a very different way of working from 'throwing out a series of grants and then doing a PR number about what you did and maybe later put out a publication.' 'It's a shift from headline chasing to using communications to promote change.' Effective communication for change involves recognizing that policy-makers and practitioners have many sources of knowledge, and that the foundation can only compete in the market-place of ideas on the basis of relevance and credibility. Building a sound non-partisan research reputation is part of the formula, but so too is ensuring relevance by testing out ideas with practitioners in innovation sites. Communicating at different levels and through different channels is also seen as important. For example, in addition to publishing national surveys and research results, the foundation also produces shorter, more focused policy briefs, as well as providing multi-year support to leading trade, general and broadcast media.

Building Reputation

'You can have the best ideas in the world, but without credibility, they're going nowhere.' Credibility requires reliable, high-quality knowledge; and a lack of perception of bias: 'The last thing Wallace wants is to be typed as liberal or conser-vative. We want to be identified with ideas, not ideology.' Credibility also means admitting what you don't know and telling people where else to go instead. Credibility involves usefully informing without alienating, and using evidence to promote informed discussion.

Reputation-building is a slow process, and foundations often have very little real knowledge about what their reputation is, especially among non-grantees. Issues to do with credibility, reputation and relevance also raise tricky issues over quality control in relationships with contracted researchers.

Getting Used: Understanding Obstacles

To be adopted, innovations have to have a comparative advantage to users. That means having better ways of understanding audience needs. Old ways of bringing grantees in are of little use because the grantee–grantor relationship gets in the way. The foundation is now investing in more market research to understand what the issues really are. Thus it faces the dual challenge of learning how to do things better, and understanding the learning issues and needs of leaders in the field. 'We can do terrific work that people are not going to pick up because other concerns are getting in the way. If people don't use it, you might as well not have done it.' 'Research has to generate application. The test of the value of research is whether people find it useful.' Many of the assumptions in the field are built on the existing system, so one challenge is to understand where the mismatches and good examples really are. Getting used involves asking, and answering (from the viewpoints of potential users/adopters) five key questions:

1 Relative advantage: Is it better than what I'm doing?
2 Compatibility: Does it fit with how I do things?
3 Complexity: Is it hard to learn to use?
4 Divisibility: Can I try it out?
5 Observability: Can I see it in action?

Innovation sites provide an opportunity to find better ways of doing things, to learn how they fit with other parts of the system and to overcome obstacles, to experiment with the simplest ways of introducing a new approach, to enable people to try it out and, crucially, to demonstrate it in action.

Maintaining Relevance and Getting it Right: The Role of Innovation Sites

Working on the ground in innovation sites plays an important role in building credibility and providing examples of where things are working. Equally important, in the foundation's eyes, innovation sites provide learning opportunities and constant challenge. The relationships created in innovation sites enable the foundation to understand tensions, obstacles and resistance to change.

Innovation sites may also correct popular assumptions. For example, when the foundation entered the field of education leadership, it was widely assumed that there was a looming principal crisis and thus an urgent need to train more principals. However, more research revealed that there were plenty of trained principals, but conditions in schools were not good enough to retain them. Innovation sites provided the opportunity to explore ideas for change, and likely reasons for resistance, with principals.

'Innovation sites are not just visible examples we can point to, but a constant challenge where we learn what's going to work. They are our reality-check, and a way of spotting trends and emerging issues.'

An Explicit Theory of Change

Informing the foundation's approach is a theory of change. From the outset of any initiative, each team creates strategies that respond to three key questions: (1) Who is in a position to bring about the changes we seek to support? (2) What do these people need to know and learn in order to make change happen? (3) What action strategies and learning efforts should we support that these people will find useful and will be motivated to use to bring about the change we are seeking to create?

These questions have led to the foundation adopting a range of strategies beyond grant-making. These include evaluations, communications and awareness projects, field-building activities, multi-site initiatives, knowledge development, helping to inform development of standards, new approaches to training, state government partnerships, university partnerships, and provision of sound information on key issues for policy-makers and community leaders. The theory is that the foundation's innovation sites inform its knowledge development and outreach, and vice versa; both innovation sites and knowledge development and outreach feed up and out to produce nation-wide benefits for people through both grantees and non-grantees.

Implications and Issues

Governance

For the first 15 years of the foundation's existence, legal and structural matters were continuing concerns for the trustees (particularly the legal and financial separation of the foundation from the corporation whose stock represented its original financial assets). At the same time as they were reorganizing the foundation's financial base and legal structure, a stable and long-serving board took a series of actions intended to focus the foundation on achieving large-scale change in a small number of specific programme goals, in place of the 100-plus programme-funding areas that were in place in 1999. This movement to adopt a creative approach to philanthropy took place gradually, beginning with the increased attention to the results of the foundation's grant-making in the mid-1990s, followed by the trustees' 1999 decision to focus on two specific large-scale outcomes (supplemented by a third in 2001).

From 2001 to 2004, the board deepened its engagement in the now sharpened programmatic areas, and expanded its membership to ten, while two directors retired. In recruiting new directors, the board sought a gradual evolution of the mix of skills and perspectives needed for the foundation's new approaches to its work. They continued to look for people who could make an input at the strategic level rather than the level of implementation, and who could provide broad nationwide and state-level perspectives on issues the foundation is addressing. 'It was less that they could open doors and more that they could provide guidance, and how to avoid pot holes, and to ensure that we hear different sides of issues.'

Board Motivation: Change not Charity

Everyone on the board is there because they want to do more than approve the giving of charitable gifts; they want to achieve real change in the education and the opportunities available to children. 'People on the board grasp that at such a fundamental level, it's almost visceral.' 'Achieving change is a very different motivation for joining the board from the usual motivation in a traditional foundation where it's more about helping your favourite charity. I don't get board members slipping me proposals to fund.'

Team Building to Question

The CEO worked hard on building the board as a team – as hard as on staff team-building – and creating 'the comfort to ask questions'. The CEO sees her role as making the board comfortable enough with the staff and subject matter to ask tough questions. 'My role as leader in this place is like a woman with one foot on each of two galloping horses. My job is to make sure that the two horses – board and staff – are running in the same direction at the same speed.' 'One of my measures of progress is the level of discourse at board meetings – we've moved well away from questions about how many principals are being trained to much more significant strategic questions.'

Keeping the Board on Board

The board is kept very well informed of what foundation staff are doing. Whereas in many foundations the board suddenly hears about things they have never heard of before, at Wallace the board hears four times a year about how each of the three teams are evolving. 'This is very, very different. It means that the board gets very involved in thinking about and planning projects at the strategy level, and then monitors implementation through regular updates.'

Managing Multiple Perspectives and Pressures

Knowledge as the foundation's key currency required a profound cultural shift, including the departure of grant-making staff involved in programme-funding areas the foundation was no longer supporting, and a broad shift from staff who worked in relative independence and isolation from other each other to a highly interdependent, team-oriented approach. Achieving the cultural change necessary to make the transition from a charity grant-making model to a knowledge-focused model is acknowledged to have been very demanding. Some of the pressures have been external. nonprofit organizations were quite happy with the foundation's old, traditional grant-making approach and 'no nonprofit leaders are pressing the foundation to be a knowledge center'. Programme staff are said to have felt this pressure to remain a traditional grant-maker most keenly. Other pressures were internal, arising not least from the meeting of different perspectives. The very different backgrounds and skills of staff working in each team mean, among other things, that although 'they want the same things, they don't talk the same language'. Nevertheless, cultural change is happening – in part because of the multi-skilled, multi-perspective teams. Now the foundation sees itself as working on how that cultural shift plays out – in questions such as who should be involved in particular meetings or decisions.

Developing Trust: Evaluation for Learning

One early tension within staff teams was around the role of evaluation staff. It soon became clear that to have real honesty and learning potential, programme and evaluation staff had to trust each other and develop genuinely collegial relationships. It was essential to ensure that the evaluation staff focused on learning and did not become an internal audit department. All evaluations are made public on the foundation's website, and most are aggressively spread to field leaders. But evaluation is seen as being about learning, moving towards solutions, and not about 'did it work or not?' 'If you are seeking practical ideas and knowledge based on experience then you almost can't fail. Mistakes are invaluable if your aim is to understand and communicate your learning.'

Constant Learning and Change

The CEO is conscious that this is a field in which there are no outside forces to critique what a foundation does; government regulation is a very blunt instrument and the board may or may not question what the foundation does. 'The internal quest for continuous improvement is the only force for change, and that hangs on the people you hire.'

Whereas in many foundations evaluation occurs (if at all) at the end of a programme, staff and board at Wallace are constantly reviewing, learning and changing. For example, when SAELP programme officers monitored the first-year grants to 15 states, they found little innovation occurring in most of the states because the states' governors, and other senior officials with the authority to make things happen, were not involved. Too much of the first year of activity was of limited importance and scope, and lacked a sharp-enough focus. The design of the second phase of the project was thus informed by the evaluation of the first phase.

The second phase has revised objectives and structures, new kinds of technical assistance provided by national service organizations, the addition of several states chosen for their use of innovative approaches, larger roles for senior leaders, greater use of assistance from experts, and a requirement for clearer plans for achieving desired results (Pauly 2005). The second phase of SAELP will continue grants to the original 15 states, provided they make progress on these updated goals, and will make grants to six new states selected through a competition among the 25 that applied, with new plans that are both more ambitious and more concrete than was the case for the original 15 SAELP states. States selected to participate in SAELP II had to demonstrate solid commitment of their top leadership, including governors, and a willingness to combine improved training of leaders with changes in the working conditions that can improve their performance in raising student achievement. Conditions include offering incentives to attract leaders to where they are needed most, creating do-able job responsibilities, and providing the authority to get the job done.

Leverage and Leadership

The SAELP programme illustrates the foundation's current thinking on using leadership to lever change. Initially the foundation asked grantees to map out all of the things they wanted to do with grant funds, but this led to them doing too many things to do any of them well. The foundation also 'did not fully analyze the politics behind the changes it wanted to achieve. That included the big P politics and the little p politics of organizations, power and incentives to change.' Now the foundation pays much greater attention to these.

The request for proposals (RFP) has come to be seen as a very powerful strategic tool in the way people think about a problem. To be effective, however, this requires considerable clarity in writing RFPs. In the new round, school districts and states work on the proposal on all levels. New states are required to put in joint applications with a network of districts to create mutual incentives to work together, and have conversations around the model and the issues that the foundation has identified. By asking for a network of districts there is greater likelihood of trickle-down diffusion. Under the old scheme only one district was involved, so it was easier for others to dismiss the ideas and the work. RFPs also require the governor's signature on letters of intent, a concept paper of three to four pages, and attendance at a conference to discuss the proposal.

The foundation has heard that states that failed to get a grant nevertheless have a plan they are working on as a result of engaging in the process and the internal conversations required by the RFP. A next step may be to invite these states to come and 'look over the shoulders' of successful grant applicants. Another step may be to start talking with other funders about contributing to funding a state or a district; the foundation has already entered into an arrangement with the Gates Foundation for co-funding of education leadership in six states. New investments have been made to capture knowledge at innovation sites. New strategies with the media have been developed to encourage debate about national strategies and impact. 'We're getting smarter about making the connection between leadership and learning.'

Flying Above the Radar: 'This is Show Business'

The foundation is moving away from the belief that it can work in the shadows, and is increasingly interested in media coverage. 'We've realized we are in show business, competing in a very crowded market of ideas, and the stage is often the media.' 'If you want to transfer knowledge you can't do that if no-one knows who you are.' But there is also an anxiety that 'you cannot control the media and how they handle complex ideas'.

In the past the foundation produced five to six publications per annum, but in 2004 it produced a dozen. 'But we're not a publishing house – or maybe we are?' Simply managing and implementing the volume of work to produce publications is one problem, as is the issue of how to time publications to have maximum impact. As one person commented: 'I guess we're just beginning to live with the reality of saying our currency is knowledge'.

Branding

In the past the foundation was reluctant openly to brand its publications and other products. Now it has evolved a range of publications from no branding to co-branding to speaking clearly in its own voice. Lately it has taken on a logo and started putting this on products, as well as using 'A policy brief by The Wallace Foundation' as a strapline on some publications. Moving to clearer branding has been difficult for at least two reasons. First, traditionally within the foundation world there has been cultural resistance to branding. Second, branding – flying above the radar – is seen as giving the foundation less freedom and increasing the revelation of possible failure.

Identifying Key Target Audiences

Given the foundation's emphasis on knowledge as its main product, the relevance of the knowledge it produces and how to communicate that knowledge have become more and more pressing questions. Who potentially might be listening, how we can reach them, and what their needs are, are seen as key questions and have led to more and more market research. The foundation is currently working on the question of its key target audiences. Target audiences currently include policy-makers and practitioners, other private and public funders, and thought-leaders at policy or practice level. There is a view that 'the most promising way to get attention is to focus on thought leaders and funders/resource providers'.

There is, however, increasing interest in engaging with the political agenda, dealing with governors, mayors, legislators, 'trying to inform political discourse with ideas that are relevant and credible'. The public is not yet seen as a key audience, although it is acknowledged that it may become necessary to engage the public for social change. Contact with the public would necessarily be mediated through the media.

Developing Appropriate Performance Measurement

The new, active and younger people added to the board have brought urgency, impatience and greater pressure to measure effectiveness. As one person suggested: 'urgency without measures is just panic'. But the measures have to be appropriate. Board members understand that change takes 10 years or more, but have encouraged the development of a scorecard of leading indicators of effectiveness. The CEO believes the foundation is making progress in developing relevant and appropriate performance measurement. Umbrella questions under which measures are presented each January include: are the sites 'working their plans'?; are the sites institutionalizing the changes they are making in the way they conduct their work?; are the people in the sites benefiting?; and are we producing and effectively promoting useful knowledge?

One effect of the foundation's emphasis on identifying and sharing effective ideas and practices was increased expenditure on evaluation and communication. With a current staff of 48, the board is conscious of staff size and overheads, and has constructed measures to compare staff size with peer foundations in order to have some measure of their effectiveness. 'Board discussions are constantly anchored in what brings about results.'

Results

Results of the creative approach the foundation has been using since 1999 include:

- The first evaluation monograph on the START initiative appears to have triggered widespread use by *non-grantee* state arts agency leaders of the 'public value' framework for planning agency priorities.

- The 2001 publication of the RAND study *A New Framework for Building Participation in the Arts* has led to widespread sharpening of participation-building activities by arts organizations, intermediaries (local and state arts agencies), and arts leaders.

- The national education reform debate was essentially silent on the roles of principals and superintendents and how those roles needed to change; this has shifted so that leadership issues are now 'on the radar', although they are not yet a top priority.

- The national debate on after-school programmes had been focused on money (how much more to spend) and effects (whether or not such programmes produce higher test scores); recent Wallace efforts have added the topic of demand – what do parents and kids want from after-school programmes? – to the topics in the debate.

- In 2000, if you asked an education policy-maker about the big issues in regard to school leaders and leadership, they would have told you about a nation-wide shortage of school principals. Now the assumption that there is a shortage of leaders has virtually disappeared, and the debate has shifted to the role of leaders in education reform.

Ongoing Challenges

Like all creative foundations, Wallace is an evolving organization that continues to face major challenges. In the President's message for 2002, the following new challenges are identified:

1 How can we work effectively with our grantees to help find solutions to pressing social problems, balancing risk and reward, flexibility and focus?
2 How can we use multiple means to capture the ideas and experiences of our grantees and others in ways that are authentic and authoritative, but also intelligible to non-specialists?
3 How can we become better at listening to the 'marketplace' so that we are not imposing ideas, but meeting genuine needs?
4 How can we credibly measure the impact of our investments, balancing the need for evidence with understanding that, often, the most important things may defy ready measurement?
5 And how do we become more effective at sharing what we, our grantees, and our research partners have learned by engaging with those in the world of policy and practice?

To those challenges some within the foundation would add additional ones that go beyond the specific case of Wallace but are likely to affect all successful creative philanthropies: how to balance the role of the foundation in promoting social change with its accountability to the general public? This challenge is most pronounced for foundations that address political topics, social problems and issues that have become politicized. The Rosenberg Foundation, to which we turn next, is a case in point.

2   The Rosenberg Foundation

'Much of the last 40 years has been about old ideas. There's a declining rate of return on old ideas and the argument that you need more money for old ideas is not convincing any more.'

The story of The Wallace Foundation was one of adopting a creative approach through self-criticism and constant learning. By doing so, its role evolved from being a conventional grant-maker supporting worthy causes to that of a change-agent and social innovator. Unlike Wallace, however, some foundations, such as the Rosenberg Foundation, are born tied to the critical social issues of their times, and by virtue of deed and mission, share a close interest in aspects of social justice and politics. How can foundations in the United States become creative actors in political or politicized fields, when the regulatory regime imposes some dividing lines between philanthropy and politics?

Indeed, The Wallace Foundation, like many US foundations, feared being or appearing partisan in its choice of topics and approaches in generating and disseminating knowledge for social change. Nonetheless, the foundation felt that its mutual independence of market and state positioned it well to act as the non-ideological and honest broker, and in serving as a neutral 'transmission belt' between local innovation sites and state-wide and national solutions. Yet what if the policy issue itself is so entangled in politics that little non-ideological ground seems left, and attempts at honest brokerage and dissemination are likely to encounter fierce opposition, and might well lead to litigation and other forms of legal action? Is creative philanthropy in intrinsically political fields possible, and if so, how? The case of the Rosenberg Foundation is instructive in approaching these questions.

History and Background

Max Rosenberg, a San Francisco businessman and philanthropist, was the co-founder, president and major shareholder of Rosenberg Brothers & Co., a firm packing and shipping dried fruit from California. The company became the largest concern of its kind in the world, with packing houses and mills throughout the agricultural areas of California and Oregon and sales offices in 65 foreign countries. When Max Rosenberg died in 1931 he left the bulk of his estate to establish a foundation with broad charitable purposes and wide latitude in how the foundation might be operated. The Rosenberg Foundation was established in 1935. In late 1936 the new foundation opened an office in San Francisco, hired its first staff and began making grants. In 1938 it published the first report of its activities and began to diversify the composition of its board of directors. By the end of World War II, the foundation had started the process that led to the sale of the company and the diversification of the foundation's investments.

The foundation currently (2004) has ten trustees, of whom four are women and five are members of minority groups. None of the ten trustees is related to the donor or the donor's company. The foundation employs five staff.

In 2003 the foundation had assets of $59.8 million and spent $2.7 million in grants.

Mission

Max Rosenberg gave a list of purposes the foundation might pursue, mainly oriented towards social justice and the 'conditions of the working man', but added a clause giving trustees discretion. No pattern was laid down in advance for the type of grants that the foundation should make. The greatest influences on the direction of the foundation were interest in the agricultural areas of the state, the character and diversity of the population of California, and the impact of national events within the state.

From the outset the directors of the foundation recognized that they would have to focus their grant-making in a limited number of fields to be effective. The foundation's early grants were concentrated in the fields of public health, inter-group relations, education and community planning. In each of these fields the foundation had a particular interest in applications to rural California and the well-being of children in the state.

At the end of World War II the foundation undertook the first of a series of regular reviews of its work, and planned the foundation's programme in the context of the changing circumstances of the post-war period. From the experience of its first decade, and after wide consultation with leading Californians, the directors defined the programme focus, grant-making strategy and geographical scope of the foundation in 1946. They decided to focus on the health, education and recreation of California's children and communities, and grants for programme innovation and demonstration projects. The directors also concluded that the foundation should make grants throughout the state of California. The 1946 policies guided the foundation for nearly 25 years.

Programmes have evolved over the years in response to constant review of the wider social, economic and policy environment, and the activities of other foundations. An external evaluation in the period 1955–57 sharpened the foundation's focus on children and youth. In the 1960s concern for civil rights provided increased opportunities for grant-making related to social movements involving youth, farm workers, minorities and women.

The Tax Reform Act of 1969 changed the regulatory environment in which foundations operate, and the growing volume of proposals forced the foundation to review and narrow its programme. After a year of internal discussion, the directors of the foundation established new programme priorities in 1973. These priorities continued the strategic approach based on innovation, but narrowed the programme focus to early childhood development and older youth involvement. The 1973 policies were modified by the creation of a rural programme in 1976 and an immigration programme in 1980, as well as a growing focus on public-policy outcomes in each of the foundation's programmes.

The foundation is recognized for its influential policy work on behalf of immigrants and minority communities. 'Rosenberg's work on immigration policy began in the 1980s, when it supported background and public education work leading to the passage of the US Immigration Reform and Control Act (IRCA) of 1986. IRCA provided opportunities for millions of undocumented immigrants to legalize their status and begin the process of naturalization. Through its networking and grantmaking, Rosenberg helped build a coalition of community groups, churches, employers and unions to help immigrants take advantage of this onetime opportunity' (Siska and Lamb 2003). In the 1990s, Rosenberg supported a successful legal battle to overturn California Proposition 187, which prohibited state public health and education providers from serving undocumented immigrants, and later an effort to prevent with-drawal of welfare benefits. 'Through its work, more than 50,000 people were able to obtain US citizenship and protect their welfare benefits' (Siska and Lamb 2003).

In 2003, the Rosenberg Foundation was one of three foundations that received the Paul Ylvisaker Award for Public Policy Engagement of the Council on Foundations.

Current Programmes

The foundation's current programmes were formulated following yet another review in 1984–85. New programme priorities were adopted concentrating on the changing population of California and the economic conditions of low-income and minority families. These two programme categories enabled the foundation to devote significant resources to the legalization of immigrants after the 1986 immigration law, and to the support of projects designed to preserve the affordability of housing in California. In 1993 the foundation added child-support reform as a third programme category (this was phased out in 2002). The Rosenberg Foundation currently has two main programmes under the head-ings of Changing Population of California and Economic Security of Working Families.

Child-Support Reform Initiative

From 1993 to 2002, the Rosenberg Foundation supported a programme initiative designed to reform the child-support system in California. The goal of the initia-tive was to improve the economic well-being of low-income children by increasing child-support collection. From its inception, the initiative emphasized policy advocacy at local, state, and federal levels. In later years, the foundation added a communications component, research, and strategic convening of grantees. In all, the ten-year initiative included grants to:

Grassroots organizing and advocacy (two grantee organizations)
State policy analysis and advocacy (three organizations)
Federal policy analysis and advocacy (three organizations)
Research (three organizations)
Communications (two organizations)
Child-support assurance development (four organizations)
Strategy development and convening by the foundation.

The child-support reform initiative contributed to the restructuring of the child support programme in California through the creation of a new state department, reorganization of child-support responsibilities in the state's 58 counties, and the creation of a framework of uniform state-wide standards, accountability and financial incentives. Over the 1993–2002 period, the initiative also increased the amount and uniformity of the California child-support payment formula, established a hospital-based paternity programme, strengthened the enforcement tools available to child-support agencies, and expanded the participation of tax-collection and other agencies in child-support enforcement.

Changing Population of California

This programme aims to promote the full social, economic and civic integration of immigrants and minorities into a pluralistic society. Priority is given to projects designed to achieve change in public social policy regarding immigrant integration through employment, language access and immigrant rights.

Grants in the five years to 2004 have included:

- Asian Law Caucus, San Francisco – garment and low-wage immigrant worker advocacy project for worker education, consumer awareness, capacity building, litigation, and policy development to reduce exploitation of garment workers and improve labour practices in the garment industry in California. (Sixth year of grant support, $85,000.)

- California Rural Legal Assistance Foundation, Sacramento – temporary foreign worker project to monitor the supply of seasonal farm labour in California and disseminate information about the availability of labour, labour conditions and proposed guest-worker programmes to policy-makers, advocates and the general public. (Seventh and eighth years, $150,000.)

- Employment Law Center of the Legal Aid Society, San Francisco – language rights project for multi-lingual community outreach to increase awareness of language discrimination in the workplace, legal representation of limited-English-speaking workers with wage claims and litigation to establish that language-based discrimination in employment is a violation of existing civil rights laws. (Eighth and ninth years, $298,000.)

- Farmworker Justice Fund, Washington, DC – agricultural guest-worker project for education, policy monitoring and advocacy to improve the wages and working conditions of all farm workers by assuring that any guest-worker programme for agriculture includes worker protection and opportunities for temporary workers to obtain permanent status. (Ninth and tenth years, $280,000.)

- Sweatshop Watch, Los Angeles – garment worker centre for organizing, policy advocacy, case management and public education to empower workers and eliminate sweatshop conditions in Los Angeles. (Third year, $50,000.)

- The Urban Institute, Washington, DC – Immigration and the Changing Face of Rural California project to examine the effects of immigration on rural areas in California and the prospects and mechanisms for the economic and social integration of immigrants in rural California. (Ninth and tenth years, $120,000.)

Economic Security of Working Families

The goal of this programme is to strengthen the economic well-being of working families. Priorities include projects designed to improve economic security through increased wages and earned income and projects designed to achieve public policy promoting good jobs and good wages.

Grants in the last five years include:

- California Budget Project, Sacramento – living-wage project for policy research and public awareness to improve public policy regarding working poor and low-wage workers in California through living wage, unemployment insurance, access to health-care, job training, and creation of state-earned income tax credit. (Sixth and seventh years, $200,000.)

- Center on Policy Initiatives, San Diego – living-wage and accountable development project for research, public education and advocacy promoting living-wage standards and equitable public economic development policies in San Diego. (Fifth year, $90,000.)

- Consumers Union of the United States, San Francisco – electronic benefit transfer equality and access project. This is a state-wide project monitoring the development of Electronic Benefit Transfer programmes to distribute food stamps and, in some counties, cash assistance to low-income people and assisting community-based organizations to participate effectively in designing county systems that meet the needs of low-income residents. (Second and third years, $167,000.)

- Institute for Labor and Employment, Berkeley – worker centres' conference to convene leaders from California worker centres, researchers and labour organizers to strengthen the capacity of individual centres and link them to a network of other centres and strategists. (First year, $25,000.)

- Labor Project for Working Families, Berkeley – child-care organizing project to mobilize a network of work–family coalitions involving labour and community groups promoting county and state policies to improve the wages and working conditions of child-care workers. (Third year, $65,000.)

- Los Angeles Alliance for a New Economy, accountable development project to improve the accountability of public economic subsidies in Los Angeles through research and analysis, technical assistance to community–labour coalitions, and increased public understanding of economic development and community benefits. (Seventh year, $50,000.)

- Strategic Actions for a Just Economy (SAJE), Los Angeles – welfare-to-work banking project to increase the accessibility of banks and mainstream banking services in low-income communities and enhance self-sufficiency of low-income people unfamiliar with mainstream banking services. (Third year, $130,000.)

In addition to the two programmes above, the Rosenberg Foundation also gives grants under the heading of promoting philanthropy. It has a longstanding commitment to the advancement of private philanthropy and the promotion of effective and responsible practices in the field. Through membership contributions and grants, the Rosenberg Foundation supports a variety of services to the public, services to and on behalf of private philanthropy, and joint grant-making activities. The foundation provides basic operating support to six programme and population affinity groups within the field of philanthropy, and two collaborative funds that are administered by Northern California Grantmakers, an association of philanthropic bodies. Since 1976, the foundation has also provided basic support grants to the National Committee for Responsive Philanthropy.

The foundation has funded Grantmakers Concerned with Immigrants and Refugees, a project of Northern California Grantmakers to promote increased awareness within philanthropy of the needs of immigrants and refugees and related policy issues, and Hispanics in Philanthropy, a national programme promoting awareness among grant-makers of the needs of Latino communities.

Drivers of a Creative Approach

In interview, the foundation's current President attributes its adoption of a creative approach to five key factors:

- 'Being the only game in town' when the foundation was started meant that there was no dominant model of how foundations work and, at the same time, lots of proposals and ideas coming through.

- The fact that the foundation began during the Depression, which heightened awareness of the nature and roots of poverty, especially in rural areas.

- Having a diverse board with a few strong personalities willing to take risks.

- Having a board made up of people who had the confidence to act creatively, and who did not feel that their personal positions were threatened by doing so.

- The recruitment of energetic staff who went out to look at projects and conditions, practising 'philanthropy as an interactive art'.

Other factors may include:

- The space, and permission, to behave in the way it saw fit that Max Rosenberg gave to the foundation.

- The early commitment to adapt to the changing external environment, including the activities of other foundations.

- The practice of regular reviews of the foundation's work, involving grantees and ex-board members.

- A tolerance of complexity: 'There's a culture of complexity here. The board are willing to listen to complex ideas and issues.'

Today the foundation is driven in its creative approach partly by its history and culture and partly by recognition that there is a growing ideas deficit among policy-makers, practitioners and funders. 'Much of the last 40 years has been about old ideas. There's a declining rate of return on old ideas and the argument that you need more money for old ideas is not convincing any more.'

Elements of a Creative Approach

Long-term Commitment

As the lists of grants above illustrate, the foundation works on issues and gives grants for the long term, often staying with an issue for 10 years, and extending its involvement when necessary.

Getting to an Outcome

Even when a programme is initially seen as being for a shorter period, the foundation will continue funding until the desired outcome is achieved. For example, the child-support reform programme was initially seen as a four-year, $2 million initiative but ended up taking $6 million over 10 years. However, as discussed below, the foundation recognizes that there are dilemmas in this approach.

Accepting the 'Political'

The foundation accepts that 'everything we do is political', commenting on the way in which many foundations tend to act 'as though there is nobody on the other side', assuming that 'if people just knew what was right then they would act right'.

Adaptability and Learning

The foundation has always been conscious of the need to adapt to the wider environment. Today it continues to stress that. 'Within each of the two priority programs, the issues addressed and program strategies are reviewed and adjusted annually to accommodate changes in the public policy environment, changes in community needs and emerging opportunities for significant and lasting social improvement' (www.rosenbergfdn.org). The foundation also remains flexible in its programmes and strategies, adapting to environmental changes and circumstances. Opportunism is part of the strategy. As illustrated below, even the way in which the issue is defined may be adapted as the foundation becomes more involved and knowledgeable.

　　The foundation's own analysis of what it learned from the child-support reform initiative provides an insightful analysis of the elements of an effective creative programme (Wilson n.d. All quotes in the four following lists come from Wilson's paper unless otherwise indicated).

The initiative confirmed some things that the foundation already knew:

- The effectiveness of a programme strategy involving multiple organizations and multiple approaches (the foundation describes itself as trying to use 'the whole tool box' and 'attacking the issue from all sides' in all of its programmes).

- The potential benefits (synergies) of active collaboration among organizations, and the time and effort such collaboration entails to operate smoothly.

- The necessity for flexibility in programme strategies, to take advantage of opportunities and to revise expectations.

- The value of persistence and the need to maintain focus on programme goals.

- The danger of becoming too committed to an idea (such as child-support assurance).

In addition, the foundation learned some new lessons:

- 'Communication strategies can play a central role in unifying a movement, enhancing other strategies and creating opportunities' (the initiative had achieved only incremental programme improvements until October 1998 when the *Los Angeles Times* published a week-long series of investigative reports on the failures of the California child-support system).

- Strategic collaboration among grantees can be difficult to sustain but can significantly increase programme impact.

- There is distressingly little interest in the reform of government among elected officials, the media or taxpayers, however costly the programme.

- The rhythm of policy reform is unpredictable (in this case three years of incremental improvements followed by two years of relatively little progress before a year of fundamental reform and restructuring and four years of reorganization and implementation).

- Adopting a strong position on a specific policy ('the child-support system in California is failing children and requires fundamental reform') exposes the foundation to controversy and attack by opponents of the proposed reforms.

- From outside government it is exceedingly difficult to reconceptualize a programme (from the emphasis on recovery of tax funds expended on welfare to the strengthening of the economic security of children in single-parent families).

With the benefit of hindsight, knowing now that an anticipated four-year, $2 million programme would become a ten-year, $6 million programme, the foundation would have:

- Strengthened the research base for the effort (initially, performance data were entirely from government sources, but they proved increasingly unreliable and were eventually used by the government to discredit the reform proposals).

- Broadened involvement in the reform by establishing grassroots organizations (particularly some based in minority communities), creating alliances with other organizations concerned with children and economic justice, strengthening relationships with the family-law bar and the court system.

- Considered a more aggressive litigation strategy (despite the involvement of several public-interest law organizations, the initiative involved very little litigation).

- Devoted more effort to collaboration with other foundations.

- Increased early investment in communications.

- Phased out the investment in child-support assurance earlier (it was not essential to the system-wide reforms, failed every market test and diverted resources).

Overall, the foundation feels that it learned some important lessons from the initiative:

- *Issue definition is critical*: the foundation's child-support reform was inadequately – and as it turned out inaccurately – defined during the early years. By focusing on incremental improvements, the foundation neglected the fundamental problems of poverty, unmarried parenthood and administrative torpor.

- *Some issues may be resistant to foundation strategies*: the foundation's eventual analysis was that the performance of the child-support system in California could only be improved through reform of the administrative system. Broad administrative reform, in contrast to policy reform or innovation, may be beyond the capacity of foundation grant-making. Unless grant-making can rely on significant support from elements within the system, it is vulnerable to vested interests that control performance data (and criteria) and shape the understanding of the issue among the general public and policy-makers.

- *Some issues may be premature for foundation intervention*: the trajectory of the foundation's child-support programme was one of several early victories followed by several years of little or no progress until the *Los Angeles Times* articles created momentum for reform. While the articles were instigated by the foundation's grantees, and much of their content was provided by grantees, the reform efforts were stalled until the articles created a policy environment supportive of reform. (This point underlines the importance, noted in other case studies, of working on issues where policy windows are already opening.)

- *The strengths of the foundation's approach also create vulnerabilities*: the strengths of the Rosenberg Foundation are its tolerance of complexity and willingness to make relatively large and long-term commitments to a particular issue. These strengths, along with the foundation's efforts to work closely with grantees, may result in relationships that lack sufficient objectivity. The foundation is, to some extent, at risk of becoming a captive of its own grantees. 'Unless the foundation can identify external measures of progress, the primary sources of information and assessment are the grantees.'

Tensions and Dilemmas

As in the case of Wallace, learning and incremental, even radical, changes in programme implementation and development became necessary. Long-term engagement in bringing about social and political change carries with it a number of challenges that can easily lead to inter-generational tensions and dilemmas. Specifically:

Maintaining Board Confidence

The foundation's President suggests that foundations 'can be pretty thin-skinned; it doesn't take much to scare them off'. During the child-support reform initiative a coalition of fathers sent a dossier on the foundation and its trustees to every member of the state legislature. 'But the board members' reaction was to say "We must be doing something right if they're getting this upset". That reaction goes back to having board members with confidence.'

Keeping the Board on Board

'There are two things we owe board members: a window to ideas ahead of time, not yet visible, and some sense of accomplishment – something that reflects back on them.' The first is accomplished by in-depth briefing sessions and background readings prepared for board members. Staff attempt to accomplish the second by 'working on making grantees and their work accessible to board members – that gives concreteness'. The dilemma is that each one of these learning opportunities only lasts for a short time and 'the board wants to get on and see something new'.

Performance Measurement

Performance measurement over the long time-scales involved in foundation grants presents challenges. Identifying interim performance measures and being able to judge whether there is any movement in the right direction are regarded as particularly difficult. As in the case of Wallace, performance evaluation serves an educational rather than a controlling function.

Costs of Collaboration

Although, as discussed above, the foundation is convinced of the value of collaboration, there are also costs involved. One cost is that of maintaining and 'feeding' a collaborative relationship. Another is the uncertainty of who did what: 'Do you each take one fifth of the credit, or each take all of the credit? If everyone takes all of the credit then we're all happy as clams, but that may come back to bite you.'

Costs of Multiple Strategies

Again the foundation has no doubts that attacking an issue from several directions with several different tools is a sound strategy. The dilemma is the danger that multiple strategies may counteract each other, and also increase costs.

Defining the Issue

The importance of issue definition has been discussed above in relation to the child-support reform programme. Apart from the difficulty of getting issue definition correct at the start of a programme – before you are familiar with all the intricacies of the issue – there are other dilemmas. One is that while most issues are complex, there is an appeal in the tidiness of 'single-shot discrete things. Defining the problem more narrowly can lead to a quicker sense of accomplishment, mitigate problems of impatience, uncertainty and performance measurement. But successful resolution of a narrowly defined problem may be deceptive because the underlying and larger problems may remain' (interview).

The Time and Place for Innovation

The foundation attempts to be at the forefront of issues, ahead of its time. But it also recognizes that it is very difficult to move an issue that does not already have some momentum – an opening policy window. Apart from the effectiveness of being 'too innovative', the foundation is also conscious of a moral and political dilemma to do with how far ahead of the consensus it should be. 'Do we jeopardize the existence of foundations if we are too bizarre? Foundations depend on the grace and favour of Congress – we keep forgetting that.'

The foundation has also learned that some situations may be more favourable to innovation than others: it is easier to be effective in the start-up, planning phase of a new policy measure than it is to change an existing system with all the obstacles presented by established bureaucracies and interests.

Exit Strategy

Programmes rarely show clear and consistent progress year by year. There are often early gains and then a period of little apparent progress. Without interim performance measures, and given the board's desire to see things happen, this can create significant dilemmas for the foundation. On the one hand, it accepts that things take time and are under pressure from grantees to give for 'just one more year'; on the other hand, when, and on what grounds, should the foundation cut its losses and accept that, for whatever reason, the programme is unlikely to succeed?

Using the Whole Tool Box

The foundation attaches considerable importance to using all the tools at its disposal. Communication and litigation are two of its newest and most powerful tools. However, litigation, in particular, creates dilemmas. For example, by late 2004, the foundation was involved in a lawsuit against Wal-Mart challenging its employment practices on behalf of 1.6 million women. 'There's obviously the sheer cost, complexity and scale of this, but there are other issues. In these bigger cases the dealings between the lawyers become more and more complex and there's the issue that the lawyers' interests and the plaintiffs' interests may run apart.' Community organizing – another foundation tool – raises similar dilemmas. Is the purpose of the grant to strengthen the organization or to achieve a certain outcome? 'Sometimes those coincide, but sometimes they don't.'

Achievements

In addition to the achievements documented above, the foundation sees itself as having been successful in strengthening the low-wage sector of the labour market by enforcing labour laws and reducing the likelihood that immigrant workers will erode wages and conditions for all workers, via:

- Limiting the scope of the Supreme Court decision regarding workplace rights and the protection of undocumented workers;

- Persuading the Social Security Administration to modify its practices regarding discrepancies in Social Security numbers to reduce unnecessary termination of immigrant workers;

- Obtaining substantial awards of unpaid back wages and overtime for low-wage and immigrant workers in several industries and expanding the concept of joint employer liability for substandard practices;

- Increasing the use of wage- and job-quality criteria for the allocation of public subsidies for economic development.

- In pursuing its goal of the cultural, economic and social integration of immigrants, the foundation has achieved increased access to public services for language minorities in California.

In conclusion, while the foundation has clearly been successful in promoting social justice and changing the lives of many people for the better, it is conscious of the potential effects of its actions on civil society and the political process. 'Are we unbalancing the local political process? Do communities have more or less capacity to solve their problems after a foundation intervention? How did we get to be there in the first place – is it a bit like a game-show with some lucky participants selected to receive the prize?' These questions point to the wider implications of the foundation as a political actor, of which the Joseph Rowntree Charitable Trust in the United Kingdom is another example.

3   The Joseph Rowntree Charitable Trust

'There's a can-do sense around, and we can-do because we have the resources and a unified sense of purpose between trustees and staff – people, time and money. What else could you want?'

Like the Rosenberg Foundation in California, the Joseph Rowntree Charitable Trust (JRCT), located in York, England, has a reputation for involvement in often-contentious policy issues. A recent study of the trust's work in support of the Campaign for Freedom of Information, the successful campaign to incorporate the European Convention on Human Rights into UK domestic law, and the Democratic Audit (which aims to strengthen democracy and political culture in the country), suggests that it has indeed been effective in influencing policy debate. The study concludes that 'by investing a comparatively small sum of money in the right place at the right time, the JRCT influenced policy debate, notably when Labour was open to reforming ideas in the early to middle 1990s. It enhanced the capacity of grant holders, helped them to push issues up the political agenda and enabled them to influence legislation . . . The JRCT is an important policy actor' (Davies 2004: 283–84).

Unlike the Rosenberg Foundation, however, which uses specific and targeted programs, and which works typically through grass-roots mobilization and using the US legal system, JCRT also operates at the larger policy level and is closer to the actual process of policy-formulation and policy-making. This makes it an eminently more political organization.

History and Background

The Joseph Rowntree Charitable Trust is one of four trusts (one of them non-charitable) created a century ago by Joseph Rowntree, the Quaker chocolate manufacturer. The trust is the sister of the higher-profile Joseph Rowntree Foundation. The trust currently distributes around £5 million per year.

The trust sees the way in which it earns its money as integral to its mission and work. As one person remarked: 'There is an untold story of creativity around how we get the money to do what we do.' All of the trust's endowment is held in equities, all of which are subject to its ethical policy, published in its triennial report. Trustees are advised by the Ethical Investment Research Service (EIRIS) on companies in the portfolio or being considered for it. Some industries (arms manufacturing, for example) are ruled out altogether, but in other cases the decision is more complex. Indications of improving practices or other positive features might lead to investment in borderline cases. If a company in which the trust has investments fails to fulfil its ethical criteria then the trust writes to tell them why it is withdrawing and, in some circumstances, might make that public.

In some cases the trust may remain as a small shareholder in order to continue to press for change. The trust's benchmark is that its portfolio should perform at least as well as the FTSE All Share index. 'It seems to be working. In the difficult period from 1999 to 2003 when the FTSE index fell by an average of 1.1 per cent per annum, we experienced growth of an average of 1.4 per cent per annum.'

The trust is governed by 14 trustees, all of whom are members of the Religious Society of Friends (the Quakers). Originally, all trustees came from the Rowntree family or the firm. In recent years, however, the trust has developed a range of recruitment methods to ensure that trustees constitute a balanced and diverse group drawn from within the Religious Society of Friends. The trust employs six full-time and four part-time staff.

Mission

The trust's work is inspired by two key quotations from Joseph Rowntree: 'Charity as ordinarily practised, the charity of endowment, the charity of emotion, the charity which takes the place of justice, creates much of the misery it relieves, but does not relieve all the misery it creates'; and from a memorandum in which he set out his intentions for the four trusts: 'the need of seeking to search out the underlying causes of weakness or evil in the community, rather than of remedying their superficial manifestations, is a need which I expect will remain throughout the continuance of the Trusts' (Joseph Rowntree Charitable Trust 2000–02: p. 3).

The trust's current aim is 'to show that, with Trustees and staff working together, a foundation like JRCT can stay at the forefront of creativity and innovation, can continue to take risks in tackling difficult and contentious issues, and can be a challenge to the status quo . . . [and] continue to be a powerhouse for social change to create a fairer and more just world' (Joseph Rowntree Charitable Trust 2000–02: p. 5).

Current Programmes

The trust describes its 'core work' as 'making grants to people with passion and expertise'. It currently funds under the following headings: peace, racial justice, Ireland, South Africa, the democratic process, corporate responsibility, and Quaker concerns.

Racial Justice

The trust describes the policy underlying its racial justice programme as follows: 'The Racial Justice programme supports projects and individuals working to: promote issues of racial justice with policy shapers, decision makers and opinion formers; empower black and ethnic minority people to contribute to policy development; challenge racism and racial injustice and promote communication and co-operation between different racial groups. The Trust seeks to encourage work aimed at furthering its objectives in the European Union (EU) as well as in the UK' (Joseph Rowntree Charitable Trust 2000–02: p. 24).

The trust was one of the main funders of the Commission on the Future of Multi-Ethnic Britain, which published its report (known as the Parekh Report) in 2000. This was undertaken in the context of the Macpherson Report following the Inquiry into the death of Stephen Lawrence. The report of the commission 'redefined Britain as a multicultural society in a way which cannot now be undone. It describes Britain as both a community of citizens and a community of communities, a place where conflicting requirements sometimes need to be reconciled' (Joseph Rowntree Charitable Trust 2000–02: p. 24). The report made a series of practical recommendations for public institutions, including religious bodies, government and schools.

The West Yorkshire Racial Justice Programme was set up in 1993 'to oppose racism in all its forms, and to empower the disadvantaged communities in West Yorkshire, so that they may be able to participate fully in civil life and promote racial justice' (Joseph Rowntree Charitable Trust 2000–02: p. 28). The programme arose in part from a challenge to the trust from black activists who pointed out that its interest in national policy development meant little to communities facing disadvantage and discrimination at a local level. The programme is described as 'unique for the trust'. The programme has a dedicated development worker (on the staff of the trust). In addition to making grants, the programme enables community organizations to access training and consultancy, and initiates conferences, seminars and working groups on key issues; it also commissions research. The programme was given added impetus by the disturbances in northern English towns and cities in 2001, the growth of far right parties, and the growing persecution of Muslims following 11 September 2001. Most recently, the trust has launched a new project within the programme bringing together key community activists from West Yorkshire to focus on racial justice issues in the region and to develop practical strategies for bringing about radical and lasting improvements. The thinking behind the creation of this 'network think tank' was that 'the actions of grassroots organisations are fundamental to change, but there is an urgent need for strategic responses to racial injustice' (Joseph Rowntree Charitable Trust 2000–02: p. 28).

Unlike many British foundations, the trust takes a keen interest in the rest of Europe, seeing racial justice as an international issue, and recognizing that the locus for policy development is increasingly moving to the EU stage. The trust has funded a number of Brussels-based groups in order to make an impact on the EU's developing legislative agenda on immigration, asylum and integration. In addition to other grants with a European element, the trust funds the UK Race and Europe Network, which works to raise awareness of the implications of the UK's membership of the European Union in black and ethnic-minority communities and to identify their concerns. Recently, the organization has focused on implementation in the UK of the European Race Directive.

South Africa

The trust has been involved in work in South Africa for many years. In the 1980s and 1990s the trust supported a range of organizations that contributed to the eventual transformation to democracy. Since 1994 the trust's focus has shifted from civil and political rights to social and economic rights. In 2004 a new five-year programme was initiated to focus on one province (KwaZulu Natal) and to concentrate on rural poverty and conflict resolution. The trust itself is a member of the South African Grant-Makers Association.

Northern Ireland and the Republic of Ireland

The trust has a long and distinguished history of involvement in Northern Ireland. Long before the peace process emerged, the trust was supporting peace-building initiatives. Throughout the ongoing peace process it has supported work on difficult and contentious issues such as prisoners, parades and the role that paramilitaries might play in a future civilian-based society.

In the 1980s the trust funded the first integrated school in Northern Ireland; in 2002 the province's (Sinn Fein) Minster of Education offered support to the then 47-strong network of integrated schools. In the 1980s too the trust helped a small group of human rights activists to found the Committee on the Administration of Justice (CAJ). Twenty-one years later the CAJ was co-ordinating a coalition of voluntary organizations working on the equality and human rights aspects of the 1998 Northern Ireland Act.

Outside the Belfast area the trust has funded the Duncrun Cultural Initiative (DCI), which seeks to build confidence within the loyalist (Protestant) community so that it can play a greater role in creating a new pluralist society and reach a genuine accommodation between the different traditions in Northern Ireland.

The trust also disperses funds in the Republic of Ireland. This programme developed out of its search for peace and justice in Northern Ireland and the realization that resolution of the conflict depended on building new partnerships on both north–south and east–west axes.

Democratic Process

The trust seeks to fund work that 'encourages people to take seriously their democratic rights and obligations, exercising them in ways that make them real rather than merely theoretical' (Joseph Rowntree Charitable Trust 2000–02: p. 42). Since the passing of a Human Rights Act 'the Trust is concerned to see that its provisions are used to enforce the human rights of people who are without privilege, rather than simply those who are well-connected and know how to "work the system"' (Joseph Rowntree Charitable Trust 2000–02: p. 42).

One example of a long-standing (over 10 years) grant in this category is that to Democratic Audit. In 2002 Democratic Audit published *Democracy Under Blair* providing a comparative audit of the quality of democracy and political freedom in the UK with previous audits in 1996 and 1999. Democratic Audit's methods for measuring democracy are now widely used abroad. Another grant is for grassroots Citizen's Juries designed to provide models for democratizing science-related policy.

The trust believes that one of the greatest challenges is the increasing sense of alienation and disaffection from the political process felt by many sections of the community. Although national change such as voting reform and regional devolution are acknowledged to be important, the trust believes that change must also be encouraged at local level and is considering how this may best be achieved. It has recently commissioned a study into the state of local democracy in two towns in northern England.

Corporate Responsibility

The trust has worked in this field for over 30 years, demonstrating its capacity for being ahead of popular opinion. There are few British trusts that give priority to encouraging public and private corporations to take their responsibilities to society seriously. The trust provides a variety of grants to encourage more responsible business practice and to work on reforming company law. 'The Trust believes there is a continuing role for individuals and organisations within civil society to provide independent monitoring and analysis of (these) developments, give voice to the concerns of under-represented or marginalised stakeholders, and act as a source of radical ideas' (Joseph Rowntree Charitable Trust 2000–02: p. 52). In an important sense, its ethical investment policy adds to its legitimacy in taking on issues of corporate responsibility.

Developing Strategy: The Move to a Creative Approach

In many respects, the trust has always qualified as a creative foundation. In its early years it supported the path-breaking poverty studies by its founder's son, Seebohm Rowntree, which were influential in the creation of the welfare state (Timmins 1995). Adult education, and support for educational settlements was also a major part of the JRCT's early work. The trust's involvement in funding issues around poverty and welfare continued into the 1990s. In this period the trust funded the Child Poverty Action Group, itself a radical departure at the time from the usual style of voluntary organizations, and one of the first examples of trust funding for groups explicitly working to change policy. The trust's current secretary suggests that in its second 50 years the trust has been more creative than in its first half century.

Drivers of a Creative Approach

Maturity

The trust's greater creativity in its second half century is attributed by the current secretary in part to maturity and learning, time to reflect and develop (and for this reason he has doubts about the wisdom of the wider current debate within philanthropy about 'spending down' endowments).

Sisterly Rivalry

It would be possible to attribute the trust's new phase of creativity to the intro-duction of trustees from beyond the family. But this would be over-simple. One key trigger for greater creativity came in the 1960s when the Joseph Rowntree Village Trust (JRVT) became the Joseph Rowntree Memorial Trust (and later the Joseph Rowntree Foundation). JRVT's sole purpose had been to look after the village of New Earswick (Joseph Rowntree's model-housing scheme on the outskirts of York). By 1959 the JRVT had too much money to use solely for that purpose. Having acquired a wider brief and a new name, the Joseph Rowntree Memorial Trust decided to spend its money on similar things to those that the JRCT had tradition-ally done. 'There were all sorts of ructions – they were usurping our role.' These events are said to have given JRCT trustees 'the push to change, to doing rather than just researching', and to move into new areas.

New Blood

New trustees and new staff have contributed to the trust's regeneration. Joseph Rowntree was keen that the most appropriate people were appointed as trustees. Over time this has led to a gradual lessening of the connection to his family, to the extent that no trustees are currently family members. On the other hand the continuing connection to the Society of Friends (Quakers) is seen as an important factor in the trust maintaining its radical edge. Not only does the Society provide a constantly replenished pool of people from which to choose new trustees, but it also provides a touchstone for the value-base of the trust. In the 1980s another, major factor in the new phase of creativity was the appointment of a young trust secretary. 'That gave the trust new leadership and a new edge because that's the sort of person he is. But then the trustees obviously wanted that [too], so it's hard to separate.'

Freedom Given by the Founder

Throughout the trust's life, Joseph Rowntree's founding memorandum has been a source of guidance but, it was suggested, in the last twenty or so years 'it may have become more of a source for radical creative ideas than it used to be.' Joseph clearly laid out his vision for the trust, but also gave the trustees explicit permission to adapt it to changing circumstances. The memorandum provides the trust's ongoing sense of purpose and legitimacy. This clear sense of purpose provided by the memorandum was said to be part of the reason why the trust feels free to be constantly learning and changing.

Elements of a Creative Approach

Diversity within Common Values

One factor in maintaining creativity is the combination of a strong common value-base with a diversity of trustees in terms of age, gender, interests and experience. Trustees 'are incredibly different; Quakers aren't all the same – one trustee demonstrated at Greenham Common, whereas another believes that you should do things by the parliamentary process'. But while trustees are diverse they also share a common value-base that 'makes them more adventurous as a group than they might be as individuals. It's about confidence in numbers of like-minded people. It gives them a common purpose, a common bond, we're all in it together so we can take risks. Trustees talk about the trust as a family.'

Keeping the Board on Board

Trustees are very involved in all stages of the grant-making process. 'Trustees' regular engagement on assessment visits means they know what we're doing. Without that it might sometimes be very hard to convince them about the more adventurous applications – the more contentious things – because often in these cases the written applications aren't that good – some of our best grants have come out of weak applications.'

Rich Networks

Continuing creativity is also attributed to the trust's rich networks. Trustees and staff are active in a number of areas outside the trust. For example, some trustees are involved in local politics, and this was one source of ideas for work related to the rise of the far right. In addition, in most of its programme areas the trust draws on the knowledge and experience of co-opted members.

Looking Out

Staff play a crucial role in creating and maintaining diverse networks, getting out and about as much as possible, maintaining a good website, keeping in touch with grantees, sending out the regular *Bulletin*, and attending grantee occasions and conferences. Staff activity in meeting and talking to groups leads to new issues being raised and new strategies for the trust. The trust also places great store by its accessibility when people make contact with the office. Applications too are a source of renewal and 'edge'. And 'if trustees identify an issue that really needs addressing they ask staff to go out and explore what might be possible'.

A Reputation (by Association)

The trust believes that its reputation is, indirectly, another element in the creative process. People bring creative ideas to the trust because 'We have a reputation – people have a sense of where we are. For example, the Islamic Human Rights Commission contacted us recently because, they said, "we know the sorts of things you do."' The trust also acknowledges that part of its reputation comes from the name Rowntree, and from the confusion between it and its better known sister organization, the social-research oriented Joseph Rowntree Foundation. 'This confusion can be frustrating for both sides but we probably gain more from the association than we lose.' A reputation for creativity and challenge can sometimes be a disadvantage, attracting attention from regulators and leading to others arriving at a view on ideas before they have been heard.

A Big Informed Fish in Small Funding Ponds

Part of the trust's creativity is its involvement in a number of areas not addressed by other foundations, or by other foundations only years later. For example, the trust has been involved in both racial justice and corporate responsibility for around 30 years, long before these were on the agenda of many other UK foundations. Being ahead of the concerns of other funders means that the trust tends to be a significant player in the areas in which it chooses to be involved. And when other funders enter the field the trust already has a strong knowledge-base and an established track record. Both factors enable it to have an influence disproportionate to the resources it contributes.

Long-term Involvement

The trust accepts that achieving change is a slow process. The trust does not change its priorities every five or even 10 years. In several of the areas in which it funds, it has been there for at least 30 years.

Regular Reviews

The trust is well aware of the dangers of stagnation and complacency. It undertakes regular reviews of its work and adjusts policies and practices accordingly. All committees meet quarterly to review aims, grants and issues arising. In addition to these regular reviews the trust is required under its deed to review every 10 years whether to continue; this may be used as a review of the mix of all programmes, but it was suggested that regular reviews are actually more useful.

Scanning the Environment

Considerable time is spent reviewing the wider context, including the political context. Discussion about the wider context may lead to not re-funding projects or a programme if the context has changed, or to the identification of new issues. For example, recently the Trust has reviewed its programme in South Africa with a view to winding it down in a changed political context. It has also started exploring work in response to the rise of extreme right-wing groups in parts of the UK.

Going Where No Funder Has Gone Before

One factor that adds to the trust deciding to engage in a programme area is if other funders are not involved: 'We don't need to get involved if other funders are already there. We see our particular role as being where other funders are not – if an applicant has a government grant then we would question why we should be there – but there might be strategic exceptions.' Generally, however, the trust finds that its social-justice orientation leads it towards programmes not attractive to many other funders.

Exit Strategy

When other funders enter a field, or the policy environment changes, then that may be a reason for the trust to withdraw. For example, the trust had significant programmes around development education, but ended those when government and the large international aid agencies became more active. Similarly, in 2001 the trust terminated its poverty and economic justice programme because other large funders were putting in large sums of money, and good applications were no longer coming through. This was a particularly painful decision because poverty and economic justice were a crucial part of the history and tradition of the trust. The length of time the trust tends to stay with programme areas makes the issue of exiting particularly difficult.

Constant Adaptation

Even though the trust tends to maintain its involvement for decades, this does not mean that programmes stand still. Programmes are constantly being re-shaped. In some cases, this happens as key recipient organizations re-invent themselves as issues change. In other cases, the changing context indicates a need for more fundamental review. For example, the trust has been active in South Africa for decades. Prior to 1994 the trust had a clear role focusing on civil and political rights, but now the key issues are the much broader ones of economic rights. As a result, the trust has re-focused its South Africa programme for the coming five years, after which the programme will end.

Theory of Social Change

The trust is clear that it is about social change, but there are a variety of inherited models: 'Sometimes it's a community development model; sometimes it's "fund bright individuals who can make change happen." In the fields of peace and racial justice generally, the theory of change isn't very clear. Racial justice operates across the whole spectrum – grassroots, national government, EU.'

Although social change is talked about, staff could not remember 'having a big discussion about it'. However, it was suggested that 'maybe we are discussing it when we say "we don't think this project will make a difference" or that it's not on the right time-scale. But it's done on a case-by-case basis only.' One reason for the variety of approaches may be, as one person suggested, that trustees have different perspectives on how social change happens.

The West Yorkshire programme on racial justice was based on the idea of change from the grassroots but there were doubts about whether it was sufficient; it was suggested that the programme needs a two-pronged approach, both bottom-up and top-down. Arguably, however, it is this willingness to work at a variety of levels from local to the EU that contributes to the trust's creativity and effectiveness in achieving social change.

Dig a little deeper and the trust does have a theory of change in which flexibility and pragmatism are central. One key factor in this theory is that social change is not about rationality and logic. For example, on the issue of migration the Trust believes that if the aim was to produce a rational and just immigration and asylum system there would be few problems. 'But the challenge is far more complex. It is how to provide a just system that has some chance of being adopted and of surviving in the context of the prejudice that exists, that is being fermented by the tabloid press, the political pressure this creates, and the reflex which seems to impel politicians to respond by demonstrating toughness to the point of ruthlessness. Logic and rationality are not enough for this' (Stephen Pittam, speech to EFC Annual General Assembly, Athens, 31 May 2004: p. 3). Meeting this challenge involves staying with issues, being idealistic and pragmatic and opportunistic all at once, funding both 'insider' and 'outsider' organizations and using the trust's position to bring people together at critical times.

Space for Creativity

Staff emphasize the importance of allowing space for responsive creativity. For example, when the government introduced a bill to remove benefit entitlements and other rights from asylum seekers, and to fast-track it into law, the trustees told staff to take £50,000 and 'see what you can do'. Working with a range of other organizations including service groups, refugee councils, church bodies and other funders, the trust created an alternative forum, chaired by a retired high-court judge, to ensure debate in the public arena.

The trust attributes part of its effectiveness to the fact that it has a minimum of bureaucracy. Most effort goes into deciding which groups to fund and then to build relationships with them. The main evaluation is done at the application stage: 'If we believe it's going to make a difference then we give them the space and freedom to do that. We make the grant and trust people to do the work.'

The trust aims to create a partnership with those funded, 'liberating groups to take risks and to follow their vision rather than jump through hoops of our creation'. But, at the same time, the trust sees its role as 'critical friend' to grantees, helping them to refine strategy, stay on target, and assess the impact of their work.

Space for maximum creativity also comes from the way in which budgets are allocated and managed. At the level of programmes and grants, 'if we decide we want this to happen then we make sure we make it happen – even if that means moving between budget heads'. At the trust level, a sustainable income formula has been developed that smooths out the peaks and the troughs of the markets over a long period and allows the trust to plan on a steady growth of expenditure. As one member of staff commented: 'we're very privileged, we don't have to worry about the money.'

Flexibility Within Core Values

It was also said that creativity is maintained because the lack of tight definitions for programme areas allows new issues to arise out of existing programmes.

'We focus on core values rather than programme boundaries – that's our strength.' Because the trust tends to have long-term relationships with its grantees, it may continue funding as an issue is re-defined or develops into another phase. This was the pattern in its work on freedom of information over a number of years.

Limits to Involvement and Focus

The trust's creative approach was also related to its self-imposed limits on areas of funding: 'If we were working locally in welfare it would be very hard to maintain that consistency because old people would need to be cared for.'

Issues and Implications

Ensuring Diversity

As noted above, all trustees are members of the Religious Society of Friends. Trustees are recruited by a variety of means including advertising. The trust aims to have an age and gender mix within the short-list. When recruiting by advertising, the short-listed applicants are invited to spend a weekend at the trust. The criteria for selection tend to vary depending on the trust's current skill-balance and needs. In general, it likes to have one trustee in each age decade.

Potential new trustees are first invited to 'sit in' on trust meetings for a year, during which time they are able to join in all aspects of the trust's work. Trustees are appointed for a maximum of 30 years, with a maximum age of 70 years old. The original trustees all served their full 30 years, but now, for various reasons, the average period of tenure is declining. One third of trustees are currently in their 40s but some are in their 50s and 60s, so this provides for some natural turnover in trustees. Change is also introduced via the practice of trustee sabbaticals.

Some within the trust acknowledge that there is a tension between the desire for openness and the restriction of board membership to Quakers. Requiring all board members to be Quakers is seen as a different issue from that of maintaining Quaker values, which is clearly seen as an essential element in the trust's philosophy and a powerful source of creativity.

Openness and Meeting Trust Needs

There is also seen to be a tension between open advertisement and meeting trust needs. Whereas advertising is seen as a very good method of finding generic trustees, it is not seen as wholly satisfactory in finding trustees from a particular niche, or with specialist skills, or people from a younger age group.

Demands on Trustees

The trust has high expectations of trustees. General criteria for short-listing include: a wide interest in national and international issues, the ability to read quickly, good communication skills, and the ability to offer at least 10 hours per week to trust business. Trustees are involved in considering applications and going on visits, as well as in policy-making and review. As a result, 'trustee time is a scarce and very valuable commodity'. Trustees generally sit on at least two sub-committees and spend 1.5 days at each of the quarterly board meetings. The trust has recently introduced a new pattern of quarterly meetings involving three meetings for business and one for reflection, analysis and for 'bonding'.

Creative vs. Conservative – Old vs. New

Although trustees are more than willing to be creative in their approach to grant-making, it is acknowledged that there is a conservative tendency when it comes to change within the organization. The trust's commitment to staying with programmes for a decade or more is recognized as valuable, but this creates some tensions with the time and resources needed to introduce new areas of work. The trust's practice of focusing its evaluation at the application stage, and then leaving grantees a high degree of flexibility to be creative in what they do, is seen by some as being in tension with the ability to learn from grant-making after the event.

Managing Exit

The trust exited from its work on poverty and economic justice, despite the pain involved, on the grounds that it had to be prepared to dig up its roots when changing circumstances meant it could no longer be most effective. But exiting from programmes remains a topic of concern, and the trust is currently exam-ining how 'we discern the time to take up new work and refocus or lay down programmes that may have become tired'.

Adding Value

The trust is considering ways in which it can make links between programmes, drawing out cross-cutting issues to add additional value to its activities. For example, it is currently discussing ways of focusing its democracy programme on accountability and transparency, and merging this with the corporate responsi-bility programme, as there are obvious links between the two areas of work. The trust enjoys thinking about how to make the best use of its resources. It often puts grantees in touch with others working on similar themes, and occasionally arranges gatherings of grantees in a programme area to discuss the changing context or to explore the bigger picture.

Working at the Boundary

The trust is always conscious of the need to stay within the confines of charity law, but feels that its niche is to be on the ever-changing boundary of what is considered to be charitable. Sometimes this was said to be a constraint on the trustees' adventurousness, but in the main was seen as a creative tension to be worked with.

Branding

Unlike its better-known sister, the Joseph Rowntree Foundation, the trust does not typically adopt a high profile in much of its work. It does not, for example, so clearly promote and brand the products of its work. The trust's working model is, rather, to empower others – its grantees – to achieve change. Empowerment is a key concept in the trust's overall philosophy, but this creates some tensions.

The trust currently has a somewhat ambivalent position on branding. On the one hand, it is argued that the trust has no brand, and that this is an advantage: 'We don't try to build up our brand, so don't worry about our brand being damaged . . . It means we can take more risks, and we can fund both sides of an argument, or we can fund the sound evidence side as well as the placard wavers.' On the other hand, the trust recognizes that the Joseph Rowntree Foundation has been hugely successful in influencing policy because of its strong branding of the work it funds. 'We say we're not like that, we're more about empowerment; we fund and empower other people to push for change.'

Some argued that although the Trust says it does not have a brand, in reality it does. 'We say we don't have a brand but really we do. Creativity is part of our brand. Trustees generally like to be at the cutting edge. Part of our brand is about being adventurous and taking risks – but we do have boundaries.' It was also suggested by interviewees that the trust is becoming more proactive in taking and pushing issues in its own name.

Recent JRCT Key Achievements

The trust describes trying to work out its key achievements as a very complex task. 'Our basic business is to give money to others to try to achieve change. The organizations we fund exist in a wider context, and it is just as difficult for them to attribute change directly to their interventions.'

Accepting these caveats, it may be possible to argue that the JRCT played a small part in bringing into being:

- The Human Rights Act 1998, through its support for the key organizations in the *Bill of Rights Consortium*, and in particular the Human Rights Incorporation Project.

- The Public Interest Disclosure Act 1998, through its support for Public Concern at Work.

- The Freedom of Information Act 2000, through its support for the Campaign for Freedom of Information.

- The trust is currently funding individuals and organizations involved in the Task Force working with the Government to create a Commission for Equality and Human Rights.

These initiatives are measurable, insofar that legislation has been introduced or agencies may be created. Much harder is the task of assessing impact in other areas, such as in getting ideas into the mainstream. The positive economic benefits of migration are now openly discussed, whereas when the JRCT was funding the Institute for Public Policy Research (IPPR) to work on these issues, this was a taboo subject. The idea of community mediation is now widely accepted, yet it wasn't when the JRCT was funding early projects in this field. Conflict transformation and peace-building are now words in the wider lexicon, but they weren't a few years ago. The JRCT may have played just a small part in helping organizations to bring about changes in the environment such as these.

> Are the people of West Yorkshire better able to engage with civic change because of interventions funded through our West Yorkshire Racial Justice Programme? To what extent has the peace process in Northern Ireland been supported through the trust's long-term backing for peace-building initiatives there, often on contentious issues? It is impossible to say, and yet some of these types of low-key initiatives may well have been just as significant in making the world a fairer, more just and peaceful place as the higher-profile work on legislation.
> We fund organizations operating on both the outside and inside tracks – groups proposing radical solutions as part of a long-term vision, and other groups working to influence short-term government policy. We fund think-tanks and campaigning organizations working on the same issue. Occasionally we bring these different strands together, especially when a window of opportunity arises to create change.

Being a political actor and trying to influence the political agenda is a risky and long-term strategy, and one that would require a certain size and resource-base, and room for the creativity needed for flexible programme and exit strategies. Yet foundations can also become involved in policy change through smaller, targeted programmes that put a premium on collaboration and networking. This is the case of the Carnegie United Kingdom Trust, our next case study.

4   The Carnegie United Kingdom Trust

> 'Being creative isn't about money. It's about getting ideas, evidence, people, networks, thinking, motivation and so on together.'

Like the JRCT represents the creative foundation in the realm of policy-making, the Carnegie United Kingdom Trust is an example of a relatively small foundation in terms of endowment, that through focus, networking and tenacity nonetheless manages to achieve significant policy change. It illustrates that creative philanthropy is not limited to sizeable fortunes and large programme staff, and that the creative use of partnerships and different forms of collaboration are important modes of philanthropic engagement.

Background

Established in 1913 by Andrew Carnegie, the Carnegie United Kingdom Trust is one of an international family of trusts founded by Carnegie and now working more closely together. Carnegie specified that the UK Trust, located in his birthplace of Dunfermline, Scotland, should be governed by trustees drawn from across the UK and Ireland, with a proportion of trustees coming from Dunfermline.

In 2003 the trust's total income was a modest £1.44 million. Recent annual reports stress the declining income of the trust due to a combination of a falling investment market and the effects of withdrawal of tax rebates on income (the latter was a Labour government financial reform that inadvertently damaged foundations' investment incomes).

The trust has 14 trustees, of whom the deed stipulates that 50 per cent must come from Dunfermline and the remainder from across the UK. Three of the trustees are women.

The mission of the trust at its founding and today is: 'the improvement of the well-being of the people of Great Britain and Ireland, by such means as are embraced within the meaning of the word "charitable", remembering that new needs are constantly arising' (Carnegie United Kingdom Trust 2003: p. 4). It is by any measure a very broad and open mission, and one that has been, and continues to be, carried out in the context of changing circumstances, as we will see below.

Current Programmes

The trust supports research, public policy analysis and grassroots social-action initiatives. In 2003 the trust concentrated on three major areas: rural community development; 'creativity and imagination which fosters innovations, particularly those which cross borders between art, science, heritage, community and the environment'; and young people's active involvement in public decision-making (Carnegie United Kingdom Trust 2003: p. 4). Within these three areas, much of the trust's work involves a more-or-less integrated strategy of combining knowledge-based work designed to influence policy with what looks, on the surface, very much like traditional grant-making.

In the 1990s, one of the trust's major contributions was the Third Age Programme, designed to put issues of ageing on the policy agenda. The Third Age Programme worked on four major fronts: age discrimination, employment, learning, and public services for older people (Carnegie United Kingdom Trust n.d.). Highlights of the programme included: a debate in the House of Lords on the programme's first major publication; a series of conferences with local authorities throughout the UK and in Ireland; a series of major national conferences; the appointment by government of an inter-ministerial group on older people, subsequently elevated to a cabinet committee; publication of a report by the Cabinet Office's Performance and Innovation Unit, with trust involvement, on actions by government concerned with active ageing; the appointment of a champion for older people at cabinet level; the government's commitment to age-discrimination legislation; and the establishment of permanent 'Better Government for Older People' structures. It would be no exaggeration to suggest that 'the combination of the Trust's original research, its subsequent campaigning and the many alliances which have been formed, have together played an influential role in bringing third-age issues firmly onto centre stage in public policy' (Carnegie United Kingdom Trust 2002).

Developing Strategy: The Move to a Creative Approach

The trust explains its creative approach partly in terms of its very broad remit. '"The benefit of the masses as they progress, meeting new needs as they arise . . ." gives you plenty of scope.' But a wide remit merely allows space for a creative approach, which took a discernible leap forward in the early 1990s. Drivers of this move towards a creative approach included the following.

New Blood and Free Spirits

The new phase of creativity was driven in part by a new chief executive and in part by the trustees. The UK trustees are described as a collection of 'free spirits';

they come from diverse backgrounds and are involved in various fields and issues ranging from the voluntary sector to business and the trades unions. Although these people might now be seen as members of the Great and the Good, 'they often joined before their gongs – we have a tradition of tapping into able people, talent spotting'. Most recently, being ahead of their time in spotting new talent has been illustrated in the involvement of a then 22-year-old researcher who is now one of the rising stars of policy-thinking and -making in the UK. While the trust has taken positive steps in recent years to widen the age and ethnic diversity of its board, it recognizes that more still needs to be done, particularly with regard to gender diversity.

The Appeal of History

The new phase of creativity involved increasing the proportion of resources going into the trust's strategic, policy-related initiatives, as distinct from its traditional grant-making. Some trustees were more enthusiastic about this than others. In overcoming resistance, being able to place a creative approach within the foundation's history may have been important. In its early years in the 1920s, the trust engaged in diverse and, for the time, innovative grant-making, setting up baby clinics and encouraging new musicians and music; in addition, although Carnegie is known in the UK primarily for his endowment of libraries all over the country, in the United States he started the first pension fund for school teachers, established an endowment for peace, and was interested in scientific innovations. Thus it was argued that from its birth the trust has involved people who wanted to influence change rather than just helping the poor.

Elements of a Creative Approach

Beyond Money: The Value of Independence and Voice

Given its very modest income it is perhaps not surprising that the trust sees one of its greatest assets as being its independent voice, emphasizing 'the importance of trusts and foundations as a truly independent force with the freedom to experiment and be creative'. 'Independence gives trusts an authentic voice in a sound-byte world – a voice which enables them to speak to government and act as a neutral ground for dialogue among groups with passionately held beliefs and interests' (Carnegie United Kingdom Trust 2002: p. 9).

Long-term Commitment

In its major programmes the trust works for as long as it takes to achieve and embed change. For example, the trust's Third Age Programme was sustained for 11 years.

Taking Risks

The trust's then CEO illustrated taking risks with the following story. 'The Nerve Centre in Derry (five out-of-work musicians at the time) sent a 42 page application (we ask for about 4 pages). A meeting . . . convinced me that he would either change the world or fail gloriously. About six years later the Nerve Centre was nominated for an Oscar' (Carnegie United Kingdom Trust 2002: p. 10). The trust aims to have a portfolio of grants with different levels of risk. 'Enough "blue-chip" grants enable you to have some much more risky, less well-formed projects.'

Regular Review: Looking In and Out

Although a quinquennial review has a longer history, the introduction of a mid-quinquennial review appears to have coincided with the new phase of creativity. The mid-quinquennial review examines the progress of all current grants, as well as what is going on in their wider environments. The quinquennial review focuses on governance, broad direction and future priorities. Review papers are compiled by a working group involving staff, trustees, key stakeholders and others in the field, including external evaluators.

Diverse Viewpoints

Reviews always have an outsider as an enabler and speakers on key issues or areas in which the trust is involved, or which are bubbling up in the wider environment. One person commented that these outsiders are selected to be stimulating, to bring different viewpoints and 'may be slightly zany'.

Open and Participative Governance

At its 1997 review the trust recognized that its governance needed to be more transparent, 'more diverse and more frequently refreshed' (Carnegie United Kingdom Trust 2002: p. 10). The trust no longer appoints trustees for life, and half the trustees are recruited by public advertisement. By these means the trust seeks to 'stay in touch' and keep its governance, and creativity, 'fresh'.

Dissemination

The trust disseminates the results of its work widely in an array of often influential publications. For example, the trust's publication of *Life, Work and Livelihood in the Third Age* (1993) was hailed as highly authoritative, and set in train a long series of events culminating, among other things, in the government's acceptance of the

EU's Equal Treatment Directive and a commitment to introduce age discrimination legislation by 2006 (Carnegie United Kingdom Trust 2002: p. 14). Research publications emanating from the Carnegie Young People Initiative are recognized as having shaped much of the Labour government's approach to supporting the 'voice' of young people in public decision-making (Carnegie United Kingdom Trust 2003).

Evaluation and Learning

The trust commissions evaluations of key programmes, and attempts to build learning from evaluations back into strategy and practice. For example, the Carnegie Commission for Rural Community Development, established in 2004, is the result of review of decades of learning from grants to village halls and other rural organizations. In other fields, evaluation of a project is often the trigger for replication on a wider scale.

Scanning the Environment: Wide Horizons

In looking for ideas of ways in which to improve its work the trust casts its net widely. For example, it recently commissioned a study of young people's participation projects in the United States, and a scoping study of rural community development policy and practice across Europe, to inform its work in the UK and Ireland.

Being One Step Ahead

In choosing its priority areas the trust has demonstrated its capacity for working ahead of current agendas, and thus being able to join emerging debates on an informed footing. For example, the trust's focus on young people, which began in 1996, was later confirmed by analysis of the following year's general election that demonstrated a crisis in British democracy in the form of huge alienation among voters, especially among the under-25s. This gave extra point and context to CYPI's [Carnegie Young People's Initiative] UK Report published only weeks later, which charted both young people's alienation as well as good practice in involving young people in public decision-making. It made a series of recommendations subsequently adopted by government. Similarly, when the trust decided to focus on rural community development, rural issues were neglected by the media, policy-makers and foundations alike, in favour of a concentration on the seemingly more dramatic problems of urban areas. Shortly afterward, Britain was hit by a foot-and-mouth epidemic, leading to a new focus on rural matters.

Adaptation and Consultation

In the case above, subsequent events, including the entry of government with new resources, and increased media attention, further increased the difficulty of decisions in this area. 'We didn't leap onto that, we stopped to draw breath and see how funding structures changed and played out.' In late 2003 the trust undertook extensive consultation with key players in rural community development, in the public, private voluntary and academic sectors. As a result of that consultation the trust decided to launch the Carnegie Commission for Rural Community Development in 2004.

Following Through to Implementation: Hanging AroundWaving the Flag

Having succeeded in changing the terms of public debate, and in some cases having achieved policy or legislative change, the trust does not immediately back out, but rather follows up on reports and ideas to ensure that they are implemented and become embedded. In the Third Age Programme, for example, the trust continued its work for another six years after its key ideas had been widely accepted. In other cases, widespread acceptance of new ideas may take longer than anticipated to achieve. In both getting ideas into popular currency and ensuring that they are properly embedded, 'surfing the ideas of the time is fine, but sometimes you have to hang around in the field waving your little flag'.

Working on Several Fronts

In its major programmes such as the Third Age and CYPI, the trust works on several fronts at the same time, carrying out research, generating debate, producing publications, and networking widely. For example, the CYPI programme engaged in a series of studies mapping activity aimed at engaging young people; a range of partnership initiatives, including work with the National Consumer Council resulting in a presentation by young people at 11 Downing Street; a survey of, and subsequent service for, support of participation workers; a study of the potential of e-participation; and a seminar for other funders on grant-giving to groups led by young people (Carnegie United Kingdom Trust 2002). During 2004, the Carnegie Commission for Rural Community Development organized a major practitioners' conference and engaged in focus-groups consultations with grassroots practitioners, government ministers and civil servants across the UK, Ireland and at the European Commission. In 2005 it initiated six major UK and Ireland-wide action-research programmes designed to inform sustainable policy and practice. Significantly, the trust's rural community development action-research programme has been designed from the outset as proactive, where the trust is seeking partners rather than responding to open grant applications.

Combining Knowledge and Action

The Trust is seen as 'punching above its weight' (Carnegie United Kingdom Trust 2001: p. 7). It attributes this to combining 'strategic policy research and action with grassroots grant-making; it commits itself over a sustained period; its policy recommendations are based on research; and it is willing to take risks' (Carnegie United Kingdom Trust 2001: p. 7). The trust has 'always made a point of combining its grant-giving with policy work to develop ideas and good practice in fields in which it is working' (Carnegie United Kingdom Trust 2002: p. 4). Grant-giving is tailored to reflect and enhance the trust's strategic policy initiatives. 'Grant-making and strategic initiatives reinforce one another, thereby enhancing impact and communication' (Carnegie United Kingdom Trust 2001: p. 7).

Top-Down and Bottom-Up

The trust disclaims any clearly articulated theory of social change, although it is generally perceived as being socially progressive, 'but if we had one it would be top-down and bottom-up.' However, it was also suggested that: 'If there's a trustee paradigm it's that we make an evidence-based argument'.

From the Micro to Macro: Focus on Causes

The mid-quinquennial review may highlight the need to move from grassroots grants to a strategic programme examining the bigger picture, including issues underlying the need for grassroots grants. It may also throw up new areas of work, or perceived imbalances in the trust's work. For example, the trust's recent focus on rural areas arose in part from the observation at a mid-quinquennial review that almost all of the trust's work was then in urban areas.

Instinct and Evidence

Creativity in the trust was described as a mixture of instinct and homework. Trustees identify new issues they see as likely to be important. 'At this stage it's about gut and instinct, a feel for the mood of the time.' This was the early source of the trust's major focus on young people's participation in decision-making, before analysis of voting patterns in the 1997 general election had revealed the extent of young people's disengagement.

Doing Your Homework

Trustees come up with a wide range of ideas from which, after discussion, a much smaller number emerge as possibilities. This is followed by considerable in-house research, looking in more depth at the issue, who else is working on it, the policy environment and so on. 'It's not a matter of saying "yes, that's a good idea". You've got to take it seriously if you're going to do it, and that means really doing your homework.' 'Trustees won't pick up radical issues just for the sake of it. It has to be thought through.' As a result of this process some ideas may be dropped. Those that survive are looked at in yet more detail, and the process of identifying key issues and questions begins.

Rich Networks From the Start

The trust creates and draws on rich and diverse networks to develop its knowledge-base and build constituencies for change. For example, in the trust's work with both older and young people the first semi-public stage involved a conference of about 50 people drawn from a wide variety of settings. The conference forms the basis for creation of a steering group, again composed of a diverse mix of people and interests. 'Right from the start it's about getting a large number of people involved with you, with varying levels of influence in different fields.' Partnership with others is seen as one of the key ingredients of creativity, and a way of making resources go further. Contact and networks formed as a result of grant-making may also feed into both the conference and the steering group.

Building Credibility and Using Reputation

'Credibility with government and the field is built on solid research, consultation and networking. Such a research foundation and network of contacts provides a basis for informed grant-giving.' The trust's independence is seen as a valuable tool in bringing people together and forming partnerships: 'Because we are independent we can act as a point of coalescence for various interests.' The trust's time-scales and its reputation are also important in bringing people to the table. 'We're not going to be around [on any one issue] for long enough to be a threat, but our work is not so short term that it's not worth being involved.' 'People come along to our consultations because they know we'll get results and because they know there are grants as well as "thinks".'

Timing and Opportunism

Timing of reports is seen as playing a part in achieving effective influence. 'It's pointless producing a report for it to go into mid-air. You want to help take the agenda forward, so you do look at timing.' But timing of the launch of a report has to remain flexible to a degree. Where obvious opportunities do not arise, 'you can't be too driven by waiting for Godot; you've got to keep the impetus going'.

Piggybacking on other events and conferences is one way of maintaining impetus, from which interviewees said everyone gains.

Opening Windows

In its creative work the trust works in three-year blocks. The argument for such blocks is that 'you can't see much further than that', and within that framework there may be open policy windows through which the trust can contribute. In the Third Age Programme such opportunities did not initially arise; later in the programme a combination of serendipity and planning gave the trust the necessary openings. In the case of CYPI the trust was confident that voting patterns in the general election would demonstrate young people's lack of involvement; the launch of the report was planned for three weeks after the election, when voting patterns would still be a topic of debate.

Iteration not Cataclysm

Despite the importance of reports and their timing, the trust sees reports as only a milestone along the way, part of a much longer, wider process of engagement and dialogue. The trust's contribution to public debate and policy is an iterative rather than cataclysmic process. 'By the time you get to the report, a lot of the ideas are already in common currency.' Promulgation does not follow consultation; rather, the two go hand in hand.

Opening Doors

One of the acknowledged advantages of having a collection of trustees from diverse but influential backgrounds is that they 'know how to work a lot of [different] systems, whose door to knock on, whose phone to ring'. As one person said, 'this trust has consciously used the Establishment to get doors open', but, at the same time, trustees are said to value 'having the nerve-end of raw real work' behind them when they knock on doors.

The way in which the trust has built its reputation, and the way in which it builds dialogue and engagement around an issue over a period of time, also have an effect on its ability to open doors. In an important sense, success breeds success. For example, in the Third Age Programme there were three major conferences, each with an audience of several hundred people; the Third Age Programme became difficult to ignore and at the last conference five ministers attended, generating an even larger audience and thus further confirming the groundswell of support for the programme.

Language Matters

Building constituencies for change involves attention to detail, including negoti-
ating the minefields of 'political correctness'. As the former chief executive
explained: 'I saw part of my job as trying to eliminate jargon and ways of saying
things that might offend people at either end of the political spectrum. Politically
correct language often puts people off even though they may agree with the idea.'

Performance Measurement and Evaluation: Space for Learning and Creativity

The trust is said to be 'not too hung up about performance measurement'.
Trustees may ask an external body to evaluate the quality of an application; the
trust may commission case studies of grant-aided projects by an external body;
and it may commission an exploration of lessons learned from a collection of
similar projects, as in its work on museums and IT.

Evaluations and performance measurement are rarely focused on establishing
what difference the trust made. 'You can never really say that if we hadn't done it,
it would never have happened.' However, this does not mean that the trust is
unreflective and un-self-critical; the quinquennial and mid-quinquennial reviews
take a critical look at the trust's achievements and continuing role in the light of a
changing environment.

Evaluation at the start of a project is in large part about establishing confidence
in the people, the organization and the broad idea of the project. Creativity is
seen as requiring flexibility to adapt, backing people and ideas, and then giving
them the space to be creative. 'Part of any creative process is backing people and
giving them opportunity.' Evaluation during or after the project is less about
'policing' and accountability and more about learning lessons and sharing that
learning, or about showing what has been done in order to create 'a culture in
which (other) people feel they can do it'.

Exit Strategies to Make Room for the New

Just as the mid-quinquennial review is the source of ideas for new work, so it may
sound the death knell for existing programmes. A grant may be brought to an end
'because it's just trundling on, or because, say, government has stepped in and
that work isn't so relevant anymore'. 'Clearing the decks is part of the creative
process, making room for new issues.'

The trust has a strong commitment to being 'a dynamic, learning organization
that people want to work for and do business with' (Carnegie United Kingdom
Trust 2004a). Since the appointment of its new CEO in 2003, the trust has incorporated an enhanced commitment to investment in staff and trustee learning, as
an integral part of its work programme planning.

Issues and Implications

As noted above, the trust combines a creative approach in a small number of key programmes with, until 2004, fairly conventional grant-making across a wider range. Perhaps inevitably, adopting two styles of working creates some tensions around the balance and allocation of resources. Some trustees may more easily see the benefits of conventional grant-giving; others may be more willing to take the risk of accepting the slow-burning fuse of work designed to influence policy.

Learning and Added Value

One benefit of conventional grant-making alongside strategic creative initiatives is the opportunity for learning and added value. Grants may highlight the need to take up issues underlying the need for and nature of grassroots grants. For example, the trust's funding of village halls provided important background for its subsequent creative work in rural areas. Just as grants may be the foundation for a strategic programme, they may follow and feed into a creative initiative providing valuable information on the way issues play out at local level, or opportunities to engage in small-scale practical 'experiments' in change. Grant-making was said to function as one of the trust's 'reality checks', keeping it and its ideas grounded in real life. In 2004 the trust undertook a review of its grant-making, and concluded that its model of generally small-scale, short-duration (up to three years) grants had 'reinforced short-term project funding dependency amongst the voluntary sector'. Through the lack of a robust system of evaluation, the trust was unable to assess the contribution of its grant programmes towards its strategic work or to measure impact either locally or in terms of wider replicability (Carnegie United Kingdom Trust 2004c). As a result of this review, the board decided to end the trust's reactive grants programmes from March 2005.

Legitimacy, Networks and Knowledge

Before 2004, the continuance of grant-making alongside creative initiatives was perceived as providing legitimacy, networks and knowledge. 'We get street credibility from the grants we give and contact with people doing the hard graft in their areas. We have relationships with good solid practitioners as well as new, raw people who tell it from the hip.' In its rural work, for example, trust credibility and networks have been built since its early funding of village halls in the 1920s and, much later, its support for more holistic rural community development programmes. The trust now believes that it can secure legitimacy, networks and knowledge through the quality of its action research and more proactive partnership approaches. It recognizes that the lessons from effectively evaluated grassroots social action can be accessed from a number of sources, far wider than the generally anecdotal and subjective evidence gathered in previous years from projects that the trust itself funded. 'The trust, through the approach it adopts for its commissions, think tanks and action research, lays great stress upon using a variety of methods to ensure that it has strong antennae out to the real world.'

Reality Check

Whatever the tensions created by different perspectives between, for example, national and local trustees, those differences are also seen as strengths. The Dunfermline trustees are seen, for example, as providing an important 'reality check'. 'The danger with ideas is that you can get carried away with a beautiful idea – having local people on the board means that they're always asking "yes, but what difference will it make?"'

Organizational Conservatism

The move from life tenure to a fixed term for trustees, advertising, job specifications and induction initially met with some resistance from within the trust, and, so far, has taken around four years to implement. There is however now a recognition across all of the board of trustees of the need for diversity of membership and for a more open approach to trustee recruitment. Interestingly this approach has also had an impact upon the thinking and practice within the local Carnegie Dunfermline Trust, which nominates half the membership of the UK Trust.

'Young, Gifted and Black': Older, Middle Class and Radical?

Although the trust has closely involved some 'young, gifted and black' people in the governance and management of its projects, the Board is (at the time of writing) currently predominantly white (two black trustees), male (one female trustee), middle class and older (two under their mid-30s). On the one hand, this is seen as having some advantages. First, it is argued that 'people on the board know how to operate change – whose door to knock on, how you do it, how you get legislation through'. Second, there is a view that age has little to do with the capacity for creativity. 'Some of the oldest, or perhaps it's because they are nearly retired, like being iconoclastic.' On the other hand, although the importance of openness is accepted, advertising for trustees has produced recent recruits in their early 30s who are described as 'spiky people, but still mainly middle class'. Both advertising and headhunting are adopted by the trust, but all applicants are subject to interview.

Costs

Although, as discussed above, the balance of resources between creative and conventional grantmaking can create tensions, the costs of creative work are not in themselves an issue partly because they are seen not as overheads but as project costs like any other.

Letting Go

Letting go of work in steering groups can create tensions. For example, the work on young people started well but then became 'too stratospheric' and had to be re-focused to avoid dominating the trust disproportionately. 'This involved an adult but very painful tension between the trustees and the people involved on the steering committee. It was a real debate, with real pain.'

Waiting for the Wave

The trust sees itself as 'surfing the ideas of the time' in spotting issues for creative work. 'Instinct gives you the ability to be one step ahead of the mood of the time. But groundswells take different lengths of time to gain momentum and can hit early or later.' One implication of this is that it is not possible to make firm plans and timetables in advance. 'You've got to be astute and opportunistic about launching reports' and, in some cases, it may be necessary to stay involved for longer than anticipated. This creates obvious difficulties in planning and budgeting. For example, the Carnegie Third Age Programme finally ended after 11 years of investment – far longer than originally envisaged.

Creativity and Idiosyncrasy

The trust accepts that the line between creativity and idiosyncrasy is a fine one. The trust resolves the potential tension here by 'managing' idiosyncrasy: 'Doing the homework, getting feedback from others and forcing identification of what the issues are and how the trust can make a difference are part of that process.' There have been occasions when one or more of the trustees were particularly keen on taking up an issue about which others were unsure. Review of existing activity in the field, discussions with others and, crucially, analysis of what role the trust could play, ensure that creativity is subject to hard-nosed reality.

To Brand or Not to Brand

The trust works on the theory that in order to get phones answered and doors opened it needs intellectual capital, and reputational capital. In building reputational capital the Carnegie brand is undoubtedly important. 'The Carnegie name has a cachet and that gets people involved. And we've been around a long time.' The tensions arise because it is felt that in the voluntary sector there is a view that funders should maintain a very low, if not invisible, profile. 'But we do want to promote our imprimatur. That's part of our recognition and building that.' Indeed, as of 2004, the board of trustees have taken a strategic decision to enhance the use of the Carnegie brand as a recognition of the almost unique selling point that distinguishes the trust in the UK from most other foundations. Few have such an iconic name and public recognition. As a central feature of this more assertive use of the brand, the current CEO, with the support of the board, is keen to develop programmes that enable partnerships with some of the 24 Carnegie foundations worldwide. Ironically, outside the United States, international Carnegie collaboration has been minimal.

Staying Independent

The trust's very success in achieving recognition and uptake of its ideas, combined with its emphasis on working to ensure implementation, means that it often has to walk a fine line between 'seduction inside the policy-making tent' and staying independent. This issue was particularly apparent when aspects of the Carnegie Third Age Programme were taken up by the Labour government. Members of the programme, in particular the chairman, were increasingly drawn into Cabinet Office policy deliberations and structures. The dilemma was resolved by encouraging new network bodies and putting a clear time limit on the programme.

Recent and Future Developments

In the future, the trust would like to develop greater synergy between its grant-making and strategic work. This will be achieved by being both more selective and more proactive in its grant-making, approaching grantees to test out an idea or approach. At the same time, however, the trust is conscious of the 'danger of being arrogant and thinking you have access to all the good ideas'.

On 1 December 2004 the trust announced that it will 'replace its grants programmes to the charitable sector after March 2005 – and step up its investment in independent national inquiries, complemented by supporting larger scale action-research designed to influence public policy and deliver longer-term change for the benefit of the people of the UK and Ireland. This new direction for the Trust builds upon the significant success that Carnegie has had in influencing public policy and statutory and non-governmental services around such areas as the Public Libraries, Social Work Services, the Third Age, the Voluntary Arts, Community Service and Youth Participation' (Carnegie United Kingdom Trust 2004b).

This change was made because the trust has become increasingly concerned that 'short-term funding, prevalent across the foundations world, has not been an effective way of addressing changing issues and needs' (*ibid.*) and has involved 'voluntary and community organisations in large amounts of time submitting complex applications for relatively small sums of money to Trusts like Carnegie. The reality is that over 90% of applications are rejected due to the competitive pressures upon our funds' (*ibid.*).

'We shall be increasingly working in partnership with other foundations, statutory agencies, non-governmental organisations and the research community, both here and overseas. In doing this we shall in particular be enhancing our links with the over twenty Carnegie foundations worldwide to address the growing agenda of global issues that have an impact upon people's lives in the UK and Ireland' (*ibid.*).

Working with other Carnegie foundations is seen as providing the trust with 'unparalleled access to some of the best thinkers and civil society players worldwide, working in such areas as international peace, human rights, democracy building, the environment and education' (*ibid.*). 'Through the work of our Commissions and Inquiries and targeted action research, we shall be working with organisations here and overseas to influence change that brings a real and sustained difference in people's lives.'

This strategy flows from the three main priorities the trust set for itself in 2003: to 'build a modern forward-looking Scottish-based foundation at the cutting edge of social change; to build a dynamic, learning organization that people want to work for and do business with; and to build an independent organization that thinks globally and is part of a wider international movement capable of bringing to the policy and practice agenda the best ideas from around the world' (Carnegie United Kingdom Trust 2003: p. 7). For a relatively small foundation, collaboration and networking is seen as a key to success.

The case of the Carnegie United Kingdom Trust is that of a foundation with a wide remit and a relatively small endowment. To be relevant and to become successful, the trust is forced to reinvent itself regularly and, increasingly, to use the power of its name and its participation in networks to multiply its impact. By so doing, the trust is moving closer to institutions that may have greater financial and organizational resources at their disposal, thereby bringing in the issue of programmatic independence and board autonomy (see above). For other foundations engaged in creative philanthropy, the challenge of independence and autonomy can be quite different: they may start as quasi-public, government-created entities that become more private and independent over time. This can be seen in the case of the Victorian Women's Trust, to which we now turn.

5   The Victorian Women's Trust

'Everyone's view of the world is partial. The more partial views you put together then potentially the better the product . . . The trick is to get a two-way flow of knowledge from expert to people and from people to expert. That's when you start to get creative outcomes.'

Like the Carnegie United Kingdom Trust, the Victorian Women's Trust is a relatively small foundation in terms of endowment and staff size. Yet it is different in two aspects that make this Australian organization an instructive case of creative philanthropy. First, the Victorian Women's Trust was not established by a private person or corporation but came into being by virtue of a government-funded endowment. Second, the trust has a diversified revenue structure that next to its endowment includes membership fees, individual donations, and grants from other foundations, and even government. However, the grants from other foundations are all special-project related, or to assist in funding of particular projects in a granting round. Business Matrix, the only women's-focused business incubator in Australia, was started with grant assistance from the federal government. This raises a third aspect of difference: because the trust's initial endowment ($AU1 million) is not sufficient to prolong an organization that seeks to take on dimensions other than an annual granting programme, the trust faces the ongoing challenge of becoming and remaining sustainable by drawing in donors not yet connected to the trust.

Background

The Victorian Women's Trust was established in 1985, with a gift of a $AU1 million endowment from the government of the state of Victoria. The gift marked the 150th anniversary of British settlement in the region that later became Victoria, and was a gift to the women of Victoria in recognition of their role in the founding and development of the state. Although initially the state government retained some rights over board selection, this was changed in 1992. Since then the Trust has been completely independent of government and has no government representatives on its board. The trustees of the charitable arm of the trust (the Victorian Women's Benevolent Trust – VWBT) are ultimately accountable, under existing legislation, to the state attorney-general (as are other trustees from other organizations).

In 2003 the trust had total assets of $AU1.8 million and an annual income of $AU656,201. In addition to income from its investments, the trust receives donations from members and donors. It also receives grants for some special projects. The trust differs from all other foundations considered here in that income from its endowment does not cover the costs of its activities.

The trust has two main entities: the VWT Ltd and the VWBT (an ancillary fund with tax deductibility). The board members wear two governance hats in that they are both directors of VWT Ltd and trustees of the VWBT (with the exception of the trust CEO who is a fellow director but not a trustee because the VWBT's constitution prohibits remuneration of trustees). The trust employs six staff of whom only two are full time.

Mission

'The Women's Trust exists to make a difference in women's lives. The Trust is fired by the vision of a just and humane society in which women enjoy full participation as citizens, free of poverty, discrimination and disadvantage' (www.vwt.org.au) The trust is 'a philanthropist, having given out over $AU2 million to over 300 projects over almost twenty years designed and run by women across the state', and 'an advocate, championing the rights and entitlements of women' (*ibid.*).

Programmes and Activities

The trust describes itself as working to improve the status of, and conditions for, women in Victoria 'in whatever practical ways it can. It uses a funding program to invest in women and effect social change; forms strategic alliances; undertakes significant action projects; advocates on relevant issues; fosters networks for the exchange of skill, ideas and information; showcases women's talents; and encourages women from diverse backgrounds to participate in social and cultural events, discussion and debate' (*ibid.*).

The trust's current priorities and programmes focus on supporting women in:

- the quest for due recognition of the value of their paid and unpaid work

- the achievement of equal access to the decision-making processes that shape our society

- dealing with violence and harassment directed at women.

Its strapline is: 'Together we are making a difference'. Indeed, since its creation some twenty years ago, the trust has achieved various 'firsts'. In 1986 it funded a publication dealing with the experiences, isolation and needs of women with disabilities. In 1987 it established the first business mentor programme for Victorian women. In 1989 it started the Guaranteed Loan Fund working with the then state bank to guarantee 50 per cent of the risk associated with bank lending to low-income women to encourage and support self-employment. The Guaranteed Loan Fund, followed by the trust's creation of the Women's

Enterprise Connection (WEC) in the early 1990s, were the two main ways in which the trust addressed the issue of economic security for women. These two programmes were the basis for the creation in 1997 of Business Matrix, the first business incubator primarily for women developing their own businesses (Business Matrix comes under VWT Ltd and is separate from the VWBT).

In 1990 the trust funded the first stage of the Women's Coalition Against Family Violence project on domestic homicides, and the later publication of *Blood on Whose Hands*. In 1992 the trust funded a project to alleviate problems experienced by isolated and ageing women that still plays a role in informing service provision today. In 1994 the trust was one of the first non-indigenous organizations to provide a Welcome to Country (modelled on the traditional aboriginal greeting ceremony) at all public events – now accepted practice across the state. The following year saw the trust funding the Consumer Law Centre to investigate whether women are discriminated against in the marketplace. In 1996 the trust funded production of a video on the exploitation of women outworkers, later developed into the FairWear Campaign. In 1997 the trust was first to fund raising awareness of issues involved in will and succession planning for rural women – *Who Gets the Farm?* In 1999 the trust funded development of a code of practice and community education campaign against sexual violence in hotels and nightclubs, a campaign titled *The Right to Party Safely*. Three of the trust's major projects have been the Purple Sage Project, Watermark Australia, and the Women in Politics project.

The Purple Sage Project

This project was set up in 1998 in partnership with five other bodies. The project was a response to 'a widening gap between rich and poor, continued high unemployment, reduced standards of community service, increased strain on local communities . . . the loss of public assets, racism and social tension, and a serious erosion of our democratic rights and culture.' (Victorian Women's Trust 2000: p. 5). The aim of the project was to create opportunities for people to come together to articulate their preferred vision for the future and to develop means by which people as citizens could engage constructively on the issues of concern to them. The project's strapline was: 'From the wisdom of the people: action for our times' (*ibid.*).

The basic philosophy of the project (and, in many ways, of the wider work of the trust) comes from Thomas Jefferson, writing in 1820: 'I know of no safe repository of the ultimate powers of society but the people themselves, and if we think they are not enlightened enough to exercise their control, the remedy is not to take from them, but to inform their discretion. To remain democratic, a society must find ways to put specialised knowledge into the service of public choice, and keep it from becoming the power basis of an elite' (quoted in *ibid.*: p. 17).

The Purple Sage Project pioneered a state-wide process of grassroots civic engagement, dialogue and action in which women played a key leadership role. 'People around the State take part in an unprecedented exercise in community dialogue describing their vision and ideas for a program of action. People come together in groups of up to ten . . . from Bairnsdale . . . to Mildura. They meet on average for three hours in their lounge rooms, kitchens, church halls, their book clubs and workplaces. Most have never done anything like this before. They are excited about the process . . . Group Leaders . . . send in written accounts that are extraordinarily detailed and carefully articulated . . . People are buoyed by the fact that they have met others, troubled by similar issues. People begin listening and talking to each other. They talk to family members. They talk outside their local primary school, to close friends and workmates, in the queue at the checkout, after the church service on Sundays' (*ibid.*: p. 13). Around 6,000 people were directly involved in groups.

From the outset the project planned to link talking with ideas for action in order to address people's feeling of being powerless. The issues people identified as of concern to them, and a range of strategies and priorities, were taken to a second stage of dialogue at which they were refined and endorsed. A publication from the project provided people with a record of the issues and a range of strategies for action designed to hold political and other leaders to account.

When the incumbent state government was defeated at the following election one leading broadsheet suggested that part of that defeat might be attributed to the Purple Sage Project's re-invention of participatory democracy.

Watermark Australia

Participants in the Purple Sage Project identified water as the key environmental issue. In partnership with the Myer Foundation, the trust, building on the Purple Sage Project, designed a Watermark Australia model. Watermark Australia aims to spark a national debate and cross-sector partnerships (at various levels from the household to the national government) around water use and management across the entire country. While it was agreed that the federal government was the only body that could co-ordinate and sponsor national water programmes, it was also argued that this would not happen without a long-term perspective and the national unity to provide that. 'Without a truly national debate, broad ownership of the issues and acceptance of proposed remedial actions is unlikely. Instead we will see a series of political fixes put in place at varying intervals.'

The trust suggested that 'successful resolution of our water resource issues requires a new and refreshing community politics, new institutional arrangements, longer term perspectives and commitments, and most importantly, a community capacity to remain engaged and active on the issue over the next decades' (Victorian Women's Trust 2001). Ownership and support by the

Australian people, at all levels, were seen as critical to providing the political will to change, and the necessary commitment to effective implementation.

Watermark Australia's aim is to involve people across Victoria (and others elsewhere online), recruited via existing clubs, voluntary organizations, businesses and networks, with direction from a secretariat of experienced, credible people. One person in each state and territory will assist the secretariat with processes tailored to reflect different organizational arrangements, styles and needs. The project is a three-year commitment, and has no political alignment.

A key element in the project strategy is to develop partnerships and strong working relationships with a wide range and number of organizations across the spectrum of water use and management, including environmental, business, government and community sectors, bringing together knowledge and expertise of both scientists and lay people. Relations with organizations in media and publishing are also central to the strategy.

Stages and tools include:

- Recruitment of project champions – prominent people, respected for their integrity, interest and commitment on water use and management, act as advocates for the project, encouraging involvement.

- Development of a Community Primer – a key project document stimulating civic engagement, educating people on the realities and providing material to support serious dialogue on water use and management.

- A website – development of an interactive, constantly developing website, but not to the exclusion of non-web users.

- Recruitment of several thousand group convenors who will facilitate the formation of small groups and the conduct of the dialogue phase.

- Dialogue – people come together in two phases of local level dialogue of approximately 3 to 4 months' duration for discussion and sharpened understanding of issues. All output would be fed back to the secretariat for processing.

- Based on trust and mutual support, local groups set goals for local action on water conservation.

- Processing all input from dialogue – output from dialogue groups processed by the secretariat and meshed with scientific and other professional knowledge and experience.

- National consolidation – the project culminates in a national Water Charter, potentially with a national media partner, to consolidate the ideas, values, vision and new directions for action that emerge from the process.

- International adaptation – the project team will work with and train people overseas to adapt the model for international use.

From the outset the project took into account risks, impact, likelihood, and response; strategies for wider/political influence, including communications strategies with key target audiences at different levels; and links with other initiatives.

Developing Strategy: The Move to a Creative Approach

In its early years the trust acted in a fairly conventional way, making grants and providing some services for women. From 1997 this began to change as the trust developed its current approach, combining grant-making, community engagement, research, communications and advocacy. Drivers of a creative approach included:

A New CEO and a Receptive Board

Twelve years after the creation of the trust a new CEO was appointed. The CEO, who came from a background in public policy and social justice, describes how she saw the advertisement and 'immediately felt excited because I knew it (the trust) hadn't reached its full potential'. In her application the CEO made the case for a change of approach. 'I later found out that the board had been having a similar discussion. Ever since then we've been on a shared mission.'

Radical Review

The new CEO and the board immediately embarked on a radical review of the trust's operation. One key starting point for the review was that with an endowment of only $AU1 million the trust was not sustainable in the longer term. If the trust was to be able to fulfil its remit as a resource for current and future generations of women in Victoria, it had to consider supplementing its investment income with fundraising. But on what basis could it currently ask people for donations?

The CEO argued that the first step was to streamline the organization to make it more efficient and productive. The next step was to build on the current strengths of the trust, consolidate those and undertake some strategically chosen initiatives that would increase the credibility of the trust among women and raise its profile – all without increasing staff expenses. Only then would the trust be in a position to undertake 'significant community leadership and be able to go out to the broader community for fundraising to give the trust a secure future for future generations of women'.

Elements of a Creative Approach

Building Credibility Through Sound Knowledge

The Trust sees its approach as being based on 'robust credibility' derived from a reputation for sound research and knowledge. Credibility does not come automatically from your name, existence or charitable status. 'You have to *do* things to be credible, you have to work hard, not just sit in your office and put out PR.' Credibility involves building a strong knowledge-base, and a reputation for having it. 'Credibility comes from being not glitzy or flimsy. You've got to work with substance, rigour and relevance – things that can't be dismissed by people thinking "what are they on about, they're myopic".' For this reason the trust sets high standards for the quality of its research, writing and relationships. This in turn requires the trust to be highly selective in the number and nature of the issues it picks up, given its very modest resources. At any one time the trust has only one or two major programmes.

Relevance and Authenticity

But the trust argues research is not enough; a sound knowledge-base has to be linked to authenticity and relevance. If the trust is to fulfil its mission, and if it is to be sustainable, it must be relevant and authentic, 'grounded in the realities women face'. This involves maintaining networks, and listening to women (via projects such as Purple Sage and regular attendance at events, large and small).

Being authentic is also seen as involving the courage to voice the concerns of women. Some of the trust's letters to the press have offended politicians of both major parties. 'If I don't get invited to events that doesn't matter because that's not where the trust's future lies. This trust belongs to the women of Victoria. The important thing is that many women emailed us to say thank you for speaking up. If the future of the trust depended on being less in-your-face, I'd be that way.'

Managing Knowledge

For the trust, being creative is about more than having knowledge. It is also about managing that knowledge, paying attention to the 'seemingly boring thing of information systems'. To be sustainably creative, the trust argues, its knowledge capital has to survive accidents, loss of staff and so on. It is currently designing a knowledge management database for the whole trust: 'There's currently too much stuff in our heads and in manila folders. We've got to capture and codify that knowledge so that it is instantly retrievable.' One small but – given the way in which the trust works – critical example is capturing and organizing its database of contacts in the media, government, business and the nonprofit sector.

Making Networks Work

Given its limited resources, the trust has had to be creative in the way it builds and uses networks. One way in which the trust does this is via its creation of complex partnerships with other funders. Such partnerships may not only provide additional funding and credibility for particular pieces of work, but may be used to resolve legal issues by, for example, locating a project involving a substantial investment in research or advocacy in an organization that can legally bear such activities as a minor part of its overall budget.

Another trust strategy is to put people and issues together in creative ways. For example, the trust is frequently approached by colleges wishing to place students on work assignments. In one recent case, the trust was offered some third-year students from the Royal Melbourne Institute of Technology. As part of their studies, they were to spend a semester designing a campaign for a client. Because of the trust's knowledge of earlier research, including a survey revealing that one-third of 14–18-year-old boys believe that it is sometimes acceptable to force a woman to have sex, the trust negotiated with the students to develop a campaign targeted at young men, encouraging respect for women. The students were seen as exactly the right sort of people to be able to communicate with young men and women, and they came up with a creative web-based campaign using a medium and language more likely to reach young men. 'Other people's brains are part of our resources.' In a further twist of network use, the trust hopes to enlist support for the campaign from a famous and respected ex-footballer whose sister was murdered as a result of domestic violence. The CEO reflects that although the use of networks, constantly looking out for creative partnerships and synergies, is driven in part by necessity, it is an essential element in the trust's creative approach.

Bridging Gaps: Putting Wisdoms Together

Underlying much of the trust's work, including and perhaps especially Purple Sage and Watermark Australia, is the notion that creativity comes from bridging gaps and bringing wisdoms together. 'Everyone's view of the world is partial. The more partial views you put together then potentially the better the product. For example, there's an enormous amount of wisdom and knowledge about water outside of the water industry. The trick is to get a two-way flow of knowledge from expert to people and from people to expert. That's when you start to get creative outcomes.' The strategy of Watermark Australia is designed to take knowledge from thousands of ordinary people to those in the water industry, research institutes and government, and vice versa, subjecting each perspective to that of another group.

Crafting Ideas into Action

But putting wisdoms together is not enough, according to the trust. It sees its job as helping to 'craft' ideas into actions that can be implemented as solutions. Actions have to be realistic, achievable and technically sound. In this respect, the trust sees its approach as very different from that of conventional researchers, many other funders and those running consultations, whose roles cease when they have identified viewpoints or facilitated acknowledgement and ownership of an issue. Again, one example is Watermark Australia, which is designed to move beyond identification of issues to implementation of solutions by ordinary people, communities and governments.

Maintaining Independence

The trust sees its independence of special interests as essential to its continued credibility and work. 'You have to demonstrate your independence through your work and the way you work.' Maintaining independence of political parties and other special interests means taking care in everything the trust does and says, and everything it does or does not support. For example, even though the trust champions the cause of more women in politics, its ethos of independence means it must champion women across the political spectrum.

People Power Plus and Champions

Next to the political thinking of Thomas Jefferson, the trust's work is informed by a quotation from Margaret Mead: 'Never doubt that a small group of thoughtful, committed citizens can change the world. Indeed it is the only thing that ever has' (quoted in Victorian Women's Trust 2000: p. 89). At the same time, the trust believes that social change involves visionary governments, political leadership, committed and inventive law reformers, progressive companies, inspirational champions, and so on. A creative approach to social change involves working at, and on, these many different forces and levels.

Informal, often high-profile, supporters are seen as playing an especially important role in the trust's work. In Watermark Australia this has been formalized in the process of building a 'stable' of champions as one of the first steps. But champions are not necessarily celebrities. They are, rather, people within a particular section of Victorian society who are revered and respected. They may come from urban or rural areas, they may be young or old, male or female, 'expert' or simply 'wise'. Use of champions and the insistence on a mix of champions is part of the trust's creative approach: 'a symbol of the inclusiveness of our work'.

Exploiting Opportunities

Although the trust emphasizes the need to choose very carefully a small number of issues and strategies, it also recognizes the value of seizing opportunities if this will contribute to the achievement of its long-term mission. For example, in 2001 to celebrate the centenary of Victoria's statehood the trust became heavily involved in producing an exhibition highlighting the extraordinary role of ordinary women in the past and present of the state. This placed a huge burden on the trust, but was seen as an un-missable opportunity to celebrate the lives and contribution of women, and to raise the trust's profile. More regularly, the trust's CEO rarely misses an opportunity to write letters to the press when issues with which it is concerned are raised.

Accepting Incremental Change

The trust's CEO describes its approach as 'visionary, with the back hooves firmly grounded'. The trust is committed to looking forward to change, but accepts that social change is a slow, incremental process. The trust's model of social change recognizes the power of the conventional view and the status quo, and sees its job as contributing to the anomalies and aberrations in thinking and practice that seek to challenge the status quo and develop new thinking and practice. 'It's like Kuhn's work on the structure of scientific revolutions. It's a long process. I don't want to feel that we've done such piecemeal stuff that it's a waste of time – but we don't kid ourselves that we've changed the world. But, I think we can say that if the trust weren't here there would be a gap for women.' For example, the trust's work on domestic violence has not ended with publication of a research report. The trust continues to keep the issue alive with letters to the press, speaking engagements, attendance at events, drawing in new voices and champions, and generating publicity in support of selected cases. The trust accepts that issues of social justice for women have been on the public agenda for over a century, and may well be for many years to come.

Sharing the Passion

The trust's CEO sees the shared passion of staff and board as crucial to the trust's approach. Without shared passion the trust could not do what it does with so little income, and could not take the risks it does. 'Even the finance officer has to understand the values and share the passion.' To date the trust has not had to face any loss of passion, and given the charisma and passion of board members and the CEO, this may not be an issue for some time.

Implications and Issues

Despite its successes, the trust faces a number of critical challenges. These include concerns about sustainability, politicization, and governance. Specifically:

Sustainability: Getting Money into Perspective

The issue of the trust's financial sustainability dominates much of its thinking about the future. 'We don't want financial comfort, but I do want some of the financial burden lifted so we can be more creative. I want to wake up with a good idea, not wake up worrying about money.' But the trust does not see sustainability simply in terms of money, but also as being about building a sustainable ethos that emphasizes independence, credibility, authenticity and relevance, and capturing and codifying its knowledge.

One of the dilemmas in building the financial sustainability of the trust is that 'to most people a million dollars sounds like a lot of money – so why would we want more?' A second dilemma is that the trust believes that it cannot expect to raise more money until it has earned the right to ask for it via its work – but the more the trust does to earn that credibility the more people are likely to 'see an organization busy doing things, supposedly without any financial problems'.

The Costs of Opportunism

Given that the trust currently has just six staff, of whom only two are full time, staff are under enormous pressure. Seizing opportunities, even if they are seen as an investment in the future, may push the organization to the very edge of its capacity.

The Costs of Being Operational

In many respects the trust comes closer to the model of an operating foundation than the conventional model of a grant-making foundation. One of the issues here is that the trust spends more on its 'overheads' than it does on grant-making. Given the expectations of the organization, and its own statements that it 'belongs to the women of Victoria', this is felt to create a short-term ethical discomfort. The trust is, however, confident that it can justify this strategy in the longer term by demonstrable effectiveness and sustainability

Managing the Political Divide

The trust guards very carefully its political independence. But it is certainly not afraid to 'fly above the radar', and its activities clearly have effects in the political domain. As the CEO notes: 'It may be good to be told that the trust helped to bring down an unpopular government, but that's a very double-edged sword.' In the process of the current CEO's initial review of the trust, it was discovered that both the trust and its subsidiary organization (the Victorian Women's Benevolent Trust) had charitable status, and the latter was also a public benevolent institution allowing tax deductibility of gifts. Legal advice suggested that the charitable status of the trust was 'dubious', and that it should be relinquished. This has meant that the trust itself (VWT Ltd) is somewhat freer of the constraints of charity law, since 'things with a sharp edge can be done by the company'. The problem is that the demarcation between different areas of work has to be very diligently managed.

Governance

The trust is conscious that it could be criticized for failing to have a fully demo-cratically elected board, and for having only limited trustee turnover. The dilemma is that the knowledge, experience, passion and stability of the board is considered essential in building the sustainability of the trust. At this stage in its development, the trust considers that retaining experienced and passionate board members gives the trust its best chance of sustainability, enabling it effectively to pursue its mission. By constantly listening to women, via projects such as Purple Sage and Watermark Australia, the trust hopes to have the best of both worlds.

A major lesson that we can draw from the Victorian Women's Trust is that diversified revenue sources can compensate for smaller endowments. More importantly perhaps is that creative foundations, driven by a passion for their mission, constant pursuit of the best way, and self criticism, are evolving and changing institutions that go through gradual and sometimes radical makeovers, as the short history of the trust has demonstrated. This lesson applies to long-established and relatively large foundations as well, as our next case study, the Pew Charitable Trusts, will show.

6   The Pew Charitable Trusts

> To 'move beyond our traditional, relatively passive role as grant givers to become catalysts, brokers, information resources, and civic entrepreneurs through strategic investments . . .'

Whereas the Victorian Women's Trust is a relatively small, single organization, the Pew Charitable Trusts are more like a system of relatively large trusts that combine grant-making with advancing policy solutions. The Pew Charitable Trusts have experienced several fundamental changes and re-organizations since they were founded, and they represent a highly instructive case on how to develop and then maintain the structure and culture of creative philanthropy in a complex organization.

Background

The Pew Charitable Trusts are a group of seven charitable funds established between 1948 and 1979 by the two sons and two daughters of Joseph N. Pew, founder of the Sun Oil Company, and his wife Mary Anderson Pew. In its early years the foundation worked anonymously, in accordance with the founders' religious principles and philosophy, which discouraged self-promotion of their good works. Nevertheless requests for support grew. In 1956 the board created the Glenmede Trust Company to take over various Trust activities, thus enabling the Pews both to establish individual funds with missions related to their individual charitable interests and to retain a direct role in grant-making without the day-to-day responsibilities of managing the funds. In 2004 the Trusts began operating as an independent public charity in order to increase their flexibility and effectiveness in carrying out their mission of serving the public interest.

In 2003 the Trusts had assets of $4.119 billion. They made 163 grants totalling $143,389,000. There are 15 people on the board of directors, of whom seven are members of the Pew family. The Trusts employ over 150 staff.

The original founders' mission for the Trusts was to contribute to the public's health and welfare, and to strengthen local communities. The Trust's current objectives are:

- 'Informing the public on key issues and trends through independent, highly credible research and polling.

- Advancing policy solutions on important issues facing the American public.

- Supporting the arts, heritage, health and well-being of our diverse citizenry, and civic life, with particular emphasis on Philadelphia.'

And the Trusts add: 'and when the case is compelling we advocate for change' (www.pewtrusts.com/ideas/area).

Current Programmes

The Trusts support work in six programme areas: culture, education, environment, health and human services, public policy, and religion. They also have a 'venture fund' allowing them to explore areas that fall outside the clearly defined goals and objectives of the six programme areas.

Policy work is seen as an important adjunct to the funding of human services. 'We do policy work to change systems. Direct services support doesn't change anything. It's appropriate to have both.' 'Money spent working on the ground doesn't go very far and the problem doesn't go away. With relatively limited money you can have great effects and impact if you're careful about where and when you intervene.'

The introduction of work on policy matters was a gradual evolution, arising from a realization that the choice of how you attack an issue is as important as the choice of the issue itself. The Advancing Policy Solutions programme works to identify solutions to policy issues at both national and state level. Its overall goal is to strengthen the institutions, processes and norms through which citizens can address issues of public concern, and to have a citizenry that participates in democratic life.

The Trusts have supported efforts to preserve America's wilderness, address the problems of global climate change and greater protection for the seas, as well as to improve access to quality pre-school and higher education, foster care and public health tracking of diseases. Current priorities include:

- Education: Pre-kindergarten education.

- Environment: Global warming, protecting ocean life, wilderness protection.

- Health and human services: foster care reform, alcohol marketing and youth, alcohol treatment policy, genetics and public policy, food and biotechnology, retirement security.

- Other areas: improving elections, death penalty reform, and medical malpractice.

The programme summarizes its way of working as identifying issues, involving experts, exploring divergent views and supporting a range of focused interventions including 'highly targeted public education initiatives, advocacy efforts and issue campaigns to inform decision makers about policy options and promote solutions' (www.pewtrusts.com). In many cases the programme will convene 'the nation's foremost leaders, thinkers, researchers and technical experts in their respective fields to produce rigorous, non-partisan research and policy analysis – all with the goal of helping decision makers form consensus around policies that will drive positive change for Americans' (*ibid.*).

Developing Strategy: The Move to a Creative Approach

The Trusts' move to a creative approach has been a gradual process. In the 1970s, after the founders' deaths, the Trusts expanded their grant-making beyond the Philadelphia area and moved away from anonymous grantmaking. By the beginning of the 1980s the Trusts were publishing an annual report, issuing grant-making guidelines and developing a more strategic and creative approach, taking an active partnership role in developing programmes designed to respond to needs in the field.

In the 1990s the board decided that the Trusts should develop their focus on 'results-orientated' philanthropy, and concentrate on a few key issues 'using the panoply of resources at their disposal – talent, intellect and dollars – to tackle those issues' (Pew Charitable Trusts 2001b: p. 36).

Promoting civic engagement – 'increased public involvement in making important policy choices' – was increasingly emphasized. This emphasis was related back to a speech by J. Howard Pew in 1953, during the Cold War: 'We are constantly being alerted to the dangers of subversive activity at work in our land, but a far greater danger lurks in what has been called "subversive inactivity". No subversive forces can ever conquer a nation that has not first been conquered by "subversive inactivity on the part of the citizenry who have failed in their civic duty and in service to their country".' (quoted in *ibid.*: p. 41). Drivers of a creative approach at Pew include:

Responding to a Changing Environment

The change of strategy is said by the Trusts to have been driven by awareness of changing environmental conditions, including more and tougher problems, more applicants, devolution, and federal government in retreat. Regular review and change to adapt to emerging issues and new structures is characteristic of the Trusts' history. For example, in the early 1990s, 'recognizing that social issues do not respect boundaries', the board widened the interdisciplinary and geographical focus of the Trusts to include grants with national and international impact in, among other areas, the environment. By 2003 the Trusts were developing state-based programmes in recognition of the fact that states had become more central in provision of many key services including, for example, education.

Awareness of Paucity of Resources

Realizing that their resources were 'minuscule' relative to those of government, the Trusts decided that if they were going to make a difference, old ways of working were inadequate. The Trusts decided to 'move beyond our traditional, relatively passive role as grant givers to become catalysts, brokers, information resources, and civic entrepreneurs through strategic investments. The Trusts have begun to think more like venture capitalists, seeking to derive the greatest benefit from every strategic investment of capital, time and talent – except . . . the return on investment is measured not in profits but in long-lasting, positive and powerful benefits to the public' ('Delivering Results', www.pewtrusts.com).

The argument was that by adding a strategic approach to their modus operandi, the Trusts could achieve more – and more sustainable – change. For example, in the environmental field, the Trusts saw a 'conventional' grant as heavily dependent on the right social, organizational and political conditions to achieve any significant effect. Under the new strategy, by contrast, working with national and regional coalitions of conservation organizations and others to design regional public education campaigns, and using state-of-the-art communication tools to encourage public participation, the Trusts could dramatically increase the acreage of protected land.

Elements of a Creative Approach

Capturing the Public Interest

Achieving its mission is, according to the Trusts, not merely about money. It is about 'capturing the public interest through good timing, good partners, imagination and creativity.' One example is the Trust's programme, 'Americans Discuss Social Security'. Aiming to inform and involve people in a debate about social security, the programme's overall aim was to 'help rebuild the voice of Americans in the political process, to engage them in discussion of a national policy issue, and to help create a dialogue between the public and the policy-makers so that public policy might better reflect public will' (www.pewtrusts.com).

The Trusts have invested heavily in independent, non-partisan research related to public attitudes and to serve the press, funding the Pew Research Center for the People and the Press, the Project for Excellence in Journalism, www.stateline.org (which provides research and public information on state governments), the Pew Internet and American Life Project, the Pew Forum on Religion and Public Life, the Pew Hispanic Center, and the Pew Global Attitudes Project. In 2004 the Trusts announced that they would be consolidating these seven projects into a new nonprofit subsidiary, the Pew Research Center, which will house all the major information projects supported by the Trusts. This consolidation is one of the benefits for the Trusts of its new public charity status (Pew Charitable Trusts 2004).

Diverse Perspectives

Programme staff are drawn from a variety of fields. They bring to the Trusts skills and experience as academics, researchers, lawyers, nonprofit managers, policy analysts, journalists, artists, scientists, educators, advocates, public administrators and so on. In addition to the diverse perspectives and skills of staff, the Trusts bring in external consultants at various stages to challenge and critique the strategies and work of programmes in a process of peer review.

Well-defined Wider Focus

Grants should be part of a programme with a well-defined goal larger than that of a single project; single grants cannot be strategic, but must be part of a cluster of grants with a focus. For example, in their work both on public-health issues and on global climate change, the Trusts provide credible research and monitoring, public education and brokering informed dialogue among players critical to achieving change: experts, interest groups, influential leaders in the public and private sectors, policy-makers and the public.

Explicit and Achievable Objectives

The Trusts emphasize the importance of explicit, achievable objectives. Directors of programme areas are required broadly to describe their ideas and purpose. They then specify the results expected, and the strategies, means and benchmarks that will be used to measure progress. These plans are then subject to external review, questioning and revision. The board reviews each programme's progress annually and sets benchmarks and expected results for the following year. 'These steps improve the chances for achieving significant and measurable results, and permit essential refinements in strategy' (Pew Charitable Trusts 2001b: p. 42).

Realism About Limitations and Collaboration

The Trusts emphasize the need to be realistic about the role of grant-makers, acknowledging that a grant-maker can achieve very little alone, or in an unsupportive climate. Acceptance that the Trusts 'are only one factor in a complex equation' radically affects the Trusts' approach to performance measurement (see below). Analysis of the funding climate, who else is doing what, and the likely obstacles are key questions from the very beginning of the programme, and are built into strategy.

This realism about the Trusts' limitations and the complexity of problems means that working collaboratively with others is essential. The Trusts have a long track record of working with other funders, including, among others, the Robert Wood Johnson Foundation on health issues.

Doing Your Homework: Scanning the Environment

The three Advancing Policy Solutions directors are responsible for proactively scanning the wider social, political and economic environment. At any one time there will be a number of possibilities being explored; more are rejected than are pursued. An issue may be explored for a year and then not taken forward because the opportunities are not there. For example, for some years the Trusts have considered developing a programme on corrections (penal) policy. After much analysis the conclusion has been that the environment is such that the Trusts could play no effective, creative role. If the environment changes, the Trusts may reconsider involvement.

Focus on Causes not Symptoms

In analysing whether to work on an issue, programme staff are encouraged to focus on causes not symptoms, and to consider whether and how these might be addressed. For example, in their work on child health the Trusts could have given a traditional grant to a hospital to support a centre for the diagnosis and treatment of chronic diseases in children. But this sort of grant would have done little to create systemic change in the public-health system, improve understanding of these diseases, and benefit children elsewhere. Instead, in 1998 the Trusts launched a major initiative to strengthen the public-health system, emphasizing understanding as well as prevention and improved treatment of chronic diseases, including environmentally related diseases, that disproportionately affect children. The Trusts are seeking to examine suspected links between environmental factors and chronic diseases by promoting a coordinated national system of tracking and monitoring that can begin to explain the apparent increase in chronic disease. This will be the basis for, among other things, a public-education campaign. 'The ultimate benefits, if successful, are expected to extend to millions of children and adults throughout the United States and beyond' (Pew Charitable Trusts 2001b: p. 39).

Open or Opening Policy Windows

The Trusts are opportunistic in the sense that they identify issues and problems on which others, including policy-makers, are ready to move. 'Attempting to make the best use of our resources typically involves attacking problems at a critical juncture, where the scales can be tipped toward a socially desirable end' (Pew Charitable Trusts 2001a: p. 7). In this sense, 'ripeness' is described as a pragmatic consideration. 'Although the Trusts are sometimes tempted to undertake major struggles for important causes against seemingly insurmountable odds, their emphasis on results – based on a commitment to effective stewardship – typically argues against doing so' (Pew Charitable Trusts 2001b: p. 40). For example, pre-kindergarten education was taken up because that part of the education system was widely regarded as badly broken; an existing body of empirical evidence was available; a growing public willingness for change was sensed, together with a readiness to consider alternatives within the policy community, and public willingness to pay.

Programme staff are encouraged to choose a problem on which they can make progress in three to five years with the resources available. This involves, among other things, analysing the relevant policy process, identifying the locus of power, assessing readiness for change, formulating a plausible theory of how change might be achieved, and points and strategies for intervention. In some cases, the Trusts may choose to work only in a small group of states that are seen as ready to 'tip'. 'There's no point in working in places where there is no interest.'

Analysing Audiences, Obstacles and Opposition in Advance

Programme staff may spend up to a year analysing the causes of a problem and identifying the audience that represents the best leverage point for change, and how best to reach and influence that audience. As part of the lengthy process of developing a strategy paper for board approval of a new piece of work, programme staff are required to consider obstacles to achieving the goal, and sources and nature of likely opposition. For example, a programme on corrections has been rejected in the past because states were seen as unwilling to move on such a politically contentious issue. In all programmes the key questions are:

- 'What is the problem you are trying to address? Based on your research, what are the root causes of this problem? Which solutions appear most feasible?

- Are there active communities working on this issue? What are their strengths and weaknesses? What resources do they command? What will they support? How do they measure up to their opponents? Are there other players not currently involved who could be brought to the table?

- Who or what might present obstacles to achieving your goal?

- If there is an opposition, who is it? What are they opposed to? What are their strengths and weaknesses? What resources do they command? What will they support and under what circumstances?

- What pieces necessary for change are missing from the field? What is not being done? What could be done more effectively?

- What are other funders doing on this issue?

- What unique strengths (beyond money) can the foundation bring to this issue (for example, credibility, visibility, experience)?' (Pew Charitable Trusts 2001a: p. 10).

Necessary Resources, but More than Money

Having decided to work on an issue the Trusts allocate sufficient resources to achieve what needs to be done, relating the duration of a grant to the tasks in hand. The resources necessary to get the job done are not seen solely in financial terms. The Trusts recognize the value of resources other than money in both the grant-making organization and the grantee. Knowledge, skills, relationships, networks and so on are all important. As noted above, what the Trusts can bring in credibility, visibility and experience are crucial early questions. In their public-health work, for example, the Trusts have employed the best skills and knowledge to produce challenging research on the understanding, prevention and treatment of diseases, used their influence and relationships to encourage a coordinated national system of state-by-state tracking and monitoring, their reputation to promote cooperation and dialogue, and their visibility, credibility and communication skills to promote a public-education campaign.

Interestingly, when the Trusts use the term 'leverage', they mean much more than getting more money. 'Leverage means enhancing a project's portfolio effectiveness through increased interest from the public, the media and policymakers, as well as support from additional organizations, including other philanthropies, and individuals' (Pew Charitable Trusts 2001b: p. 41).

Working on Several Fronts

The Trusts recognize that most of the problems on which they work are unlikely to respond to a single type of intervention. For this reason several interventions are identified that work towards the same goal from different angles at the same time. Research, monitoring, public education and policy influence all play a role in most of the Trusts' programmes.

Beyond Knowledge

The Trusts emphasize the need to work at providing knowledge resources to policy-makers – but that this alone is not enough. It is also necessary to work on the ground. 'Research doesn't create change – you need both.' For example, in their conservation work the Trusts combined research with developing regional and national coalitions involving more than 500 conservation organizations, helping them to redesign public-education campaigns, using sophisticated communication tools to gain public participation. As of 2000, more than 100 million acres of old-growth forests and wilderness areas had been protected (Pew Charitable Trusts 2001b: p. 2001).

Strategy is Not Sufficient

Despite the Trusts' emphasis on planning and strategy, they are clear that strategy is not alone sufficient for effective grant-making. It is also necessary to pay close attention to implementation, monitoring progress and making necessary adjustments. Questions regarding implementation are built into the initial design of a programme. 'Being strategic also means paying close attention to implementation, getting timely information on progress and responding to that information appropriately' (Pew Charitable Trusts 2001a: p. 11). But a narrow focus in individual grants is also not sufficient to see the wood for the trees.

Seeing the Wood for the Trees: Evaluating Strategy

The Trusts' approach to evaluation has moved from an emphasis on monitoring individual grant outputs and compliance to a focus on achievement of overall strategy and goals. A 'tracking portfolio' looks at a sub-programme as a whole, providing key pieces of information to show programme staff how their strategy is unfolding, and whether it is having the desired effect on targeted audiences. This will include external factors that may affect progress. Evaluation is therefore not so much about 'success' and 'failure' as assessing progress and the need for 'course corrections'.

A Constant Learning Loop

The Trusts aim to develop 'ambitious but feasible' programmes, accepting risks but building in learning from failure and success. Learning is seen as a constant process, continually feeding back into current strategy. The internal strategy cycle has three stages: creating a convincing plan to address a problem; turning the plan into action with grantee partners, monitoring and adjusting implementation if necessary; and independent evaluation in cluster reviews. Programme staff then feed the results of this evaluation into a revised plan, thus triggering a new round in the strategy cycle.

Opportunities for learning within the Trusts are built into various stages of the grants strategy process. The most formal learning resource is the internal educational curriculum called Pew University. Pew University courses, lasting from an hour to a day, are designed to enhance the grant-making skills and professional development of staff. The courses are constantly being updated with lessons from the Trusts' own experiences and by scanning the wider environment.

Applying Core Competencies across Areas

Advancing policy solutions is said to involve 'not a very sophisticated tool kit, and you can develop a set of core competencies and apply them across a range of areas'. Producing and promoting credible, solid, non-partisan research to inform policy-makers and the public on the nature, causes, scale and implications of the issue; using state of the art communication skills to inform and educate, promoting dialogue among key stakeholders and, where necessary, advocating for change are the core competencies underpinning all major programmes.

Maximizing Flexibility

Flexibility is seen as crucial in ensuring continued effectiveness in a changing world. The Trusts' strategies are constantly evolving as new information and variables emerge in the field. One example of the Trusts' commitment to maximizing flexibility is their planning and evaluation process; another is their use of the venture fund to fund outside their chosen priorities. Yet another example is their move to become a public charity.

The move to become a public charity was possible because of the way in which the Trusts were set up. The change was designed to give a new flexibility to try additional ways of strengthening existing work. For example, the Trusts could now operate programmes, lobby, take policy positions, and so on. Although no decision has been taken to do any of those things, the Trusts now have the flexibility to do so. There is currently some interest in running programmes, but the Trusts are also aware of their core competencies and obligations to grantees.

Goals above Power

One of the effects of becoming a public charity is that members of the Pew family, previously a majority, will become a minority on the new 15- or 16-member board. The family were said to be willing to give up control on the board because of their over-riding commitment to the Trusts' goals and desire to match the structure to the goals. This was not said to have been a controversial decision.

Issues and Implications

Balancing Levels of Intervention

The Trusts' emphasis on analysing the locus of power and effective points of intervention requires constant flexibility, as power in a subject-area shifts. For example, the Trusts are now developing state-based programmes because states are becoming more and more central to key services; at the same time, however, they are aware that as states become more powerful the national voice gets lost.

More generally, there is some tension between work at federal and state level. 'It's hard to work in every state, whereas the federal level is easier because there is only one federal [government].'

Exit Strategies

The Trusts' approach to constant review, adjustment and getting results means that exit strategies are particularly important. For example, the Trusts had a fairly large higher-education programme that is now being phased out. The decision to exit from this programme was made on the grounds that higher education is fragmented, institutionally driven, and that no obvious policy lever exists, making it very hard to achieve any change. Exit is an occupational hazard of foundations adopting a creative approach. But it is still a difficult, painful and slow process.

Staying in Touch with Opening Windows

The Trusts recognize that they need to know when to exit, but they also need to know when to enter or re-visit a field. The existence of an emerging window of opportunity is considered very important, and there are many important issues the Trusts would not tackle because that window does not exist. For example, corrections is a politically difficult issue to tackle. Five years ago the Trusts could not have gone into states and suggested discussion. Now, because corrections budgets are increasingly out of control, some states are willing to discuss policies. Spotting opportunities is a constant task, and an issue that may have been explored and dropped a year ago may need to be revived as windows begin to open.

Occupying the Middle Ground: Flak from Both Sides?

The Trusts emphasize the importance of not being seen as 'shrill ideological advocates'. The aim is to advocate based on knowledge and, where possible, create bi-partisan support by building a consensus and moving forward with incremental gains. This raises two issues. One is that this is a slow process requiring both work behind the scenes and patience. The second is that occupying the middle ground may mean that 'we get flak from both sides'. 'If you're doing traditional philanthropy everyone loves you. But with policy work some people don't like you. That's hard.'

Being Honest about Being an Honest Broker

The Trusts recognize the potential of their role as a 'nice, neutral convening ground' and their ability 'to pull people in because of our size and because of our reputation for policy work'. But they are also clear that 'once the facts are in you can't be an honest broker. Once you know what's necessary or what works you have to take a position.'

Earning and Keeping a Reputation

The Trusts have been doing policy work since the early 1990s. Programme staff are conscious of the time it takes to build a solid reputation, and the need to manage that reputation very carefully. This has implications for a range of matters, including choice of issues and levels of risk-taking. Above all, staff emphasize that managing the Trusts' reputation is 'not a PR campaign, it's about doing the work'. Like the Victorian Women's Trust and other cases, the Trusts emphasize the need for solid, credible evidence to underpin their contribution to policy issues.

Performance Measurement: Nowhere to Hide?

Staff suggest that it is impossible to work in this creative way without a supportive board. But the board are also described as 'pretty hard-nosed about getting results'. One full board meeting per year is devoted solely to programme strategy and results. One problem with identifying results is that 'stimulating change is a messy process with many uncertainties, and the Trusts are only one factor in a complex equation. How the many variables will play out can be unpredictable. It is often very difficult to establish a direct causal link between our subprograms and observed outcomes' (Pew Charitable Trusts 2001a: p. 16).

Reconciling the demand for clear measurement of performance with the 'messiness' of change involves looking for 'a chain of evidence that establishes our contribution'. Interim benchmarks are necessary to accommodate the fact that change takes considerable time. For policy work these might include: agenda setting, building coalitions, debates in the state, bills introduced, pilot funding, getting research out, getting media attention, and getting journalists involved.

While at one level advancing policy solutions may be seen as the hardest to measure, there is also a sense in which 'with policy work you can see when you win, but you can also see when you lose. In other types of work you rarely know when you win or lose.'

Resource Intensive

With a staff of over 150, the Trusts accept that their way of working is highly resource intensive, involving considerable investments in people and knowledge. The issue of overhead cost is one of which the board is constantly aware. 'Investing in ideas, returning results' (Pew Charitable Trusts 2001b: p. 44) is the criterion by which overheads are assessed.

Branding

The Trusts view branding as enormously important in building reputation. But they also brand very carefully. There are times when it is important not to be too closely associated with an issue, especially when something becomes 'politically edgy'.

For example, the Pew Commission on Foster Care generated bi-partisan and practical recommendations, attracting considerable interest and attention of great value to Pew's reputation. The commission was able to build bi-partisan support in large part because it had the Pew name as well as a strong evidence base. But when it comes to pushing recommendations through, Pew is likely to be much less openly associated, even though it may fund such work.

What's in a Name?

Family foundations may face particular problems in adopting a creative approach when this generates controversy. 'Everyone gets edgy when there is criticism, and because the name is Pew it gets personal.' Staff maintain that it is important to be sensitive to such issues and highlight the importance of both keeping board members in the loop so they are never surprised by criticism and ensuring that the Trusts' evidence base is strong.

7   The John S. and James L. Knight Foundation

> 'Nor does the support and defense of freedom begin and end with the individual, however well educated and informed. It also is vitally dependent on that great boiling stew that is the independent sector. Now as in the past, the nation's health requires that it continue to bubble over with alternative approaches and more diverse options than those prescribed by government.'
>
> (Knight Foundation, 2002:5)

The John S. and James L. Knight Foundation is an example of a creative foundation that operates at the intersection of politics, the media and society. The foundation operates in a fast-changing field in which many threads and opportunities are present and frequently collide. Its grant-making programme is informed by a passion for the free press and democracy, and its activities are characterized by tenacity and risk-taking. At the same time, it is also a story of a foundation that is rooted in local communities while pursuing national and increasingly international agendas.

Background

The John S. and James L. Knight Foundation is based on the Knight family newspaper fortune. To honour the memory of their father, the eponymous brothers established the Knight Memorial Education Fund in 1940 to provide financial aid to college students from the Akron, Ohio area. The fund existed until December 1950, when its assets of $9,047 were transferred to the newly created Knight Foundation. In the 1960s other Knight newspapers began to contribute to the foundation, leading to the practice of making grants in those cities.

In 1965 the foundation received a bequest of 180,000 shares of Knight Newspapers stock from the Knights' mother, Clara I. Knight. Given this increase in size, the board decided in 1966 to end assistance for college students and to replace it with grants to the colleges and universities themselves. In 1972 the board authorized the sale of Clara Knight's stock in a secondary offering by Knight Newspapers, increasing the foundation's assets to more than $24 million. This prompted an expanded grant programme focused on the growing number of cities where the Knights published newspapers. Journalism, especially the education of journalists, became a key funding issue.

In 1974 Knight Newspapers merged with Ridder Publications to create Knight-Ridder Inc., at the time the largest newspaper company in the United States. Jack Knight was its biggest shareholder, making Knight-Ridder vulnerable to management by outside interests and possibly a takeover. Jack Knight was therefore persuaded to leave the bulk of his estate to the foundation, requesting, at the same time, that the trustees think about the foundation's future. The trustees opted for optimum flexibility 'on the grounds,' Jack Knight wrote, 'that a truly effective foundation should have freedom to exercise its best judgment as required by the times and conditions under which they live' (www.knightfdn.org).

After Jack Knight's death the foundation received his bequest of $428,144,588, creating a 20-fold increase in its assets and making Knight Foundation the 21st-largest US foundation based on asset size. Another review was conducted. One result of this review was a formal Cities Program focusing on all the communities in which Knight-Ridder businesses were located. In journalism, the foundation built on the Knights' legacy of support for education as the cornerstone of quality journalism by establishing, salvaging or strengthening some of the profession's mid-career fellowship programmes for journalists. Programmes for education, arts and culture were established.

Under new leadership the foundation's national presence grew with, for example, the Knight Foundation Commission on Intercollegiate Athletics, a blue-ribbon body that advocated for reform of college athletics; the Knight Chairs in Journalism, a programme that sought to elevate the quality of education at the nation's best journalism schools by attracting notable working journalists to serve as educators through an endowed chair; and the National Community Development Initiative (NCDI), the largest philanthropic collaboration in US history.

In late 1990 the board undertook a new strategic planning process, given further impetus by Jim Knight's death in 1991 and his bequest to the foundation of a further $200 million. This extensive, one-year strategic planning exercise led to a decade of initiatives and more focused grant-making. On 1 January 1993 the foundation became the John S. and James L. Knight Foundation.

The immediate roots of the foundation's current programmes were developed during the 1990s. The Cities Program was renamed the Community Initiatives Program to reflect a proactive emphasis in grant-making, and seven areas of special interest were identified as funding priorities: arts and culture, children and social welfare, citizenship, community development, education, homelessness, and literacy. Among the major initiatives launched under the auspices of the revamped programme was a Community Foundations Initiative designed to enlarge or establish donor-advised funds at community foundations in cities and towns where the foundation made local grants.

In 1998 the board decided the Community Initiatives Program should cover only the 26 cities that had been eligible for local grants at the time of Jim Knight's death in 1991. This decision ended the practice of the foundation following the company as it bought or sold newspapers throughout the country.

Journalism initiatives focused on educational needs, and free-press and First-Amendment issues. In 1993 the Knight International Press Fellowships, administered by the International Center for Journalists, were established to enable US journalists and media executives to go overseas to provide professional advice and training in emerging democracies.

The education programme underwent a major shift in direction – from higher education alone to include K-12 (primary and secondary) – after the 1992 strategic plan was adopted. The foundation forged alliances with national education reform groups such as New American Schools, the National Board for Professional Teaching Standards, and Teach for America, that resulted in these and other organizations incorporating many of the foundation's cities into their activities.

The arts and culture programme launched two initiatives in the early to mid-1990s. The 'Magic of Music' symphony orchestra initiative provided grants to symphony orchestras to generate a greater sense of excitement about the concert-going experience and a more vital relationship between artists and audiences. The second initiative, the Museum Loan Network, is a collection-sharing programme administered by the Massachusetts Institute of Technology (MIT) that aims to get artworks out of storage in one museum and onto the walls of another.

A review of the foundation's strategic plan in 1995 resulted in fine-tuning, using such strategies as needs assessments and evaluation. As the decade ended, the foundation launched an in-depth, ongoing Community Indicators Project to acquire more comprehensive information about its 26 communities.

In 2003 the foundation had $1.846 billion in assets, and paid out grants of $90.4 million.

Governance and Staffing

The foundation is governed by a board of 14 trustees and officers. Trustees come from backgrounds in business, journalism, and the nonprofit and education sectors and are said to have become younger and more diverse in recent years. It employs 56 full-time and one part-time staff, some of whom are based in the communities in which the foundation makes grants.

Mission

The foundation has a dual mission: 'committed to preserving, protecting and invigorating a free press at home and abroad and to investing in the 26 US communities where the Knight brothers owned newspapers until their deaths' (www.knightfdn.org). The John S. and James L. Knight Foundation is 'dedicated to furthering their ideals of service to community, to the highest standards of journalistic excellence and to the defense of a free press' (www.knightfdn.org).

The foundation's emphasis on journalism is a continuation of the Knight brothers' interests, and is based on a clearly articulated philosophy regarding freedom and democracy.

> If the people do not constantly assert their primacy and exercise the freedoms then inherited, the system will collapse or be replaced by a more rigid model. The bad news is that there is nothing permanent about freedom, any more than there was permanence in the totalitarian model once widely feared to be the one sure survivor of the 20th Century.
>
> Freedom cannot endure in the face of apathy and neglect. Its security depends upon each man and woman speaking up for what each believes, exercising First Amendment rights to free speech, assembly and petition for redress of grievance. To put it another way, it depends on advocacy for the transiently unpopular, and uninhibited dissent from the currently popular (Knight Foundation 2002: p. 4).
>
> What the people do not know about, they cannot adequately question or meaningfully support. Freedom depends upon the news media's presentation of a rich diet of information and a wide variety of views on public policy issues. It requires that the information that is presented be put in usable context, not as 'news from nowhere' but as news with relevance to the past, the present and the future. It requires a media that does not see itself as cheerleader for power but as honest auditor of power (Knight Foundation 2002: p. 5).
>
> Nor does the support and defense of freedom begin and end with the individual, however well educated and informed. It also is vitally dependent on that great boiling stew that is the independent sector. Now as in the past, the

nation's health requires that it continue to bubble over with alternative approaches and more diverse options than those prescribed by government (Knight Foundation 2002: p. 5).

The foundation believes 'that a significant portion of our mission, community-based as it is and supportive of a free press as it has always been, is to strengthen organizations that in turn strengthen democracy and freedom. Knight believes that in a free society, more voices and more options for the solution of enduring problems are a good thing. That means on the local level and the national. It means in old forms of media and new. It means in new problem-solving associations as well as old.' 'We believe we do best by promoting journalism of excellence world-wide and investing in the vitality of 26 US communities. We occupy a unique niche in philanthropy, given the advantage of having enduring ties with these 26 cities and towns' (Hodding Carter III, President and CEO, Knight Foundation 2002: p. 5).

The commitment to democracy as a work in progress is what links the two elements of the foundation's mission. Work in communities seeks 'to incorporate all Americans into the body politic' (Knight Foundation 2003) via, among other things, civic participation and education.

Current Programmes

A review in 2000 resulted in the 'most extensive reinvention in the foundation's history' (Knight Foundation 2001). 'To heighten the impact of our grant making' the foundation decided to narrow its focus to two signature programmes: Journalism Initiatives and Community Partners. A third programme, the National Venture Fund, nurtures innovation, leadership and experimentation for community investments that might benefit Knight communities.

The Journalism Programme

This set of activities receives approximately 25 per cent of the foundation budget. It seeks to promote excellence in journalism, focusing on five categories: Education and Training; Electronic and New Media; News and Newsroom Diversity; News in the Public Interest; and Press Freedom and Freedom of Information.

Education and training initiatives are seen in the foundation's established practice of funding chairs in journalism; in 2004 it gave a $1.5 million grant to endow another Knight Chair in Journalism (the 18th), focusing on health in the US BlackBelt.

Expanding mid-career training is a key feature of the foundation's training programme. As well as highlighting issues and promoting excellence in journalism, the foundation also works to encourage the media industry to make its own investments in excellence. A foundation study for the Council of National Journalism Organizations showed that the $100 billion-a-year industry spends just 0.7 per cent of payroll on professional development (*Newsroom Training: Where's the Investment?*). One result of that project was the formation of a coalition of 40 professional groups that recommended a project to encourage greater news-industry investment in training. This in turn resulted in a four-year grant from the foundation to Northwestern University for the Tomorrow's Workforce Program. This programme will work with chief executives and newsrooms to improve training and to show how mid-career training improves newsroom quality, productivity, retention and diversity (Knight Foundation 2003: p. 13). Tomorrow's Workforce is one part of a wider, three-year foundation journalism training initiative. One of the greatest early success stories of this wider initiative has been the Traveling Campus Program, launched by the Southern Newspaper Publishers' Association. This unique travelling training course provides a model for others because the industry itself will support it in perpetuity via a $10 million endowment.

Training also extends internationally. For example, the Knight Center for Journalism in the Americas at the University of Texas is central to the Foundation's Latin America initiative, aimed at advancing press freedom and journalism excellence. So far the project has trained 500 Brazilian and Mexican journalists, and helped coordinate the activities of 30 journalists' groups. Another example of work with international impact is publication of a report and a website examining US actions in Iraq, Afghanistan, and Guantanamo Bay through the lens of international humanitarian law; this was followed by a grant of $450,000 to support an outreach programme to enable 20,000 journalists better to understand the international laws of war (Knight Foundation 2002: p. 18).

Press freedom, and freedom of information initiatives, also work nationally and internationally. For example, the Inter-American Press Association (IAPA) campaign to draw attention to the murder of journalists in the Americas led to a 500 per cent increase in traffic to IAPA's Impunidad website (www.impunidad. com), an increase in the conviction of assassins of journalists, and an agreement by the government of Colombia to reopen all its old cases; a broadcast version of the campaign started in 2004 (Knight Foundation 2003: p. 16).

At home, the foundation has funded various projects addressing the effects of the Homeland Security Act (2001) on freedom of information and government accountability. For example, the Reporters' Committee for Freedom of the Press issued *Homefront Confidential*, a study detailing the federal government's restraint of information. The National Security Archives filed Freedom of Information Act requests to challenge the new security measures by bringing test cases to court.

As important to the foundation is the establishment of two press freedom coalitions: one to mobilize journalists (The Coalition of Journalists for Open Government), the other to mobilize advocates (The Fund for Constitutional Government). These are in addition to helping the Associated Press, the American

Society of Newspaper Editors, the Radio and Television News Directors Association and others to work on the March 2005 Sunshine Sunday campaign. In all, the foundation has 33 active grants with 28 organizations working in the area of press freedom and freedom of information.

News and newsroom diversity, and electronic and new media initiatives, include Consumer Webwatch (www.consumerwebwatch.org), which has worked with some one hundred major companies, including CNN and the *New York Times* to make it easier for consumers to understand the difference between advertising and news on the web. Other projects relate to the encouragement of new high-school news outlets focusing on schools with a majority of students of colour; development of new teaching tools to help students obtain the writing experience to break into the profession, and a searchable online national calendar of journalism training projects. Published studies include *Reaching Generation Next: A News Media Guide to Creating Successful High School Partnerships* (2004).

News in the public interest initiatives stem from the foundation's fundamental philosophy, underpinning all its journalism programmes, that journalism is a public trust. 'Journalism excellence – the accurate, fair, contextual pursuit of the truth – acts in the public interest. Good journalists verify and clarify. They monitor power as fair, independent auditors' (Knight Foundation 2003: p. 16). This means, at times, reporting news that is unwelcome, but necessary to the public good. To address this issue the foundation has increased support for: TRACFED (http://tracfed.syr.edu), a Syracuse University project that provides a database tool tracking federal government spending, court decisions and agency actions; the Center for Public Integrity, a leading nonprofit investigative unit; and Investigative Reporters and Editors, which trains journalists internationally to be better watchdogs in the public interest (Knight Foundation 2003: p. 16).

Community Partners

Following the 2000 review, the foundation strengthened its commitment to the 26 Knight communities. The Community Partners Program receives over 50 per cent of the total grants budget. Through this programme each community receives a share of the total allocation based on its size. In larger communities this may amount to around $25 million over five years.

As a result of the review, greater commitment was combined with greater focus over a longer period of time on a set of locally recommended priorities. Specially created Knight Community Advisory Committees (CAC), made up of local people, were asked to choose up to a maximum of three priorities from a list created by the foundation. Choices have varied dramatically, ranging from early childhood development to race relations. In addition to the CAC, in each community the foundation works with a resident liaison officer whose job is to develop fundable strategies in partnership with nonprofit organizations. The plan is that these local liaison officers, in turn, work with a team of content officers researching and sharing what works across Knight communities.

Complementing the narrower focus of the Community Partners Program, the foundation made a commitment to invest $50 million by 2005 in expanding its donor-advised funds at community foundations in Knight communities. This gives flexibility for smaller, shorter-term grants. The revised Community Partners Program is designed to make the foundation's local grants both more focused and effective and, at the same time, more locally informed and responsive.

Knight trustees make an annual visit to projects in a Knight community.

National Venture Fund

The third arm of the foundation's current range of programmes is the National Venture Fund (NVF), which spends about 14 per cent of the foundation's total budget; this programme 'supports innovative leadership, organizations and ideas addressing our fields of funding interest; integrates their contributions into our programs nationally and in the 26 Knight communities; and communicates the knowledge gained from these investments to those who influence change on the local and national level. The long-term goal of the National Venture Fund is to deepen Knight Foundation's impact by providing models, leveraging resources and influencing decisions that create systemic change across our areas of funding interest, at the community level and ultimately across the nation' (www.knightfdn.org). NVF works on the premise that in a free society all citizens should have equal access to economic opportunities, healthy living conditions, high-quality education and social justice.

The National Venture Fund makes grants on the basis of both top-down and bottom-up factors. Bottom-up grants come about when several Knight communities are engaged in similar work and the NVF is able to amplify that work at a national level. Top-down grants originate from ideas and interests first identified at national level but that have an impact at local level in Knight cities.

The NVF takes risks, explores new ideas and offers potential for large-scale change. It puts particular emphasis on encouraging collaboration among funders, and it attempts to align the efforts of all interested parties nationally and locally. For example, CEOs for Cities is a national alliance of mayors, corporate executives, university presidents and nonprofit and foundation leaders working to advance the economic competitiveness of cities. The organization strengthens urban leadership networks across sectors and cities, commissions research on best practices, and promotes effective economic development policies and practices on the local and national level. Information and ideas are shared among urban decision-makers through conferences and policy advocacy. Similarly, the foundation is involved in Living Cities, an 11-year-old partnership of 17 national foundations, intermediaries, financial institutions, federal agencies and local leaders in government, business and community organizations.

The NVF also works to promote civic participation and education. In 2002, with budget cuts looming, the NVF made a $250,000 grant to Charity Lobbying in the Public Interest to help non-profits in Knight communities advocate more effectively for their clients and organizations. Charity Lobbying helps nonprofit leaders understand the broad legal scope for participation in the public policy process, the importance of advocacy, and how to lobby effectively.

The NVF also supports Kids Voting USA, a programme to engage elementary students and their families in discussion of current events and voting. More recently, the NVF has worked with the journalism initiative on a project to get civic education and media literacy into the high school curriculum. Gaining a foothold in the curriculum is seen as essential in ensuring that high-school initiatives are not killed off as fast as they are funded.

Following the disputed outcome of the 2000 presidential election in Florida, the NVF funded the National Commission on Federal Election Reform. In 2002, President Bush signed the Help America Vote Act, a bi-partisan effort to aid states and localities in updating their voting systems, acknowledging the work of the commission. 'Enactment of the new law illustrates the benefit that one Knight grant to a national organization can have in all 26 Knight communities and beyond' (Knight Foundation 2002: p. 3).

In 2003 the NVF gave $100,000 to Project Vote Smart, collaborating with newspapers nationwide in its effort to push political candidates to provide more issue-related information rather than more 'self-serving candidate hype'. In the same year, the NVF gave a grant to PACE (Philanthropy for Active Civic Engagement) to fund collection and analysis of data on funding strategies and to evaluate what works in civic engagement grant-making.

Drivers of Change

A Culture of Flexibility

In many respects, the drivers for change and creativity are rooted in the culture of the foundation. From the very beginning the Knight brothers and the trustees emphasized the need to stay flexible in order to respond to changing circumstances and needs. The foundation's response to recent events at home and abroad – the Homeland Security Act and events in Latin America, for example – has demonstrated the value of this flexibility.

Regular Review

As outlined above, like other foundations studied, the Knight Foundation has engaged in regular reviews of its work, and has not been afraid to reinvent itself as circumstances demanded. Regular review appears to have become part of the culture and practice of the foundation.

Increases in Income

Over the years, the foundation has experienced significant increases in income, and reviews have, if not been prompted by these, then at least coincided with such changes in resources. For example, Jim Knight's death in 1991 and bequest of $200 million to the foundation made the Board's 1990 decision to initiate a new strategic planning process even more timely. This review initiated, among other things, the foundation's more proactive approach, especially in relation to community programmes.

Changing Leadership

Change in leadership among both board and staff have also tended to coincide with review and fine-tuning of the foundation's direction. This was the case when Jim Knight died in 1991; again in 1996 with a change of chairman (W. Gerald Austen); and with the change of president two years later, when Creed C. Black stepped down after ten years and was succeeded by Hodding Carter III.

A Sense of Direction

Despite the foundation's regular reviews of its work it has retained a clear sense of direction in its core commitment to support a free press and the 26 communities in which the Knight brothers made their fortune. These commitments, built into the foundation's mission, have provided a stable anchor in changing times and enabled the foundation to build a solid national reputation based on accumulated knowledge and networks.

Elements of a Creative Approach

The elements of the Knight Foundation's approach are similar to those displayed in the other case studies so far. Perhaps what marks out the Knight Foundation is its focus on democracy, civic engagement and the role of a free and educated press in those processes, and how this emphasis requires a different approach.

Passion of the Founders

The foundation's tenacity and focus is due in part to the passion it derives from its founders' commitment to maintaining and promoting democracy and their conviction regarding the importance of a free, high-quality press. In addition to various initiatives in journalism training and activities to support a free press abroad, the foundation works to protect a free press in the United States. For example, in 2003 the foundation gave a grant to the Public Broadcasting Service (PBS) to add coverage of media issues to the Friday night television series *NOW*. The show pioneered coverage of the Federal Communications Commission plan to allow expansion of commercial media companies. After protests, Congress reduced the FCC's rules, preventing any single company owning more than 39 per cent of the television market, and is considering other changes in the FCC's ownership guidelines (Knight Foundation 2003).

Diversity in Governance

In line with its commitment to democracy as a work in progress, the foundation attaches significance to diversity in its governance, enabling it to listen and learn more effectively. Trustees have become more geographically and occupationally diverse, and younger; and in the 26 Knight communities in which the foundation makes grants, the foundation has created mechanisms for understanding local issues and concerns via both advisory committees and resident liaison officers.

Awareness of Paucity of Resources Relative to Need

Jack Knight was always aware of how very small the foundation's resources were, and always would be, relative to the issues it sought to address. Today, in spite of its increased wealth, the foundation continues to be aware of that, but sees its value as lying not simply in its financial resources but also in its staff's experience and knowledge, its capacity and space to create and engage in collaboration and research. In 2003, for example, in its journalism programme the foundation worked with a coalition of journalism groups to promote a nationwide push for improved training and mid-career education; new groups of citizen advocates and journalists to promote a campaign for free flow of information; classrooms and newsrooms on a creative web collaboration; and with news leaders to support 'news in the public interest' (Knight Foundation 2003: p. 12).

Knowledge at National and Local Level

The foundation attaches considerable significance to producing and funding research and knowledge both to inform others and regarding its own grant-making. Its work in journalism is based on research into, for example, existing training of journalists, effects of the Homeland Security Act on First-Amendment freedoms, and on global developments in support of a free press. In informing its own grant-making in Knight communities, the foundation invested in the production of community-indicator profiles.

Compilation of community-indicator profiles for each community was an essential part of the process of the Community Partners Program and its new approach to grant-making. CACs were provided with a copy of the profiles to use in their choice of priorities. The use of the community indicators was said by the committees to be very helpful: they 'provided us with a reason to act beyond our beliefs and anecdotal knowledge' (Knight Foundation *et al.* 2004: p. ii) and provided a legitimation for final choices. Other results included substantial local press coverage and interest from other decision makers; other foundations working locally have also adopted the indicators as key elements of their own needs assessments. Funding of research and knowledge production is seen as being valuable not only to the foundation itself but also as a way of providing tools of value to others.

Working at Different Levels

The Foundation attaches significance to working at different levels. For example, in its programmes on First-Amendment freedoms it works both with and on journalists and directly on public opinion. It recently gave a $1 million grant to the Ad Council to raise public understanding of First-Amendment freedoms through a campaign of public service advertising. Similarly, the NVF, as noted above, works on issues that arise from the 26 Knight communities, attempting to tie those into a national policy framework, and on issues that come from national level programmes taking those down to the local level in Knight communities. For example, Knight grantees in Miami were looking for ways to help low-income families improve their standard of living. The NVF commissioned the Brookings Institution to research the economic impact of the Earned Income Tax Credit (EITC) in Miami and in some other Knight communities. The Community Partners Program then funded a local coalition to take the research and create a county-wide effort to help the working poor file for the EITC, bringing in $62 million in EITC credits. The NVF is now offering hands-on support to launch similar campaigns elsewhere.

Evaluation and Learning

Evaluation is seen not as a 'report card' but as a means of learning and self reflection. Learning from both success and failure is seen as helpful in thinking about strategies for the future. The foundation also values its links with other foundations doing community development work as a means of sharing lessons and experience. The way in which the foundation has restructured its involvement at local level illustrates the value it attaches to listening and learning. CACs and the liaison officers are the foundation's eyes and ears in local communities, providing knowledge that a centrally based foundation could never acquire on its own.

Coalitions

At both national and local levels, the foundation seeks to build support around an outcome or an issue, bringing others to the table and focusing interest. At national level, it works through large and complex coalitions that bring knowledge, legitimacy and the power to achieve change. Similarly, at local level the foundation has organized its involvement in such a way as to build in maximum community input. Considerable effort was put into ensuring diversity in the CACs, but given the difficulties of having every segment represented, active community liaison officers were added to fill in any 'gaps'. In an important sense, CACs and the foundation's grantees act as coalitions in themselves.

Valuing the Old and Inventing the New

The foundation has a number of well-established and influential relationships. Wherever possible it attempts to work through existing relationships and collaborations, helping to make the changes they want; and, at the same time, develop new and old relationships to do something new. For example, in recent years the foundation has developed its relationships with PBS, with international journalism organizations via the Inter-American Press Association in a public campaign to draw attention to the murder of journalists in the Americas, and with the National Security Archive Fund to obtain and release government information.

Borrowing Credibility

In its journalism initiatives in particular the foundation already has considerable credibility in its own right, and it adds to this credibility via the support of the coalitions it encourages and creates. In areas where the foundation has less credibility it will underwrite research by those who already have an established reputation. Funding of the Brookings Institution work on tax credits, outlined above, is one example.

Sustainability

Programmes and grants vary in duration. For example, the foundation-endowed chairs in journalism will exist for decades, whereas the individual community programmes are scheduled to last for about five years. In general, the foundation aims to put in place sustainable change. Where the term of funding is unlikely to achieve the impact desired by the foundation the aim is to create the conditions in which independent sustainability is possible. For example, in one community the chosen issue is race relations: 'We recognize that we won't have much impact on race relations in 5–10 years, but the aim is

to galvanize the community around the issue and establish the right collaborations to make that self-sustaining.'

Promoting Ideas, Ensuring Dialogue

As illustrated above, promoting ideas, via research, investments in training,
listening and learning, and ensuring informed dialogue via collaboration, coalitions, communications and its defence of a free press are central to the
foundation's *raison d'être* and its strategies.

Implications and Issues

Risk and Sustainability

Some of the foundation's programmes involve very little risk of lack of sustainability. Other programmes may be more far reaching in their effects but involve
greater risk of lack of sustainability. For example, 'if you endow a chair or a
fellowship you know that you will train x-thousand journalists and that the chair
or fellowship will still be there in 20 years. If you spend the same amount on
trying to change newsroom cultures and companies that is much more risky. Will
it work and will the change be sustainable?'

Dilemmas of Evaluation

The foundation sees various dilemmas in relation to evaluation and performance
measurement. First, while some staff see one function of evaluation as building
data on best practice, trustees are more focused on directly improving grantees'
work rather than adding to the stock of knowledge. Furthermore, 'trustees want
snapshots – digestible bits. They like stories more than data points.' Second, while
evaluation is considered important for learning it is also the case that 'people have
only a limited appetite for more evaluation information. We're still working on
proving that evaluation has relevance for their work.' Third, when evaluation is
linked to performance measurement, problems of attributing causality inevitably
arise, and not really knowing what you achieved is never very satisfying. Fourth,
while failure may provide important lessons, there are obvious dilemmas in
'staying honest about things not working out'.

Preaching to the Unconverted

Getting information out in places where the foundation is not already preaching
to the converted, and the costs of that process, are seen as another dilemma. One
option is to communicate more directly with the public, in addition to working on
journalism education and structures.

Integration

Integrating the two elements of the foundation's mission and the different levels at which it works – national and local – is seen as an ongoing challenge. As one person commented, 'the danger is that we work like two foundations under the same roof.' To avoid this, one option is to create closer relationships between work in communities and the National Venture Fund. Similarly, there are challenges in ensuring that the work in the 26 Knight communities becomes more than the sum of its parts, adding value via shared learning. One possibility is to bring lessons from individual communities together in a systematic learning network.

Balancing Autonomy and Focus

Creation of the CACs has given a degree of autonomy to each of the 26 communities in which the foundation works. At the same time, however, the foundation has legal responsibilities and accountabilities for how its money is spent, and a desire to maintain focus in the interests of effectiveness and creating added value from the integration, at some level, of the various community initiatives. This balance between autonomy and control is currently maintained via restrictions on the nature and number of initiatives each local community can undertake, and the status of CACs as advisory to the foundation. Creation of Knight donor-advised funds in local community foundations 'sweetens the pill' of a smaller number of (larger) grants, as well as maintaining a more widespread local presence for the foundation.

The Costs of Coalitions

While the foundation is convinced of the value and effectiveness of working through coalitions, it acknowledges that coalitions entail costs in time and money. 'There's no doubt that managing the care and feeding of coalitions is very demanding – the members may not like each other, and they sometimes compete for funds, and those are just some of the problems. Trying to help them become self-maintaining is hard work.' This is a challenge yet to be resolved.

Achievements

The foundation sees its key achievements in recent years as including:

- 'Deepened connection to the 26 Knight communities, taking greater advantage of our long-term relationships as a local funder there.

- A well-branded commitment to increased training for professional journalists, with early and positive results indicating success.

- Leadership in important philanthropic collaboratives including Living Cities: The National Community Development Initiative, and in the formation of the Florida Philanthropic Network.

- An enduring commitment to reforming the governance of intercollegiate athletics through the work of the Knight Commission on Intercollegiate Athletics.

- Starting a transforming conversation among US symphony orchestras about changing their approach to their audiences through the Magic of Music initiative, and

- New programming, new collaborative leadership, new marketing approaches and new, creative uses of technology on stage are among the results of this long-running initiative.'

8   The Annie E. Casey Foundation

'For us, real success is not simply using our resources to do good for kids, but finding ways to help the far larger public and private sectors do better'

(Nelson 1999).

With the Casey Foundation, we come to a creative philanthropic institution that operates in a rather traditional field of charity: disadvantaged children and communities in distress. Yet it goes about it in very innovative ways, in particular in a programme called Making Connections.

Background

The Annie E. Casey Foundation was created in 1948 by Jim Casey, founder and CEO of United Parcel Service, in memory of his mother Annie. From the outset the foundation was committed to helping disadvantaged children. Involvement in supporting high-quality foster care, started by Jim Casey, continues via Casey Family Programs, now an independent operating foundation in Seattle, and Casey Family Services, established in 1976 as the direct operating unit of the Annie E. Casey Foundation. When Jim Casey died in the mid-1980s, he left his personal holdings in UPS (worth $800 million at the time) to the foundation. With these increased resources the board of trustees began to expand the foundation's work on behalf of disadvantaged children. In 2002 Casey had around $3.5 billion assets and annual spending of around $240 million. The foundation is UPS's largest shareholder.

Governance and Staffing

The board of the foundation is made up of senior UPS employees, along with some others from beyond UPS, such as a former governor of Michigan. The foundation employs 170 staff in its grant-making operation and another 350 through the adoptive, post-adopt, and foster-care services its provides in eight offices throughout New England.

The foundation has established a social investing initiative through which it directs a portion of its endowment (as opposed to the income that funds its regular grant-making budget) towards Program-Related Investments (PRIs) and what it calls Mission Related Deposits (MRDs). The primary goal of this initiative is to further the foundation's programmatic strategies in its Making Connections and Civic Investment sites. The initial programme has involved investments of up to $20 million, with further investments planned in future years.

The foundation uses both PRIs and MRDs to support work in the field and leverage other investments locally that grants alone may not be able to do. PRI investments are made through intermediary organizations that reinvest these funds in a range of local projects related to the work Casey is supporting in the community. An important priority is to seek co-investors with the work, rather than operate independently.

In addition to PRI-related investments, the foundation also has allocated a portion of its social investment portfolio in what it calls Mission Related Deposits. MRDs are investments into insured depository institutions in places where these resources can help poor families improve their financial well-being by better managing their debt, improving their credit, and establishing stable banking relationships.

Current Mission

The foundation's mission is 'to help build better futures for millions of disadvantaged children who are at risk of poor educational, economic, social, and health outcomes'. More specifically, the foundation aims to change 'the condition, status and the life prospects of the ten million children in this country (about 1 in 7) – least likely to succeed as adults – least likely to make a good and secure living – least likely to parent as well as they'd like, and – least likely to contribute as workers, voters, neighbors, citizens, and leaders' (speech by Douglas W. Nelson to Johns Hopkins Community Conversation Breakfast series 1999).

Current Programmes

The foundation operates three major inter-related programmes: Promoting accountability and innovation; improving major systems serving disadvantaged children and families; and transforming neighbourhoods.

Promoting Accountability and Innovation

This program has a number of elements. Assessing the New Federalism is a collaboratively funded project investigating the effects on outcomes for disadvantaged children of the shift of responsibility from the federal government to the states. The Casey Journalism Center for Children and Families acts as a resource centre to encourage more informed investigative print and broadcast reporting on matters affecting children. Developing Leaders and Leadership Skills seeks to build the leadership capacity of individuals who can help systems, institutions and communities to plan, manage, communicate and sustain long-term change. Lessons, Models and Tools is concerned to build data-driven evidence of successful innovations, and broad dissemination of them. The Place-Based Philanthropy initiative works with like-minded foundations to increase resources, develop and test approaches, and broker ideas and relationships that improve outcomes for disadvantaged children and families. Kids Count is one of the foundation's flagship projects to increase public awareness of the conditions of children, and to foster greater accountability for improving outcomes. Kids Count collects national and state-by-state data on the educational, economic, social and physical well-being of children, providing invaluable data to those responsible for services and outcomes, as well as those to whom they are accountable. Kids Count, in effect, provides benchmarks against which the position and progress of individual states can be assessed.

Improving Major Systems Serving Disadvantaged Children and Families

This programme aims to help distressed neighbourhoods become environments that foster strong, capable families. One of the key challenges is seen as changing the child-welfare, mental-health, and other public systems serving disadvantaged children and their families, which often: focus on individual problems rather than working holistically; wait for a crisis before intervening; are physically and culturally remote from the communities and families they serve; and are accountable only for the quantity rather than the quality of services offered.

Since the early 1990s, the Casey Foundation has supported a number of long-term, multi-site initiatives designed to reform specific child- and family-serving systems. More recently, the foundation has invested in policy and practice initiatives that address the related challenges of strengthening distressed neighbourhoods, alleviating family poverty, reconnecting fathers and families, providing better health care, and preventing community violence. The practice and service innovations of Casey Family Services feed into and validate learning from the programme.

The Education Reform initiative encourages better public education by working in two areas: in states and communities where there is potential for comprehensive reform, and developing and publicizing specific components of comprehensive education reform. Family Economic Success was developed by the foundation to provide a more holistic approach to helping low-income families move up the economic ladder. The programme uses a three-pronged approach, marrying strategies for workforce development, family economic support and community investment in mutually reinforcing ways. The programme has a website providing information for practitioners, policy-makers, researchers and the general public.

Other initiatives under the heading of improving major systems include Tools for Rebuilding Foster Care, Plain Talk – a sex education programme, a Mental Health Initiative, a Jobs Initiative, and a Juvenile Detention Alternatives Initiative. The Human Services Workforce Initiative is designed to confront the problems arising from the low-paid, excessive workloads and regulation that make frontline social-service workers' jobs so difficult. The foundation intends to gather evidence to raise public awareness and guide policy, promote proven practices, provide technical assistance to jurisdictions willing to address the problem, evaluate promising initiatives, and create a national commission to focus attention and action. More generally, the foundation's State and Local Systems Reform programme provides funding to a number of states to make their services work better for children and families.

Transforming Neighborhoods

Transforming Neighborhoods is a 10-year programme taking an increasing proportion of Casey resources. It has five elements: Baltimore; Making Connections; Rebuilding Communities; Reforming City Level Systems; and the Technical Assistance Resource Center. Overall, the programme aims to demonstrate ways that states, localities, and neighbourhood groups can reorganize themselves and integrate their efforts to support vulnerable families and improve distressed neighbourhoods. The challenges of this work are seen as decentralizing large public bureaucracies, pooling funding streams for children and family services across agency lines, and formalizing the involvement of communities in the design and delivery of human services.

Started in 1999, Making Connections is based on the foundation's research showing that children do better when their families are strong, and families do better when they live in communities that help them to succeed. Making Connections is based on the assumption that families matter and place matters in addressing the problems of poverty, isolation and ineffective help. Working with local groups in 22 sites across the United States, the goal is to link isolated families to employment opportunities, to positive social, civic and religious networks, and to competent service systems designed to help them succeed as parents.

There are three key strands in Making Connections' strategy. First, it provides technical assistance built around neighbourhood needs and community issues, using and building on local expertise wherever possible. Second, it creates local partners to gather and analyse data identifying the assets and challenges in each area. Third, it provides support and guidance to enable neighbours in Making Connections sites to share their experience, know-how and ideas with each other about what works with the goal of helping to support and connect a range of formal and informal efforts that promote family success. Sharing what works has itself stimulated bottom-up change, encouraging neighbourhoods to rebuild and revitalize themselves.

In addition to the above programmes, the foundation runs the Casey Strategic Consulting Group (CSCG), which is designed to build on the Annie E. Casey Foundation's systems-reform legacy by developing the capacity to consult human-service leaders and their organizations in bringing about reform. The aim is to strengthen families in the context of their communities, and to do so by working with public sector officials and agencies committed to substantially improving the lives of the citizens they serve.

Recent experience has suggested that one of the most powerful opportunities to make a difference for more rapid and durable change may occur when Casey can focus intensive and strategic consulting resources at critical times in state government. These times could include:

- System failure leading to a crisis in public confidence

- Class action litigation, or

- Leadership transition at the level of governor, mayor or major agency head.

The Casey Strategic Consulting Group seeks to help identify such moments of opportunity, establish relationships with the champions of change, and provide the strategic consulting needed to maximize the likelihood that fundamental public systems change occurs. To do so, it works to support Casey's vision for reformed human services and the public agency leaders' vision for reform as they make difficult decisions in the interest of their jurisdiction.

CSCGs provides direct, intensive, and expansive consulting support to leaders and agencies poised for significant change. The approach, shaped by both private sector strategy consulting techniques and the foundation's experience in technical assistance, is characterized by the following critical elements:

- Emphasis on clear alignment of results sought by the agency with foundation principles, approaches, and expertise;

- Diversely expert CSCG teams that provide ongoing, hands-on, and sometimes day-to-day assistance in change efforts;

- Close collaboration with a parallel team of dedicated site staff;

- Planning driven by analytic use of data, guided by strategy tools and frameworks, and supported by excellent back-office research capacity;

- Defined phases of work clearly delineated and punctuated by clarifying products (assessments, plans, etc.) and by renewed commitments by both the system leaders (Governors, Mayors, Secretaries) and the Foundation' (interviews/correspondence).

Developing Strategy: The Move to a Creative Approach

This case study concentrates in particular on Making Connections, one of the foundation's newest and most ambitious place-based initiatives. Drivers of a creative approach in the Making Connection project include:

Radical Review

Eight years ago the foundation became increasingly dissatisfied with how it was working and embarked on a two-year review to look at what it had learned and to think and talk about how it could do things differently. This led to a realization that 'traditional grant-making was not really working'. Closely related, data from the review suggested that silo programmes were not effective because problems are inter-related. The foundation therefore looked at ways in which it could try to build new connections, putting its resources and work together in new ways.

Board 'Outsiders'

Some see the fact that the board is not composed of child-care professionals as having been an advantage in driving the move away from conventional grant-making. The board's business, rather than nonprofit, background is also seen as having been important in introducing the conversation about accountability for results, which has had a 'profound' effect on the foundation. Holding itself accountable for impact, influence and leverage has affected not only what the foundation does but also how it plans, manages and monitors its work.

Awareness of Paucity of Resources

The move to a creative approach was also driven by the foundation's awareness (despite its considerable assets) of the paucity of its resources relative to its mission. Casey's president remarks: 'That $240 million is also less than we Americans currently spend on gym shoes for our teenagers each year. It's only enough to run the New York City schools for a few weeks. It's only enough to pay for the incarceration of juvenile delinquents in California for about 3 months. It is only enough to meet the needs of two percent of the foster-care kids who are currently in foster care in the US. Indeed, $240 million is only enough to subsidize one football stadium in one city' (speech to Johns Hopkins Community Conversation Breakfast series 1999). Awareness of the foundation's large, yet tiny, resources is an important factor in understanding the foundation's approach.

Focus on Facts

The drive towards a new approach was also closely tied up with a systematic statistical analysis of where children in need were located. This showed that the most disadvantaged children were not randomly distributed throughout the United States but were concentrated in about 900 neighbourhoods. Combined with the desire to get away from a silo approach, awareness of the foundation's paucity of resources, and a revised theory of social change (see below), this analysis led the foundation to move to a 'place-based philanthropy' programme (Making Connections) and to test this new approach in 22 neighbourhoods.

Elements of Effectiveness: A Creative Approach

Listening to and Involving Others

The foundation adopts a stakeholder approach via the 'consultative process' developed initially for its Transforming Neighborhoods/Family Development Initiative in the mid-1990s. More than 600 practitioners, family members (including youth), community organizers, business leaders, Casey grantees, researchers and others participated in 24 sessions over a two-year period. The process was especially designed to obtain input from people who are knowledgeable but ordinarily do not have opportunities to provide input to philanthropy.

A stakeholder approach was used to design Making Connections. Stakeholders had emphasized that the initiative would need to be more accessible to neighbourhood groups, more likely to attract other investors, and more accountable to families than in the past. This led to the development of a place-based approach in which Casey works behind the scenes to encourage local planning and action, including involvement of both individual and institutionalized philanthropy (Backer and Smith 2003).

Long-Term Commitment

From the outset the foundation board committed to a ten-year investment in Making Connections. The board recognized that achieving sustainable community change in social and economic systems would require sustained investment.

Changing the Environment / Focus on Causes

The foundation believes that it cannot change the futures of at-risk children until it changes the present for their parents. 'Nothing determines or predicts the future of a child more strongly or more profoundly than the condition, the capacity and the values of their mother and father' (Nelson 1999). In Making Connections, this philosophy underpins the emphasis on connecting families to the economic, social and other supports they need, and promoting the provision of those supports.

Leading with Ideas

Making Connections is one element in the foundation's commitment to investing in knowledge, leading with ideas not money. 'Lasting change comes from good ideas. Money is necessary to support ideas, but it shouldn't lead the charge. And foundation funding should never overshadow local investments and resources' (www.aecf.org). This in turn led to a decision to have more in-house staff to do research, and to a strong emphasis on technical assistance to Making Connections sites.

Identifying Solutions

The foundation sees its role as investing resources in learning 'what investments, what innovations, what partnerships, what service system reforms are most likely to connect the families who live there to the work, relationships, and help that will enable more families to raise their children more successfully' (Nelson 1999). For example, in addition to its site-based local work, Casey co-sponsors the 'Families Count' Family Strengthening Awards, which identify, reward and communicate exemplary initiatives. The awards and partnerships with national groups are seen as creating an 'echo chamber' of messages and models for family strengthening (Casey Foundation 2002: p. 1).

Working Top-Down and Bottom-Up

'Making Connections has never labored under a romantic notion that the neighborhood and institutional transformation needed to strengthen families and improve outcomes for disadvantaged children will happen solely from the bottom up . . . The initiative has held that the engagement of a broad base of stakeholders from the top down, bottom up and everywhere in between is needed to catalyse family strengthening movements of sufficient scope, scale and impact' (Annie E. Casey Foundation 2003a: p. 1). The foundation believes that without resident organizing it is impossible to achieve sustainable scaled-up change, and it therefore combines work on resident organizing and capacity building with work with institutional stakeholders. However, it is recognized that one of the difficulties in translating community mobilization to system change is 'a disconnect on policy issues'. Systematic thought and effort has to go into making that connection, taking into account the fact that the site team and residents will probably have uneven levels of engagement with different systems, and systems themselves may differ in their resistance to change.

Multiple Strategies

Both in its wider work, and more specifically in Making Connections, the foundation works with multiple strategies at different levels. So, for example, compilation and publication of Kids Count is the pre-eminent example of the foundation's commitment to and use of knowledge transfer and management at all levels, from federal to local. Grantees in 50 states develop the data and work with whoever is in a position to influence outcomes on children's well-being. Casey lays out the state of progress and enables the change-makers to address system reform at various levels. An in-house consultancy service offers states ways to address system reform.

But system reform is only one part of the strategy. In order to stimulate real, long-term change, Making Connections works with a three-pronged strategy: leveraging additional resources and partners to create and sustain long-term change in neighbourhoods or in families on a large scale; influencing systems and policies affecting families and neighbourhoods; and helping develop and support a mobilized community that can propel and sustain change over the long term.

Catalysing Change

The Foundation accepts that there is very little it can do alone, as a single institution. Knowledge, demonstration, communication and creating partnerships all play key roles. 'We can: help catalyze a clearer understanding of the problems that face young families; we can mobilize partnerships; engage in research and development; take risks with new approaches that others cannot afford to take; incentivize innovation and new investment by the public and private sector. We can collect and disseminate honest data about what's working and what isn't. We can broadcast and applaud the most positive achievements of schools, cities, programs, neighborhoods, and other foundations' (Nelson 1999). In addition to catalysing change at local level, the foundation works with a range of national partners. Some newer partners include the National Assembly for Health and

Human Services and Corporate Voices for Working Families, made up of over 30 leading national corporations.

Adding Value Beyond Money

Recognizing its limitations as one institution, the foundation sees its role as adding value by using its resources, credibility, networks and staff to help local partners explore new ideas, strategies and practice that strengthen families and communities. This 'grants plus approach' often involves working behind the scenes, out of public view. For example, its role in reforming the child-welfare system in New York City could not have worked had it been restricted to grant-making: 'This is the kind of work that is not amenable to just a grant. The institutional credibility we lent to the effort, the hands-on involvement of senior Casey staff, and the network of experts we were able to draw on – all this mattered at least as much as the flexible dollars we provided' (Annie E. Casey Foundation 2004: p. 95; Silverman 2004: p. 98).

Collaboration Across Boundaries

Partnerships across boundaries are central to the foundation's way of working. In many cases, it is the lack of collaboration across systems and boundaries that is part of the problem the foundation seeks to address. For example, Making Connections does not invest in a sole strategy or lead agency at any site. It seeks out a wide range of partners across sectors and at different levels to attack a group of related problems. Partners include residents, local government, employers, financial institutions, large and small businesses, faith-based groups, community-based organizations, cultural clubs, hospitals, universities, schools, law enforcement officials, and grassroots community groups. A broad base is seen as generating more ideas, energy and ownership. Recognizing that alliances may be difficult to build, the Making Connections support service assists site participants in this task.

One example of the power of collaborations is the story of the campaign against predatory lending in Des Moines, a Making Connections site. With support from the foundation, Citizens for Community Improvement (CCI) helped residents in the Making Connections neighbourhood to expose the prevalence and effects of predatory lending. This led to a partnership between CCI, local families, city and state officials and legislators, financial institutions and housing advocates, who all worked together to stop financial predators. The result was the passage of a city ordinance enacting new protections for homebuyers, and a state law requiring contract dealers to disclose certain information to buyers. Some other Making Connections sites have since taken up this issue with similar success in making changes.

Flexibility: Not All Communities Are the Same

Although certain key principles and strategies run through all of the foundation's work, there is no single blueprint for action even within a single programme such as Making Connections. Because not all communities are the same, each Making Connections site works with a team to help promote family neighbourhood strengthening in a variety of ways. It is up to those involved to decide how best to proceed in their community. What matters is not what is done, how, or in what order, but rather that work is concentrated around the foundation's three key premises: creating the opportunity to earn a decent living and build assets; building close ties with family, neighbours, kin, faith communities and civic groups; and having reliable services close to home.

Learning and Innovation

The foundation emphasizes the need to learn from and build on past experiences, while at the same time continuing to break new ground. It attempts to apply this to its structure and grant-making, as well as its practices in the field. For example, working with the Center for the Study of Social Policy in Washington, DC, the foundation has arranged peer matches. These are structured opportunities for teams of people from different places and organizations working on similar issues to exchange experience and practical knowledge to resolve a particular challenge identified in advance (see, for example, Annie E. Casey Foundation 2003b).

Mistakes are Fine – If They are New

The foundation accepts that taking risks is a necessary part of learning and innovation. It accepts that it will make mistakes – but only if they are new mistakes; repetition means that the organization has failed to learn from past errors. Old 'mistakes' have included impatience to get going in local sites; now it is accepted that building trust is a long, slow process, and may take 2–3 years.

Promoting Knowledge for Change

The foundation attaches enormous importance not just to investments in system reform and community building, but also to promoting findings, ideas, and strategies that help others create and sustain family-supporting communities. This involves supporting a range of activities that provide the best available data and analysis on critical issues affecting disadvantaged children and families, as well as the knowledge and tools that practitioners, policy-makers, and citizens need to advance their efforts on behalf of children. Kids Count is the cornerstone of the foundation's strategy in increasing awareness of the conditions of children, but the foundation publishes a range of other reports, identifying practical strategies and solutions (see www.aecf.org).

Beyond Foundation Money

The foundation's emphasis on communicating knowledge is related to recognition that even its large resources are not big enough to achieve the outcomes it seeks: 'For us, real success is not simply using our resources to do good for kids, but finding ways to help the far larger public and private sectors do better' (Nelson 1999). In addition to partnerships at local and national level with private and public sector organizations, provision of state-by-state benchmarking data, peer matches, and publications to highlight needs and exchange knowledge, the foundation also works to improve public political understanding via the media. The Casey Journalism Center for Children and Families is an independent, nonpartisan resource centre for journalists; it holds a week-long conference for journalists covering specific children's issues, administers an awards programme honouring distinguished coverage relating to children and families, and acts as a resource centre for journalists.

Communication

Having an effect beyond its immediate programmes and grantees requires the involvement of others. Thus communications are central to all of the foundation's work, including the Making Connections programme. 'Effective communications about Making Connections must do more than simply state our mission, values and goals. Instead, we must help focus public attention on – and build support for – policies, practices and investments that are most likely to result in improved outcomes for children, families and communities' (Nelson 1999).

The foundation sponsors a wide range of research, publications and partnerships that help Making Connections sites develop messages, use print, video and web-based communications tools, and improve relationships with local media. These range from very practical communications toolkits to partnerships with the Frameworks Institute and the Center for Communications and Communities at UCLA to promote communications strategies that help reframe negative perceptions and common assumptions about at-risk children, isolated families, and disinvested communities. The Media Outreach Initiative brings local public television stations together with Making Connections sites to convene community forums around national PBS broadcasts of documentaries with family-strengthening and community-building themes.

Being Accountable

The foundation holds itself accountable for three goals: impact, influence and leverage. 'Being focused on impact, influence and leverage forces us to establish milestones and benchmarks that allow us to track progress.' Key questions are: What did an investment achieve for the people whose lives they are hoping to affect? How are they better off? Who is behaving differently as a result of an investment? Are policy-makers, decision-makers, and opinion-leaders saying different things and making different decisions? Did the investment help stimulate other investments? In Making Connections each site develops its own assessment of current issues, and then identifies clear short, medium, and long-term targets, as well as indicators (along the lines of the questions above) of what would count as success at different stages.

Issues and Implications

Balancing Interference and Change

One of the issues arising from place-based work is the danger of negatively affecting existing relationships, ongoing work, and local partnerships. To avoid this, the foundation invests time and resources in understanding local politics, cultures, and systems. But as one person pointed out: 'You can't say you're into change and then say you're not going to change anything.'

Time to Build Trust, Local Relationships and Ownership

In the past, Making Connections worked with lead agencies in each site; this practice was dropped because it did not solve the problem of enlarging the scale of the initiatives beyond the pilot project. All sites now have a local person as co-ordinator, employed via a grant to a local organization or independently, depending on the needs and resources of the particular site. This move away from working with one lead agency has increased the onus on the Making Connections team to build trusting relationships at every level with people who can get things done. In most cases this has taken 2–3 years. Only when relationships are judged to be sufficiently solid, and there is seen to be a willingness to change, does the foundation start work on capacity building.

Place-based work is time consuming, slow, and involves accepting dependence on the willingness of others to co-operate. The Making Connections agenda may not resonate with everyone in a community, and some partners are being asked to make major changes. Finding common ground, building local ownership and strong alliances requires skill, persistence and time – with no certain results. The investment required is very different from that involved in conventional grant-making.

Working At the Right Level

One of the conundrums of place-based work is that the 'place' has to be right, and what may be the right place to effect one sort of change is not the right place to effect another. Making Connections has come to realize that the local level is too low to affect some types of change; work at higher levels is also necessary. But making relationships with county-level bureaucracies has proved challenging.

Another dilemma in achieving institutional change is that it can be a moving target, and the change temporary. Change achieved one year may have dissipated the next year, and while you are busy changing one part of the system, another part may be deteriorating further. Recognition of this has obvious implications for the complexity, and uncertainty, of performance measurement.

Integrating the National and the Local

The place-based work of Making Connections is part of a larger programme – Transforming Neighborhoods – that works on big national non-profits and big national family-policy issues. How all of those involved can converse with each other is an ongoing issue, as is the consistency and integration of the ideas and findings from work at different levels. The foundation's knowledge management system is an effort to deal with this problem of integration.

Living with Local Autonomy

The foundation is committed to respecting the autonomy of Making Connections sites and local neighbourhoods. But Making Connections is only one part of the foundation's wider work, which is driven by a national perspective and a strong, clear value-base. There is a worry that place-based work may take the foundation in a direction that is not consistent with its very clear commitment to the family as an institution.

Managing Knowledge

Because the foundation's major resource is not defined as money but as the knowledge generated by its money, organizing knowledge is seen as crucially important. The foundation's knowledge management has three phases: (1) system access for staff; (2) opening up knowledge to informed publics; and (3) opening up knowledge to the general public. Stage 1 is now largely completed, with 2005 targeted as the year to move to Stage 2. This will be a major undertaking 'because people are perhaps not sure they want to share, perhaps because the knowledge is not firm enough and perhaps because there's a reluctance to allow other people to see us saying that, for fear of negative reactions'.

Knowledge Costs

The foundation's decision to move away from traditional grant-making and to focus on knowledge and learning led to an increase in 'overhead' costs, including the number of staff employed. The foundation invests around $4.65 million a year in producing Kids Count Data, providing state-by-state data on key measures of children's well-being. Its internal consulting group spends about $2 million a year advising state and local government agencies about welfare and juvenile justice reforms. It also invests in technical assistance to support grantees, and in peer assistance. In 2003 $16.5 million was invested in documentation and evaluation.

The board accepts the high level of staffing and non-grant investment, but keeps up the pressure to track and show results. In the last few years there has been some pressure to introduce cost-cutting measures (e.g. around staff benefits and travel) to reduce the foundation's overhead. 'Non-grant activities allow us to achieve results that otherwise would not be possible . . . Part of the challenge now is trying to help the public and the policy-makers understand that the contribution of foundations ought not to be measured simply by how many grants are given in any year.'

Maintaining a Bi-partisan Position

The foundation's board is said to be largely conservative, but is nevertheless willing to support what some see as a radical, or at least liberal approach. This is put down to several factors, including the fact that Republicans 'support our family focus', and 'perhaps because we address causes on which there is greater consensus, rather than solutions that are more politically contentious.' Maintaining a bi-partisan position and the distinction between advocacy and lobbying are seen as important factors in keeping the board happy.

The Casey Strategic Consulting Group emphasizes that it provides non-political consulting resources to states that are receptive to change. For example, the foundation was involved in Louisiana in discussions about shutting down a prison for youth. The foundation's role was to identify the issues and the available alternatives to prison. Based on its reputation as a knowledgeable player, the foundation was seen as providing an informed basis for change rather than as being a political player.

Branding

In general, despite its emphasis on knowledge, learning and leverage as its key resources, the foundation is said 'to work under the radar', partly to ensure that it maintains a publicly bi-partisan position and partly because of a fear of creating expectations and skewing conversations. In some cases, however, the foundation is prepared to clearly brand its products. Kids Count, for example, is very clearly an Annie E. Casey Foundation 'product'. This was explained in terms of a willingness to brand only when 'things are tested and proven and we're very, very sure of our position'.

Openness — A Mixed Blessing

The foundation's commitment to sharing its knowledge and learning with others raises issues about accountability and political positions, and may not be altogether helpful in generating bi-partisan support. The implications of this have yet to emerge.

Rethinking Communications

The foundation produces various regular and one-off publications in a variety of formats, including the *Casey Connects* newsletter, *AdvoCasey*, the data book *Kids Count*, as well as publications and other forms of communication from individual programmes. But there is a view that the foundation 'still needs to have a conversation about what our message is, who our target audiences are and the best ways of reaching those audiences'.

Performance Measurement

While the board demands performance measurement, it also recognizes that achieving social change is different from delivering parcels. In the case of Making Connections, each site works within a framework of six core results. The prescribed Core Results framework helps to frame the work as each site defines areas of common ground between the foundation's required results and local priorities.

From the outset, Making Connections works with local residents and institutional stakeholders to lay out goals, and interim and longer-term results. Laying out 1-year, 3–5-year and 10-year results both allows for some things happening faster than others and enables the team and the foundation to identify and distinguish more clearly between outputs and outcomes. This is said to have no deterrent effect on risk-taking, because the focus is on results, rather than on prescribing a particular strategy.

Results

The foundation sees Kids Count, one of the foundation's flagship projects, as successful in increasing public awareness of the conditions of children, and fostering greater accountability for improving outcomes. The Kids Count collection of national and state-by-state data on the educational, economic, social and physical well-being of children provides invaluable data to those responsible for services and outcomes, as well as those to whom they are accountable. Kids Count provides, in effect, benchmarks against which the position and progress of individual states can be assessed, and thus tools for local and other groups to advocate for change.

The recent emergence of the foundation's role via its Strategic Consulting Group has helped build on earlier successes to support changes in the child welfare system in New York City. The Strategic Consulting Group seeks to help leaders improve outcomes for children and families at key 'opportunity moments' by coupling private-sector management consulting strategies with the foundation's system-reform expertise to make significant, measurable, and lasting changes in public systems. Finally, the foundation's role in the campaign against predatory lending in Des Moines (a Making Connections site) is one example of the potential of an effective place-based focus to address the needs of disadvantaged kids and families. One result of the latter campaign was the passage of a city ordinance enacting new protections for homebuyers, and a state law requiring contract dealers to disclose certain information to buyers. Some other Making Connections sites have since taken up this issue with similar success in making changes.

9   The lessons of success: conservative foundations and the Robert W. Scrivener Award for Creative Philanthropy

More recent lessons on innovation in the policy arena come from the conservative foundations, widely accepted as some of the most successfully innovative foundations in the later 20th century (see Paget 1998; Stefancic and Delgado 1996). Following Barry Goldwater's presidential defeat in 1964, conservative foundations began putting money into conservative think tanks in order to counter what they saw as the better organization of the liberals, based in part on liberal foundation funding.

These foundations were not large in number, nor were they particularly wealthy at the time. What was it that made these conservative foundations so successful in embedding conservative paradigms within the broader policy arena and beyond? Arguably, part of their success lay in the fact that they were attempting to persuade the country's conservative elites to adopt ideas and values that were already congenial. But it is also true that conservative foundations' tools and strategies went against the grain of conventional foundations' wisdom and practice.

The National Center for Responsible Philanthropy (NCRP) conducted a study of conservative foundations, and found that their high level of effectiveness was related to seven factors (NCRP 1997: p. 5):

1   Clarity of vision and strong political intention.
2   A focus on building strong institutions by providing general operating support rather than project-specific grants.
3   Attention to state, local and neighbourhood policy environments rather than focusing solely on the federal level.
4   Investment in institutions and projects geared towards the marketing of conservative policy ideas.
5   Support for development of conservative public intellectuals and policy leaders.
6   Support to a wide range of policy institutions, recognizing that a variety of strategies and approaches is needed to advance a policy agenda.
7   Long-term funding for grantees, in some cases for two decades or more.

A later study by NCRP (2004b) confirmed and amplified these findings. Conservative foundations:

- Fund a small number of organizations with the same strong passion and commitment as themselves.

- Emphasize long-term grants to give grantees the stability to concentrate on their core work, thereby acknowledging that achieving social change is a long-term process.

- See themselves as funding institutions and ideas, rather than tightly defined projects.

- Believe that flexibility to adapt to the constantly shifting policy environment cannot be achieved within the constraints of conventional grant-making cycles.

- Emphasize core grants to build organizational capacity, freeing the grantee to develop their own agenda, adapting as necessary to the changing policy context.

- Trust grantees to do what is necessary to achieve their goals.

At the same time, there is a high level of interaction between foundations and grantees, with informal meetings several times a year. With very small boards and staffs, conservative foundations can more easily schedule fast-response decisions to enable grantees to react to unanticipated changes in the policy environment. Nevertheless, all of these factors – long-term grants, core operating support, wide discretion and flexibility – require a very high level of trust in grantees.

High trust also plays out in relation to performance measurement. Conservative foundations have generally resisted the wider pressures for formal methods of performance measurement. By the same token, in terms of their own performance measurement conservative foundations accept that the very fluid and complex nature of the policy formation and decision-making process makes it difficult to gauge success as well as failures back to a particular funder, let alone a particular grant. For the conservative foundations, success meant that their 'staff members are motivated by a desire to see major policy changes develop and take place over time rather than their own career advancement' (Russell 2005). Conservative foundations are unlikely to have in-house communications programmes, and rarely brand the products they fund; they prefer to enable grantees to communicate their own successes and not have the spotlight on the foundation.

Conservative foundations fund work at a variety of levels from local to federal, and invest in grantee organizations that help set the policy agenda. They do so through informing and mobilizing the public, lobbying lawmakers, and generally disseminating conservative ideas through a variety of media, court and legal action in multiple jurisdictions, and keeping a key on policy implementation throughout the country (Russell 2005).

One of the broader lessons of these foundations is that policy innovation is not necessarily direct, discrete and traceable. Nevertheless, the combined effect of foundations working together or on parallel tracks can be hugely powerful not so much in influencing particular policies but rather in the broader politics of knowledge, changing the way in which domains think and work. Writing about the establishment of social and economic research as a policy tool, Smith (2002: p. 6) notes that foundations were key participants in this process, 'building institutions and shaping fields of knowledge that have a bearing on policy decisions, giving prominence to individual experts and to groups working in particular policy domains, structuring the lines of communication between experts and the public and, through training and education, fostering access to those knowledge-producing elites' (see also Lagemann 1999).

More specifically, Russell (2005) and others such as Smith (2002) and Lagemann attribute a large part of conservative foundations' success to their willingness to take a passionately ideological stance, combined with high levels of risk-taking, and trust in grantees. The research by the NCRP (1997; 2004b) and Smith (2002), among others, suggests that several factors are critical to the impact of conservative foundations:

- *Time* – many of the ideas considered common in today's policy debate were once considered too radical even to consider, and it took years to get them into the mainstream. Flexible long-term funding proved key to successful policy change.

- *Focus* – concentration on a small number of grantees. The aim is to sustain existing grantees, not replace them by new ones before goals are achieved.

- *Initiative* – developing affirmative ideas rather than simply reacting to liberal social policies.

- *Inclusive* – presentation of changes as bi-partisan to help build a larger constituency by recruiting conservative Democrats.

- *Allegiance* – conservative foundation boards stand by their grantees no matter how controversial their research, because they hold the same beliefs.

- *National outlook* – conservative foundations understand that policy-making does not just happen in Washington; policy expertise and engagement is critical at state and local levels as well.

Smith (2002) suggests that conservative foundations illustrate what can be achieved when various actors work to the same goals and focus on building institutions rather than piecemeal projects. But the author highlights three other important lessons from the success of the conservative foundations' strategies of innovation:

- Large ideas and values matter.

- Politics is a relentless intellectual contest.

- Ideas can be propagated, marketed and sold.

Part of the creative thrust of the conservative foundations was to recognize the way in which the framework of policy discourse had changed, and to adapt accordingly. Policy discourse is no longer the sole preserve of political parties, interest groups and elite opinion makers, but is now shared with the media, direct mail, talk radio, the web, and so on. But 'these new realities of the policy process have posed continuing, bewildering challenges to mainstream foundations whose work has been grounded in problem-oriented, field specific and, above all, pragmatic work' (Smith 2002: p. 25).

The Scrivener Award

While the case of the conservative foundations and the Robert W. Scrivener Award for Creative Philanthropy appear different at first sight, they do indeed share many common features. The Council of Foundations gives the Robert W.

Scrivener Award for Creative Philanthropy annually to someone who has achieved 'a creative response to a particularly important problem in society' (Brousseau 2004: p. 14). The award is focused on a grant-making programme, and is not a career achievement award. To qualify for an award the programme must:

1   Be sufficiently developed so that its use as a paradigm is possible.
2   Demonstrate an entrepreneurial spirit.
3   Build on and take full advantage of existing networks.
4   Be a creative departure from past grant-making.
5   Ensure that the sum is greater than the parts.

Brousseau (2004) interviewed ten recipients of the award, and the results highlight a range of themes, including: spiritual belief and operational wisdom; transposing knowledge to solve problems; moving the marginal towards the mainstream; taking on tough issues; creativity as an iterative and incremental process, and as a constant collaborative process of learning; creativity from crossing social divides, and through a group process; and the role of principles (such as trust, respect or flexibility). From the award recipients' individual stories, Brousseau (2004) identifies five common themes central to creative grant-making, which resonate well with the characteristics of creativity from Chapter 3:

1   A motivating belief that drives philanthropic activities.
2   A range of cognitive skills – sifting information, translating between contexts, staying grounded and learning from grantees, seeing patterns, synthesizing, being flexible to make changes as new data emerge.
3   Interpersonal competence – not getting caught up in the distorting lens of the grant-maker–grantee relationship.
4   Crossing boundaries and 'mixing worlds'.
5   A sense of journey – continuity of effort in the long term, sometimes for as long as 20 years.

Brousseau (2004) concludes that creativity is rarely the linear step-process often assumed. In reality, creativity is messier and more repetitive, involving evaluation and iterative learning, good feedback, staying close to people and programmes, and a calculated balance of methodologies and strategies. In Gardner's terms (1993: p. 43), creativity can sometimes be 'paradigm shifting', but more often it is a matter of 'forward incrementalism'.

Part III

Implications

6   What makes for creative philanthropy?

Why do foundations adopt a creative approach? Only one of the cases studied, the Joseph Rowntree Charitable Trust (JRCT), saw itself as 'having been born like that'. All of the other foundations saw creative philanthropy – whatever they called this approach – as being a more or less conscious and deliberate change. In most cases, the approach had evolved through various iterations; in other cases, the change was more dramatic.

While it may be reasonable to assume that a dramatic increase or decrease in income or endowment triggered a review, and subsequent change of some sort, this was not the major factor for change in any of the cases we studied. At first sight, this seems remarkable, as changes in economic fortunes are frequently the cause of re-organization in businesses and nonprofit firms; among foundations, however, the greater stability afforded by endowments makes such an impetus less likely, although we could well imagine that greater resource uncertainty may lead to a search for new ways and means of conducting philanthropy, including creative approaches. For example, at the Knight Foundation development of a creative approach coincided with increases in income (while at the Baring Foundation in the UK – not one of our cases – a dramatic decrease in income necessitated significant change in the foundation's programmes).

Another reasonable explanation of change would be a major turnover in board or staff leadership. Although in our cases the board and CEO undoubtedly played a crucial role in the move towards a creative approach, this does not tell the whole story, for at least two reasons. First, an explanation in terms of 'new blood' does not explain why the new blood was introduced – is the 'new blood' the result of a positive decision to change, or simply the result of previous incumbents moving on? Second, although it is true that in some of our cases change did coincide with appointment of a new CEO or new members of the board, in other cases, change came from an existing CEO and board. Indeed, in some cases, such as The Wallace Foundation, change was attributed to the longevity of board membership.

Although the particular combination of factors leading to adoption of a creative approach was somewhat different, even distinct in each case, there were some common themes across the foundations studied. At some level, the factors driving adoption of a creative approach form a complex, interacting, reinforcing web that make it difficult to identify which are causes and which results. At the same time, it is nonetheless possible to point to a number of factors we see as common among the cases presented in the previous chapters.

Commitment to Mission. One of the striking characteristics of foundations adopting a creative approach is their commitment to the foundation's mission, and a value-based vision that in some cases amounts to a passion. In some cases, this commitment is derived from a personal connection with the original founders, whether as family member, friend or close business associate. In other cases, the passion for mission is rooted in a wider value-base. For example, the JRCT's passionate commitment to its mission is said to stem from Quaker values and the fact that all board members share this faith. The Victorian Women's Trust's passion derives from the board's deeply felt commitment to promoting social justice for women.

A Culture of Self-criticism. This commitment to the foundation's mission is combined with a culture of self-criticism. In some respects, the culture of self-criticism is part of commitment to the mission, and helps keep the foundation in line with its wider vision. For these foundations, doing good is not good enough – only the very best the foundation can do is acceptable. In some foundations, this self-critical culture was explained with reference back to the style and vision of the founder. For example, the Knight Foundation explains its constant search for 'the best' in terms of the tenacity, focus and passion of its founders for maintaining and promoting democracy and ensuring a free, high-quality press. Similarly, at Pew Charitable Trusts the development of programmes to promote increased public involvement in making important policy choices was related back to a speech by J. Howard Pew in 1953 warning of the dangers to democracy of 'subversive inactivity' by citizens.

Regular Radical Review. This culture of self-criticism was most clearly manifested in radical reviews of how the foundation puts its vision and mission into practice. All of the foundations studied had undertaken at least one, usually more frequent (and sometimes even regular) radical reviews. These reviews were more thorough and wide-ranging than conventional foundation reviews typically are. Reviews went well beyond performance assessments of what the foundation had done in the last few years – although this obviously formed part of the process. Some reviews lasted a year or more and covered the foundation's mission, priorities, activities, policies and processes, staffing, structures, costs and so on.

But these foundations not only looked inward, but also outward to the wider environment. Events and trends in the social and political environment especially – though not only in the foundation's key areas of interest – and in the foundation and nonprofit worlds were included. What were the key issues to be addressed, what was the foundation currently doing, what had worked and what had not, who else was doing what, where and what were the gaps, where and how could the foundation most effectively intervene, what resources could it apply, and what could be learned from past programmes and ways of working, were among the key questions. These were reviews where no holds were barred.

Dissatisfaction with Existing Ways of Working. Dissatisfaction with existing ways of working, and what the foundation had achieved, was sometimes a cause and sometimes an effect of a review. Dissatisfaction was obviously closely related to the passion for mission, and the culture of self-criticism discussed above. The key issue was not so much 'have we been doing it wrong', but rather, 'how can we do (even) better'.

In some cases dissatisfaction with current ways of working and the quest for constant improvement were said to have been in part a result of new blood (whether the CEO/senior staff or on the board) and partly the involvement of people who took none of the traditional shibboleths for granted. For example, at the Annie E. Casey Foundation the quest for improvement – and the willingness to undertake radical reviews – was attributed in part to the fact that board members were not child-care professionals with established notions of what and how things are done. Similarly, the Carnegie United Kingdom Trust attributed its quest for better ways of doing things to the diverse collection of 'free spirits' it attracts to its board.

Interestingly, however, at The Wallace Foundation dissatisfaction with existing ways of doing things was said to be a result, in part, of the stability of the board. Precisely because the same board members had been in place for 10 years or more, they could see that programmes they themselves had approved had not delivered quite as much as anticipated, and that the same sorts of applications in the same sorts of areas kept being received.

Awareness of a Changing Environment. Again, it was not clear whether awareness of a changing environment was a cause or a result of regular reviews. It was, however, very clear that these foundations were outward-looking, and regularly assessed how wider environmental changes might affect, positively or negatively, the areas in which the foundation or its beneficiaries worked, as well as the foundation's own position and effectiveness. Several of the US foundations studied (for example, Pew, Wallace and Knight) were very conscious of the need to take into account the effects of government devolution and budget cutbacks in considering their activities and strategies. Analysis of the changing environment took into account not only structures, processes and activities of government, but also the changing face of the nonprofit sector and the activities and interests of other foundations.

Awareness of Paucity of Resources and Limitations of Roles. Another factor prompting these foundations to adopt a creative approach was awareness of the very limited size of their resources relative to the demands of the issues they were seeking to address. This was true even of those foundations that had, by foundation standards, very sizeable financial assets and income.

Awareness of the paucity of their financial resources encouraged these foundations to consider very carefully the range and scope of their priorities and involvement, and to be more selective in those. It also led them to consider building up resources other than money, and in some cases to actually do so. For example, The Wallace Foundation's most recent review led to a realization that one of its key resources was its knowledge. Similarly, the Victorian Women's Trust talks about borrowing 'other people's brains', and the Carnegie United Kingdom Trust adopts a similar strategy. Another common under-utilized resource 'discovered' by these foundations was their networks, or capacity to build and use social connections among people and organizations. Influence, or potential influence, was also increasingly seen as a key resource in, among other things, the ability to bring (sometimes warring) factions around a table.

Awareness of the relative paucity of their resources also commonly led these foundations to reassess their roles, and the limitations and strengths those imply. Realizing that their financial resources are only sufficient to fund a limited number of grantees or operations, these foundations looked for ways to extend their impact and the sustainability of their programmes by adopting a creative approach.

'Space' or Permission to Change. Adopting a creative approach is not, of course, only a matter of drivers or incentives but also of the absence of obstacles or constraints. Several of the foundations studied suggested that adopting a creative approach was made possible by having the 'space' to change. For example, although Joseph Rowntree left a memorandum outlining what he saw the trust doing, he also explicitly gave the trustees permission to change in the light of changing circumstances. Similarly, the Pew Charitable Trusts and the Carnegie United Kingdom Trust noted that their very broad remits allowed them plenty of space to change.

Appeal to History. Finally, several foundations commented that being able to appeal to the history of the foundation, or the personality and style of the founder, provided additional legitimation for the adoption of a creative approach – however 'stretched' this reference might be in reality. For example, in addition to the Knight Foundation and Pew Charitable Trusts cited above, the Carnegie United Kingdom Trust adopted a creative approach partly on the grounds that this is what Andrew Carnegie would have done.

Key Elements of a Creative Approach

Although the foundations portrayed in the previous chapters are in many respects very diverse in terms of age, size of endowment, revenue structure, mission, location, and mode of operation, they share certain fundamental views about roles, use and allocation of resources, planning, organizational and policy change, grantmaking practices, communication and dissemination, evaluation, and relationships with others. These views relate to each other to form a complex and in many ways distinctive approach.

Role: Beyond Service Provision to Creative, Constructive Conversation and Change

As noted above, these foundations do not merely want to make a difference, they place significant emphasis on making a sustainable difference with an impact beyond their immediate grantees. They maintain a clear, strong and critical commitment to their missions, bolstered by diverse perspectives within a framework of common values. They see their independence as a vital element in this process.

In some cases, including the Annie E. Casey and Knight foundations, they adopted a creative approach in making grants to provide services. But they see themselves not primarily as service-providing grant-makers, but rather as change-makers. 'Charity' and local grant-making are a way of staying in touch, developing, refining and demonstrating solutions. But they also know that foundation funding will never be enough to achieve sustainable change.

To achieve sustainable change with an impact beyond their grantees, foundations adopting a creative approach go way beyond conventional grant-making for demonstration projects. They seek to contribute and effectively communicate new, informed perspectives on issues and problems, and proactively to encourage conversation and action by others. Grant-making is only the beginning of a usually long-term process and may be only one strategy in a complex toolbox.

Foundations vary in the extent to which they adopt an explicit policy advocacy role. But they share the view that, for most issues, sustainable change will require

---

Box 6.1

The nonprofit sector and philanthropy have become very acquiescent. The partnership model (usually with Government) needs to be revisited. Philanthropy has been captured – despite the rhetoric. How free are foundations from government influence? Whatever the correct answer, we have more freedom than we exercise! However, we are fundamentally quite conservative with some exceptions.

Creative philanthropy's role is to Test, Inform, and Influence Public Policy (TIIPP). However, philanthropy is not always that. Philanthropic dollars are important to bolster service delivery systems – particularly innovative ones. The poor cannot always wait for policy change! Sometimes we need to forget about innovation and seek out what works best – not always innovative but well practised and tested.

Ray Murphy
Charles Stewart Mott Foundation

change in the policies and practices of other organizations, including government. Variation comes in the extent to which these foundations see their role as attempting directly to influence government policies, or rather to provide 'enlightenment' and to stimulate creative, constructive conversation and debate. What they have in common is that they are not afraid of talking about policy and implications for government.

Conventional foundations usually start with a mission and a handful of programme priorities, and move from there to a programme of grants. Strategies are often determined by the foundation's pre-determined rules and procedures. Creative foundations start with an outcome they want to achieve and work back towards the strategy needed to achieve it. Creative foundations are not afraid to do things themselves if necessary. Contracting out tasks to others, typically through grant-making, may not always be seen as the best way of getting things done and reaching the desired outcome.

Assets and Resources: Beyond Money to Credibility, via Knowledge and Networks

We have already touched on these foundations' awareness of the paucity of their resources – however large some may seem. For foundations adopting a creative approach, knowledge, networks, influence and an independent non-partisan voice are seen as key resources. For creative foundations, having money is not enough: money alone does not earn you a seat at the table, influence, or the right to be listened to. The ability to contribute and effectively communicate informed new perspectives requires, among other things, building reputation and earning credibility in a particular field. For example, the Annie E. Casey Foundation has systematically built its reputation in child welfare, the Knight Foundation in journalism, and The Wallace Foundation in educational leadership.

A Theory of Change

Starting with an outcome encourages creative foundations to think hard about how that could be achieved. In the process of identifying what would have to be different for the desired outcome to be achieved, creative foundations, in effect develop a theory of change. The theory of change identifies who or what would have to change, how those organizations, institutions or people could be reached, and what sort of information (and in what format) would be required. Identifying and overcoming obstacles was another important element in a workable theory of change. The desired outcome and the theory of change influence all subsequent decisions, including what is funded, to what amount, and for how long.

Foundations adopting a conventional approach, insofar as they seek to achieve change, rarely appear to have thought through a theory of how change happens, whether generally or in their field of interest specifically. Their practice typically suggests that they implicitly believe that change can be achieved in the short to medium terms, that grant-making alone is a way of triggering change, and that change happens from the bottom up, encouraged by an infusion of cash.

Foundations adopting a creative approach included in this study generally saw social change as a matter of iteration, not cataclysm – as a slow, long-term process. Creative foundations work on an issue for as long as it reasonably takes to achieve the desired outcome – often ten years or more. Social change was rarely seen as either uniformly bottom-up or top-down, but more as a mix of both, requiring work at various levels and multiple strategies, and certainly involving more than the transfer of cash. They also generally saw social change as neither logical nor predictable nor linear and, for that reason, maintained a degree of flexibility and opportunism in programmes and strategies.

In some cases – for example the Pew Charitable Trusts, the Joseph Rowntree Charitable Trust, and the Rosenberg Foundation – the theory of change underpinning the strategy may change as the foundation assesses the results of its approach, develops new understanding of the complexities of the issues and the obstacles to change, and finds new points of leverage. In some cases the major obstacle is lack of information or workable solutions; obstacles may also include lack of local or national political will. Unlike some social-change foundations, creative foundations recognize that building political will may involve not only influencing policy-makers but also their constituents, winning hearts and minds to create support for policy change.

For foundations adopting a creative approach there is no 'one size fits all' theory of change. What and who needs to change, and how that can be achieved, has to be worked out anew for each and every case. Because social change is rarely linear and rational, the theory of change is itself constantly changing – but acceptance of that is part of the overall theory. Foundations adopting a creative approach know that they have to be ever-vigilant sailors on the often turbulent seas of policy change – adjusting their routes and speeds, tacking and weaving, and accepting periods of being becalmed or in choppy waters, in order to reach their destinations.

The Power of Rich Networks

Foundations adopting a creative approach value their independence and voice but, at the same time, recognize that they are relatively 'powerless' alone, or at least not as effective as they would be as part of a wider circle of actors. They see relationships as one of their key assets and work to build rich networks of different types at various levels, very much along the patterns of heterophily and homophily suggested by sociologists and students of innovation and diffusion (Rogers 2003).

Box 6.2

Creative philanthropy analyzes the structures of injustice, crafts strategies to address them, and helps to organize constituencies who will take action to create a fairer world.

Creative philanthropy is transparent, collaborative, accountable and committed to diversity in all that it does, from board structure to grant making practice. Transparency can generate more accountable practices, stronger learning, and better results.

Working together, a variety of funders can leverage more resources, develop a deeper analysis, spread risks, and craft a more effective strategy in which the "whole is greater than the sum of its parts." For example, the "State Fiscal Analysis Initiative" involves national and local foundations in creating a network of policy think tanks in 27 US states. This is a great model for the future.

Michael Edwards
Urvashi Vaid
Christopher Harris
Governance and Civil Society Unit, Ford Foundation, New York

A creative approach is hungry for ideas and perspectives – the more diverse the better. A creative approach also requires relationships to test out ideas, to build legitimacy, to recruit champions and to make things happen. Creative foundations may work with government but they do not see their role as substituting for, or subsidizing, government; rather the aim is to provide new ideas and perspectives and to stimulate creative, constructive conversations and programmes. These foundations build relationships with a wide variety of other people and organizations in academia, the nonprofit world, government, the media and so on. The breadth and depth of relationships are dictated by what is necessary to achieve the desired outcome. Networks are rich in scope and number, as well as rich in knowledge, influence, access and sometimes money.

For example, the Victorian Women's Trust's Purple Sage and Watermark Australia projects are founded on building wide and rich networks from the start; and the Carnegie United Kingdom Trust maintains that 'being creative isn't about money. It's about getting ideas, evidence, people and networks, thinking, motivation and so on together.' Annie E. Casey's Making Connections programme seeks out a wide range of partners across sectors and at different levels; partners include residents, local government, employers, financial institutions, large and small businesses, faith-based groups, community-based organizations, cultural clubs, hospitals, universities, schools, law enforcement officials, and grassroots community groups. In Making Connections, rich networks are seen as generating more ideas, energy and ownership. Rich networks may also generate more power, as in one Making Connections site where a partnership between the foundation, a nonprofit citizens' organization, local families, city and state officials and legislators, financial institutions and housing advocates together achieved significant regulatory changes relating to predatory lending.

Planning: A Work in Progress

Adopting a creative approach involves focus and flexibility. In order to build reputation and credibility, to develop sound knowledge and to build rich networks in a particular field, creative foundations have to focus on a small number of priorities in a limited number of fields.

But creativity requires space and freedom. Flexibility is also necessary to take advantage of unforeseen opportunities, and new points of access and leverage for change. For example, publication of a report, or a conference, may be brought forward or delayed in order to 'catch the wave' of interest or to build on other initiatives and events in order to maximize value and impact.

Creative foundations spend time scanning the environment, keeping up with changes and spotting trends, newly opening policy windows and new issues. Creative foundations do their homework to stay one step ahead. In spotting new issues and trends they emphasize the importance of hard evidence, but they also acknowledge that instinct plays a part. For these reasons planning is always a work in progress. The plan is a framework, not a blueprint.

For example, the Rosenberg Foundation is conscious of the dangers of defining an issue too narrowly too early – with more knowledge it may become clear that popular understanding of the issue may miss the underlying cause. Another reason why the Rosenberg Foundation sees planning as being always a work in progress is the need constantly to adapt to changes in the public policy environment, changing community needs and emerging opportunities. For Rosenberg and other foundations in our case studies, opportunism is as much part of the strategy as planning. The Pew Charitable Trusts, and others, build change and flexibility into their planning by maintaining 'tracking portfolios' that monitor progress and enable programme managers to revise strategies accordingly. Somewhat differently, the Joseph Rowntree Charitable Trust, emphasizing the need for space and flexibility for creativity, provides long-term, loosely specified funding for individuals and organizations so as to enable issues and programmes to evolve.

One consequence of accepting that planning is always a work in progress is that budgets have to be similarly flexible. For example, Rosenberg's child support reform programme and the Carnegie United Kingdom Trust's Third Age Programme involved significantly more time and money than originally anticipated.

Box 6.3

Creativity, whatever the field, is rooted in a persistent search for new insight into language, institutional structures, and prevailing habits of mind. Those insights then expand conceptual confines and break old molds. And all who come after find that they must operate in fundamentally altered intellectual and organizational realms.

This sets the bar very high for creativity within the domain of philanthropy. When and how has philanthropy has managed to transform other fields of activity? Creative philanthropy at its best would have to be measured against such work as that of Abraham Flexner and his associates at Carnegie and Rockefeller who elevated the standards of medical training throughout the U.S. in the 1910s and 1920s. Creative philanthropy would be gauged against the work of the W.K. Kellogg Foundation's Michigan Community Health Project, which began in the 1930s to re-shape children's health, education and welfare and, in the end, altered governmental relationships in the rural counties near Battle Creek. And creative philanthropy would embrace the insights and persistent efforts of the Ford Foundation's MacNeil Lowry, who in the 1950s labored to understand and change the landscape in which American cultural institutions operated.

James A. Smith
Waldemar A. Nielsen Chair in Philanthropy, Georgetown University

Show and Tell

Communication is an essential element in the creative foundation's tool-box. For foundations adopting a creative approach, the 'good' project or idea that is not communicated is like the philosopher's unwitnessed falling tree. Effective communication is essential if the creative foundation is to have a sustainable impact beyond the limits of its immediate grantees.

Creative foundations 'show and tell'; they are in 'show business'. Communication to the right audiences by the most effective routes in the right format is crucial to the effectiveness of the creative foundation. The precise strategy follows from the foundation's theory of change, but goes way beyond the conventional publication of a report, or item in a newsletter or website.

For example, The Wallace Foundation talks about getting 'more eyes and ears around a problem', getting journalists asking questions, and raising public attention, learning and coverage in order to build a more informed dialogue, rather than pushing a particular policy. In expanding awareness of the challenges and

Box 6.4

Creative philanthropy needs the right conditions. In institutional terms these conditions would include freedom and self-government – i.e. autonomy rather than close regulation. They would also include a constitution or governing instrument which did not freeze the present but enabled the future, so allowing fluidity and permeability of boundaries rather than being stuck in a particular box. The box could be an issue or need, or it could be an ideology. Either way the box could inhibit intellectual exploration, and limit the possibility of joining things up in new ways. This is inimical to creativity. On top of this, there needs to be the space and capacity to think and act. Creativity is not about processing capacity to deal with requests for money. Creativity means a minimum of people resources – human intellect, skills, experience – to enable the synapses to fire, lateral thinking to connect, ideas to flow, action to happen. And the organizational culture must permit and preferably encourage this: an autocratic-style governing body with closed minds is a barrier to creativity.

Some of the main learning from RCP includes: the need for much greater public involvement in the criminal justice system to counter public ignorance and misinformation; greater visibility and positive recognition for community penalties and what they allow offenders to put back into the community; more 'vertical knowledge integration' so that judges and courts understand better the options available and what will happen to the offender.

Margaret Hyde
Esmée Fairbairn Foundation

opportunities of educational leadership, the foundation provided multi-year funding and support to leading trade, general and broadcast media, including Channel Thirteen/WNET New York. Similarly, both the Pew Charitable Trusts and the Annie E. Casey Foundation have made considerable investments in serving the media with better information on key issues. Casey's Making Connections programme has a specific Media Outreach Initiative bringing local public television stations together with Making Connections sites to convene community forums around national PBS broadcasts of documentaries with family-strengthening and community-building themes.

Foundations adopting a creative approach do not assume that communication will happen 'naturally', or that it can be left to someone else. Creative foundations run marathons, not relay races. The majority of foundations adopting a creative approach featured in this study put considerable resources into publishing the results of their work, and actively communicating results to carefully targeted audiences.[1]

From Demonstration to Implementation

But communication alone is not enough. Creative foundations know that the market-place of ideas is crowded, full of obstacles and blind spots. If change is to be sustainable it has to be implemented. Moving from ideas and small-scale demonstra-tion projects to wider implementation requires continuing, influential champions. Again, strategies for ensuring implementation of change follow from the foundation's analysis of how change happens, who and what are the change makers, and where the obstacles are in any particular case. Ensuring effective implementation may require different networks and skills from both demonstration and communication.

Following through from demonstration to ensuring effective wider implemen-tation differs from the mainstream conventional foundation approach. Foundations adopting a creative approach do not assume that implementation will happen 'naturally', or can be left to chance. In some cases, foundations adopting a creative approach go a step further, monitoring on-going implementation by others.

For example, the Joseph Rowntree Charitable Trust is continuing to monitor implementation of the Human Rights Act to see that its provisions are used to enforce the human rights of those without privilege rather than only those who know how to 'work the system'. It has also funded Democratic Audit to provide audits of the quality of democracy and political freedom in the UK over a period of ten years.

From Evaluation and Performance Measurement to Risky Learning

Evaluation and performance measurement have become fashionable accessories in the foundation world. Foundations adopting a creative approach use both evalua-tion and performance measurement, but in somewhat unconventional ways. Because creative foundations recognize the need to work flexibly over the long term, performance measurement and evaluation have to be similarly flexible and long term. Because creative foundations seek to achieve outcomes, not merely outputs, and recognize that these cannot be achieved alone, performance measurement and evaluation have to be adapted accordingly.

Creative foundations' approaches to risk and learning underpin their atti-tudes to performance measurement and evaluation. Because creativity – generating new perspectives and finding new combinations – often involves challenging conventional wisdom, and experimentation outside the box, creative foundations have to take risks. Risk is an occupational hazard of creativity and innovation.

Box 6.5

Creative philanthropy for a grant-making foundation is the new boundary to cross in reaching significant results optimizing efforts and sources. A creative grant-maker seeks solutions facing the complexity of the problem, ready to try new approaches combining the past experiences with new perspectives. In comparison with traditional philanthropic activity, a creative approach takes risks, to find a new path leading to results

Dario Disegni
Compagnia di San Paolo

Conventional approaches to evaluation and performance measurement sit uneasily with real risk-taking and the possibility of failure. But in an important sense creative foundations do not have 'failures'. Things that go wrong or do not work out are seen not as failures but as valuable learning opportunities. Creative foundations are learning organizations in at least two senses. First, learning how to do things better and how to resolve problems are seen as key steps towards the outcomes they seek. Second, creative foundations put a high premium on constant learning within the organization and on sharing that learning with others. Sharing learning is an essential, on-going element of a creative approach.

For example, at the Pew Charitable Trusts opportunities for learning are built into various stages of the grants strategy process. The most formal resource is the internal educational curriculum called Pew University, which provides courses to enhance the grant-making skills and development of staff. Pew University courses are constantly being updated with lessons from the trusts' own experiences and from scanning the wider environment.

Foundation Characteristics and the Creativity–Innovation–Diffusion Process

A creative approach has a number of signature characteristics. In addition to the characteristics initially identified, on the basis of which we made our initial selection of case studies, foundations adopting a creative approach:

- Demonstrate a strong commitment to mission.

- Demonstrate a culture of self-criticism.

- Engage in regular review.

- Constantly search for ways of doing even better.

- Are always mindful of their changing environments.

- Are aware of the paucity of their resources and the limitations of their roles.

- See their roles as moving beyond service provision and 'science' to stimulating creative, constructive conversation and change.

- See their assets as not merely money, but also knowledge and credibility.

- Work with a sophisticated and flexible theory of social change.

- Recognize the power of rich networks.

- View planning as a work in progress.

- Value the power of 'show and tell'.

- Move from demonstration to implementation.

- Emphasize the importance of moving beyond evaluation and performance measurement to risky learning.

Figure 6.1 summarizes our insights into creative philanthropy as part of a process that begins with the initial creative act and passes through the phases of exploration, demonstration, implementation and diffusion to widespread innovation with impact beyond immediate grantees. Our thinking begins with the signature characteristics of foundations in modern society that make them truly independent, self-governing bodies with a high degree of freedom and 'room to act'. These characteristics enable them to adopt strategies and roles that address the key dimensions of the creativity–innovation–diffusion process as identified in the works of Landry (2000), Kanter (1983), Rogers (2003) and others.

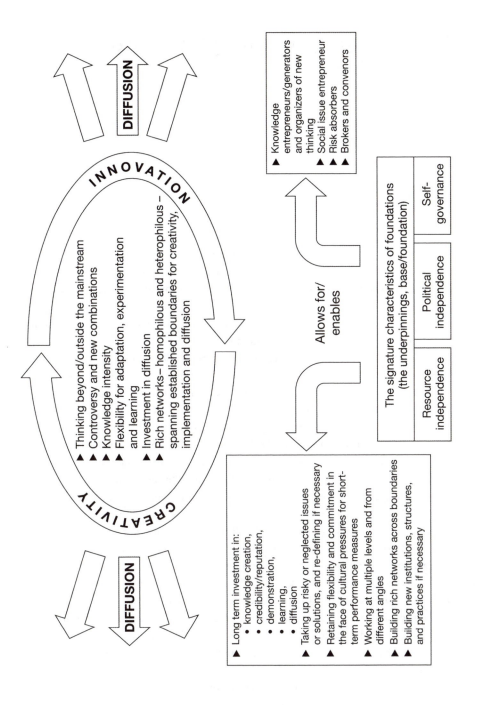

Figure 6.1 Creativity, Innovation and the Signature Characteristics of Foundations

7 Managing creative philanthropy

Introduction

In this chapter, we argue that managing a foundation adopting a creative approach involves tools, strategies, tasks, skills, structures, cultures and processes very different from those required in managing a service- or science-oriented foundation. One major difference between creative and other types of foundations is that they work on a complex set of tasks that involve higher levels of uncertainty that in turn require dynamic management styles.

However, before addressing management implications more specifically, it is useful to take a look at foundation management more generally. Typically, the foundation management literature addresses two central issues: board management – how the board makes decisions and implements them, and grantee management – how funds are allocated, disbursed and accounted for (see, for instance, Prager 2003; Orosz 2000). These foci reflect a more narrow vision of what foundations do, and casts them as seemingly insular funding agencies with set patterns of operations. By contrast, we take a broader view of foundation management, and suggest that managing a creative approach goes well beyond board and grantee management. At the same time, and in line with modern management literature (see Magretta 2002), we argue that no management model fits all circumstances equally well, and like organizational design itself, management approaches are context and task-specific.

The management of foundations, like that of any other formal and goal-oriented organization, involves three critical aspects (Magretta 2002). First, the chief responsibility of management is 'value creation' in relation to the organization's stated mission and goals. For example, if the mission is to bring about greater social justice, support the arts, or help the homeless to gain paid employment, all management activities should contribute to the stated objectives around that mission: value creation towards social justice, the arts or for fighting homelessness. In this sense, foundation management is all about how a mission is to be accomplished within the guidelines established in the deed and as interpreted by the board.

Second, within such guidelines, management involves making critical, clear and consistent choices. This means weighing trade-offs and establishing boundaries. It is as much about what to do well as it is about what not to do at all. Given a limited deed, making choices and setting priorities may be easier, but restricts the space and ways in which a foundation can grow and change over time as circumstances change. The challenge here becomes one of maintaining relevance. By contrast, having a very broad set of guidelines makes goal- and priority-setting more complex, and the challenge for management is focus and consistency around some medium- to long-term vision. At the same time, change is easier as more options are possible, and can be explored.

Third, the organizational design and management style are not only contingent upon mission and goals but also on the task environment in which the foundation finds itself. The term 'task environment' refers to the specific elements with which the foundation interacts (the 'environment') in the course of its operations (its 'task'). This includes first and foremost the nature of the product or service provided, and the grantees, clients or audiences involved. Clearly, it will make a difference for organizational design if the foundation seeks to influence long-term policy change, supports disaster relief overseas, awards scholarships to disadvantaged students, or runs homes for the frail elderly.

Within the context of the product and service range, the task environment for foundations can include the board of trustees, staff, volunteers, grantees, customers, clients, users and other beneficiaries, suppliers, competitors, collaborators, supervising and government agencies, and professional associations, but also more abstract factors such as the level of resources, technology, information, communications and logistics available to each. Each element can make different demands on the foundation and harbour varying expectations, but the key point is that the various elements can introduce uncertainty, and even instability – which the organization needs to reflect in its structure and operations.

One aspect of the task environment is central: environmental uncertainty refers to a situation where future circumstances affecting the foundation cannot be accurately assessed and predicted. Obviously, the more uncertain the environment, the more effort management has to invest in monitoring, and the more likely are decisions and operations to be short-term and tentative. The degree of uncertainty itself includes two major components (Duncan 1979):

- *Complexity* refers both to the number of elements in the organizational task environment and to their heterogeneity in terms of demands and expectations. If a foundation has few task elements and all are fairly similar, such a homogeneous task environment would be less complex than a situation with many more elements that vary in their demands.

- *Dynamism* refers to the rate and predictability of change of the elements. If the elements change rarely or slowly and are relatively predictable, then the task environment is stable; however, if they change often, fast and in unpredictable ways, then the task environment is unstable or volatile.

If we combine both dimensions, we arrive at four uncertainty scenarios, which are presented in Table 7.1:

- In low-uncertainty scenarios, a small number of relatively homogeneous elements remain the same over an extended period of time. The funeral-home industry, car registration, day-care centres, and elementary schools are examples of such situations, but also the conventional Type IV foundations identified in Chapter 3.

- Task environments with a large number of heterogeneous elements and low dynamism lead to medium–low uncertainty. The insurance industry, savings and loans associations (building societies), higher education, and culture and the arts are prominent examples. Similarly, moderately high uncertainty exists in cases where a small number of homogeneous elements change often and unpredictably, as with the fashion industry, catering, and many social- and health-care services. Type II and Type III foundations, i.e., relay philanthropy and venture philanthropy, fit into this category.

- Large numbers of heterogeneous elements with high dynamism constitute high-uncertainty task environments. Software and internet-based companies are prime examples, as are disaster relief and humanitarian assistance programmes. Our argument is that foundations are uniquely positioned to operate as Type I organizations, and that they can seek out heterogeneous and dynamic environments at lower risks than other organizational forms.

From a structural perspective, however, foundations in high-uncertainty environments are best organized as entrepreneurial organizations with a minimum of bureaucracy and a premium on flexibility and innovation. We suggest that this is the home of creative philanthropy. By contrast, foundations in low-uncertainty environments are best organized as small, relatively bureaucratic organizations; small, to maintain a relative degree of homogeneity, and bureaucratic, to enhance the efficiency of operations. We argue that much conventional philanthropy and its management style falls into this category; and we also argued in Chapters 1 and 2 that this model is not best suited for modern philanthropy, failing as it does to take full advantage of the signature characteristics of foundations.

In between are foundations that operate under moderately low or moderately high uncertainty (Table 7.1). They have the challenge of finding a balance between

Table 7.1 Task environments and uncertainty

	High Complexity	Low Complexity
High Dynamism	High uncertainty	Mixed
	Type I	**Type III**
	Creative foundation	Ad hoc new scientific philanthropy
Low Dynamism	Mixed	Low uncertainty
	Type II	**Type IV**
	Relay philanthropy	Traditional service philanthropy

bureaucracy for efficiency's sake – that is, to keep operational and grant-making costs low – and flexibility to be able to cope with changing conditions. Relay philanthropy and ad-hoc new-scientific philanthropy are characteristic models for these task environments.

In what follows, we will focus on Type I foundations, that is, foundations with high creative and entrepreneurial capacity that operate in a highly uncertain task environment characterized by high levels of complexity and dynamism. In so doing we have to move away from technocratic, rationalist management models and embrace a management concept more fully in tune with the realities of foundations. Gomez and Zimmermann (1993) suggest one such concept, which offers a useful starting point for exploring the implications for management of creative programmes. Key facets of this management concept include:

- A *holistic conception* of foundation management that emphasizes its relationship with the task environment, the diversity of orientations within and outside the foundation, and the complexity of demands put on it. A holistic view is particularly needed in the field of philanthropy, where foundations are frequently part of larger systems of service delivery or policy developments. Such systems require sound knowledge-bases, up-to-date information as well as a 'big-picture view', and search procedures to accommodate different perspectives. In other words, *managing creative programmes means managing knowledge and information.*

- A *normative dimension* of management that includes not only efficiency aspects and technical performance, but also the importance of social, cultural and political values, and their impact on policies. Thus, in addition to management in complex task environments characterized by uncertainty, foundations adopting a creative approach are typically value-based organizations, and managing them involves the ability to work with different preferences, perceptions and projections of reality as well as different assessments and implications for different constituencies. Thus, *managing creative programmes is ultimately political rather than technocratic management*.

- A *strategic-developmental dimension* that sees foundations as an evolving system encountering problems and opportunities that frequently involve fundamental dilemmas for management. This dimension views foundations as entities that change over time as they deal with the opportunities and constraints confronting them as part of a larger political economy. *Managing creative philanthropy means managing change, both internal as well as external.*

- An *operative dimension* that deals with the everyday functioning of the foundation, such as administration and accounting, personnel, service-delivery, and grant-making. This is the part that has been the focus of conventional foundation management (see Prager 2003; Orosz 2000; Oster 1995).

Against this background, we argue that managing foundations adopting a creative approach involves tools, strategies, tasks, skills, structures, cultures and processes very different from those required in managing a service- or science-oriented foundation. One overarching difference between creative and other approaches is that creative approaches work on a complex set of tasks (in theory sequential but, in practice, often contemporaneous) including:

1 Service provision
2 Demonstration and analysis
3 Influencing implementation
4 Influencing policy
5 Influencing people and opinions.

Service provision is the primary conventional foundation approach, and is characteristic of Type IV foundations. The foundation provides services and stops there, moving on to the next grant once the service is up and running. Providing the service (to a necessarily limited number of people or projects) is seen as making the difference.

Conventional foundations may accompany service provision with a demonstration aim. The assumption often seems to be that merely doing something different will demonstrate its worth to others by some organic, automatic process. Foundations that are serious about demonstration accept that, to be effective, demonstration has to involve evaluation of the model and its effects. Again, this may be the end of the conventional foundation's involvement.

A smaller number of foundations go a further step to attempt to ensure implementation of 'demonstrations'; this is likely to involve more complex tools and strategies at a variety of levels. Again this may be the final stage in the conventional foundation's involvement.

Foundations adopting a creative approach (and a minority of others) see working on individual organizations to change the way in which policy and practice are implemented as potentially ineffective and too limiting. For these foundations, making a difference means attempting to influence policy and practice in a variety of settings and at a variety of levels, adopting a variety of tools and strategies.

Foundations adopting a creative approach often also work to influence communities and wider public opinion. The assumption is that this sort of work is necessary to achieve sustainable change and to ensure an impact beyond the limitations of direct beneficiaries. Without popular support and understanding, policies will fail to be adopted or effectively implemented, partly because policy change in organizations, institutions and government requires political will, and partly because in some cases citizens are the implementers.

Other foundations may adopt one (or more) of these roles, expecting other organizations to move on to the next stage. Indeed, foundations are sometimes categorized in terms of one of these five sets of tasks. Foundations adopting a creative approach work on all five sets of tasks at a variety of levels. For example, they often build on service provision or site demonstrations to provide the learning and credibility to buttress their efforts at organizational, institutional or wider policy influence. These foundations typically attempt to integrate all five roles in the pursuit of change. Creative programmes run marathons, not relay races. They do not assume that someone else will pick up the baton if they drop out.

In terms of their key assumptions and strategies, foundations adopting a creative approach might be summed up as post-modern, post-managerialist or post-rationalist organizations. They:

- Emphasize the value of knowledge as much as money.

- Recognize the power of passion, values and other intangibles.

- Create and draw on wide networks to stimulate ideas and support.

- Work on the same issue from several angles.

- Resist the lure of the short-term and the quick fix.

- Are both strategic and opportunistic.

- Understand the complexities and power of communication in agenda setting, framing and influencing change.

- Recognize that achieving sustainable change is not just about good ideas or sound plans but about overcoming inertia, and individual and organizational obstacles.

- Adopt sophisticated performance measures that accommodate uncertainties and the serendipity of change.

Managing Creative Approaches

Managing a foundation adopting a creative approach involves both internal and external challenges, changing the way in which board and staff approach roles, structures and processes as well as changing the way the foundation relates to others outside the foundation. Internal and external challenges are different sides of the same coin: one provides the basis for the other. For example, because foundations adopting a creative approach rely not only on money but on reputation and credible knowledge to stimulate change, the foundation needs appropriate approaches to skills, tasks, processes, time-scales, and performance measures. We begin by looking at some of the tools for change that foundations adopting a creative approach need to acquire.

Given the emphasis on innovation and change in foundations' accounts of what they do, it is surprising how little attention has been paid to the strategies and tools available to them for achieving these ends. By contrast, in the public-policy literature there is a long history of attempting to classify policy instruments or tools. Hood (1983) identifies four broad groups of 'power tools' available to government, ranked from strong to weak as follows: Effectors for producing changes in cultures or behaviour such as direct government provision, education and training or regulations and mandates; Collectors for obtaining resources such as taxation, levies or appeals; Detectors for acquiring information and knowledge, such as inspection and research; and Selectors for managing, analysing and presenting information and knowledge.

Clearly, foundations are not governments and thus have a more limited range of tools and strategies on which to draw in effecting change. Even though foundations cannot raise or spend taxes; cannot make regulations; cannot mandate, requisition or impose service fees and charges; they can, and do, make direct provision; make loan guarantees; provide grants; engage in persuasion, demonstration projects, education and training; make appeals for information; use audit, cost-benefit analysis, performance indicators and measurement, cost measurement, resource budgeting, management review, scenario-building and risk assessment. Specifically:

Effectors for producing changes in culture or behaviour include:

- Operating agencies as well as the foundation's own programmes

- Contract purchasing

- Loan guarantees

- Grants-in-aid, matching grants

- Persuasion and public awareness

- Demonstration projects

- Education, training.

Collectors for obtaining resources include:

- Donations and contributions in kind

- Service fees and charges

- Return on investment, endowment building

- Appeals

- Volunteers, board members

- Collaboration, pooling.

Detectors for acquiring information and knowledge include:

- Audits, performance indicators

- Inspection

- Monitoring and observing

- Enlisting diverse networks

- Having 'listening posts' and focus groups.

Selectors for managing, selecting, analysing, and presenting information and knowledge include:

- Policy review

- Management review

- Scenario-building

- Risk assessment.

For foundations, tools for change involve three key elements: authority, incentives and ideas (Weiss 2000). Recognition and utilization of the power of these elements underpin the creative foundation's tools for achieving change with impact beyond their immediate grantees.

Authority

While governments have generalized authority to exercise control over activities and resources in some spheres, private foundations have no such generalized authority. As noted above, foundations cannot, for example, raise taxes or make laws. Unlike many other nonprofit and religious organizations, foundations cannot claim authority derived from membership or representation.

Foundations adopting a creative approach recognize the importance of authority in intervening to make a difference, and their lack of democratically derived authority. Foundations adopting a creative approach do not believe that they have authority simply by virtue of their money, or their charitable status. Although such foundations may use the composition of their board to gain or borrow some authority (and may select board members to that end), they know that this is not sufficient alone. Foundations adopting a creative approach deliberately set out to earn authority through what they know and do. They engage in the slow, arduous process of building expertise and reputation as reliable, credible authorities in particular domains.

They build their reputations as authorities in a particular domain by demonstration projects, site initiatives, research, and wide communication of the findings derived from these initiatives. Many such foundations' authority-building activities combine a variety of styles, marrying a wide, statistically robust overview with anecdotes, case studies, listening to people, on-the-ground experiments and data. This is a very different approach from that condemned by conservative foundations distrustful of university researchers and professionals (see for example, Schambra and Shaffer 2004). By combining qualitative and quantitative, the emotional and the objective, appealing to hearts and minds, foundations adopting a creative approach draw on two very different sources of popular authority: experiential ('I am an authority on this because I have been there and done that') and rational ('I am an authority on this because I have studied the facts and figures').

Foundations adopting a creative approach recognize that exercise of authority in any given policy intervention occurs in the context of other reinforcing or competing sources of authority, and in a world of other incentives and ideas – that is, authority operates in the context of many other pressures and forces bearing on target actors. Policy designers have to recognize and grapple with these multiple pressures and incentives.

Foundations adopting a creative approach attempt not only to work directly with, or on, policy-makers, but also to influence competing pressures and forces by changing the terms of the debate, or by reducing the number of competing pressures, encouraging creative, constructive conversation and common viewpoints. Because they recognize the complexity and dynamism of competing sources of authority, foundations adopting a creative approach carefully monitor the environment for opportunities to contribute to debate.

Ideas

Ideas are another tool for achieving desired changes. The basic strategy here is to use ideas to change how people (the target group) think, or what they think. Foundations adopting a creative approach work to produce and distribute timely and relevant information to key target audiences that need or want it so that they can produce the desired outcome. Information may include technical assistance, dissemination of research findings, and information campaigns. Foundations adopting a creative approach often begin with information collection and learning and, depending on their analysis of the potential for change and viable roles for them in that process, they may or may not pursue the issue.

Foundations adopting a creative style are like magpies, gathering ideas and information from a variety of sources at a variety of levels. Research, training, demonstration projects, auditing, public hearings and commissions are among their tools for generating ideas.

Again, ideas have to compete with other sources of influence and arguments supporting alternative courses of action. Thus the key question for foundations adopting a creative approach is how can this instrument make a difference in the mix of competing constraints and influences that shape the behaviour they seek to influence. As noted above, some foundations adopting a creative approach will not pursue an issue if there is little chance of competing with other sources of influence and argument.

Foundations adopting a creative approach use the different types of knowledge they have built to gain authority as a tool of organizational and policy change. To be effective in achieving change, ideas do not, of course, have to be true or accurate. But to be effective they do have to gain the attention of the target actors (those in a position to effect change) and that means first that they have to be effectively disseminated and communicated, and second, that they have to be able to compete in the increasingly crowded marketplace of ideas.

Foundations adopting a creative approach are conscious of Rogers's (2003) five qualities of innovations that help spread acceptance and adoption:

1   Relative advantage (over what it replaces).
2   Compatibility (with values, past experiences and needs of adopters).
3   Complexity (how difficult it is to understand or use).
4   Trialability (how can potential adopters 'try before they buy').
5   Observability (some aspect people can see or can be taken to see).

These characteristics help to shape communications content and strategies, drawing on the data derived from prior demonstration and research sites and projects, and their adaptation in the light of the experience of those who have to implement and use them.

Foundations adopting a creative approach attach considerable significance to effective dissemination and communication, and are willing to spend money on these processes. An idea or approach that is not widely and effectively disseminated obviously does not add to the generally available stock of solutions, and is unlikely to have impact beyond immediate grantees; to that extent, a good idea that is not communicated is a wasted investment. Dissemination not only potentially increases impact but also helps to establish the foundation's interest and legitimacy in an issue, informs others, and adds to learning by allowing for dissent and discussion (Carson 2003b).

Foundations adopting a creative approach produce their own publications and hold their own events, but they are also prepared to use the mass media and to piggyback on events arranged by others in order to get their ideas out into the public, political domain. Recognizing the power of the media to frame the way in which issues are perceived, creative foundations tend to pay particular attention to the roles of editors, journalists and other media makers. In addition to using press releases and briefings, these foundations may produce regular, carefully researched data, specially tailored to the needs of media staff. Some also fund training courses for journalists and editors.

Because the marketplace of ideas is crowded and increasingly ideologically polarized, foundations adopting a creative approach are conscious of the need to generate attention from across the political spectrum. Language matters here, as does content, which can bring in right-leaning progressives or liberal-leaning conservatives. Convening meetings of a variety of actors, from different agencies, political persuasions, professions and so on, can be an effective strategy in turning ideas into effective change interventions.

Foundations adopting a creative approach recognize that because the marketplace of ideas is crowded and contentious, ideas have to be strategically introduced in order to capitalize on open or opening 'policy windows' or tipping points. Strategic opportunism plays a part in these foundations' choice of times and places for the introduction of ideas.

Closely related, foundations adopting a creative approach know that ideas are more powerful if they provide a viable solution to a recognized problem. The Annie E. Casey Foundation, for example, has taken this insight a step further by developing an in-house consulting unit, based on the foundation's accumulated knowledge, to help governments and others in crisis moments. This borrowing of a private-sector consulting model has not only increased the foundation's contribution to policy formation but also led to interaction with a dozen states, thus further increasing the foundation's networks and reputation.

Incentives

Incentives are a third major tool of intervention for change. Incentives include the direct or indirect use of sanctions or inducements to alter the calculus of costs and benefits associated with given behaviour for the target individuals. Governments have a wide range of sanctions for a broad range of target actors. The simplest incentive is money in exchange for goods and services, such as contracts, tax relief and so on. Incentives may also be used to make some actions more or less attractive than others through, for example, grants, subsidies, charges, taxes and penalties.

While, unlike governments, foundations have no authority to wield direct sanctions, they do have control over scarce financial resources. Thus foundations adopting a creative approach may use grants as positive inducements, and withhold grants as sanctions to achieve desired changes.

Financial resources as incentives work in a number of ways. Just by announcing an interest in a particular area, the foundation may provide an incentive for change in the priority accorded to that area. Use of matching grants as ways of inducing grantees (including state governments) to adopt certain practices and standards goes back to the early 19th century. Foundations adopting a creative approach today use a variety of incentives to change, including, but not limited to, direct financial incentives. For example, the Request for Proposals (RFP) content and process may itself be used as a means of change, even if no grant is subsequently given.

The power of matching grants as incentives is demonstrated by the criticism they have attracted. For example, Kim Dennis, ex-executive director of Philanthropy Roundtable, has suggested that matching grants 'bribe government to take on projects they would not otherwise do' (quoted in Roelofs 2003: p. 69). Similarly, a Pennsylvania House of Representatives select committee accused foundations of using their money to buy public policy. The sub-committee argued: 'It is one thing to seek change, it is quite another when changes in public policy are influenced by the offering of private money to state governmental institutions' (quoted in Roelofs 2003: p. 70).

A Variety of Levels and a Mix of Tools

In some cases, foundations adopting a creative approach identify a wide range of groups at different levels whose behaviour bears on the outcome they seek to achieve. In these circumstances, creative foundations use a mix of tools at a variety of levels, across a range of sites, in attempting to explore the potential for, and barriers to, change with a diverse groups of actors. Other foundations tend to use only one of these tools. Foundations adopting a creative approach tend to use not one but all three tools in varying and complex combinations.

Many foundations have traditionally worked on the assumption that knowledge via 'demonstration' projects would be sufficient to achieve change. Some have realized that demonstration without active, targeted dissemination is unlikely to be effective. However, even demonstration or knowledge plus dissemination may not be enough. First, facts rarely speak for themselves; they have to be interpreted in the 'right' way. Second, knowledge alone will not overcome obstacles to change, including self-interest and the power of the status quo. Some argue that those required to change need to 'own' the problem and want to change; others maintain that even ownership and commitment may be insufficient without positive incentives and the removal of disincentives such as extra work, loss of status, or incompatibility with payment or performance reward systems.

Resources are one, often powerful, incentive to change (for example, actions, programmes, and practices often follow the money), just as lack of resources can be a powerful disincentive. Again, however, it is vital to identify the 'right' targets. Resistance to change may lie at the individual or group level, or at a wider organizational or system level. Focusing change efforts, via incentives and penalties, at the individual or group level alone is therefore unlikely to be effective if the organization, structure, or wider policy continues to encourage and reward other practices. For these reasons, foundations adopting a creative approach frequently attempt to achieve change via influence over organizational, institutional or wider public policy.

Marketing of information and potential solutions to issues, and encouragement of debate around them, plays a crucial role in these foundations' tools and strategies. Like all successful innovators, foundations adopting a creative approach know that good ideas are nothing without active dissemination to the right people, at the right time, in the right place and by the right means. When necessary, such foundations use the tools of marketing – publicity and publications, demonstration, face-to-face communication, and careful analysis of target audiences (Meffert 2005).

8 The practice of creative philanthropy

Managing a creative approach requires different skills and strategies from conventional management. Drawing on Koestler (1989), the creative manager has to be artist, sage and jester. To be creative it is not enough, or always helpful, to be unconventional and unorthodox; creativity is an intellectual discipline and a business tool (De Bono 1996). As noted in the previous chapter, in order to develop the tools and strategies required for an effective creative approach, managers of such foundations face a number of internal and external challenges.

Changing Roles

First, the manager and board of a creative foundation need to encourage a new approach to the roles of the foundation. Whereas conventional foundations see their primary role as spending money by making grants to provide services or discover causes, the foundation adopting a creative approach sees its role as stimulating sustainable change by providing new perspectives, new ideas, new solutions, and new conversations and debate.

The Board: Values Are Not Optional

A creative approach requires radical change in the way some board members see the roles of foundations, since it is very different from conventional expectations of charity or philanthropic work. Board members need to be able to resist the blandishments of 'giving to the poor', and be prepared to forsake the easy glow and immediate satisfaction of patronage. Board members need to understand that everything the foundation does reflects social values and assumptions about social change – whether examined or unexamined: 'Every grant reflects a social value about what a foundation believes and how it would like to improve the community in which it works' (Carson 2003b).

Re-Thinking Resources

Board members may be encouraged to adopt a creative approach through a real-ization of the paucity of their financial resources relative to the issue they seek to address (and, in some cases, to the resources of other foundations). Awareness of the paucity of their financial resources, coupled with recognition of their power to access and build other resources, are important tools in changing board members' perceptions of the strategies available to them. Taking a longer-term view of finan-cial resources may also contribute to a different perception of potential strategies. For example, thinking not of $0.5 million over one year but rather $5 million over 10 years for a particular programme may change the mind-set of board members, liberating them to think more widely and creatively.

Diversity, Creativity and Criticism

Board members of the foundation adopting a creative approach need to be willing to think outside the box, bringing diverse interests and perspectives to the foun-dation. Co-option of new board members, as well as advisory committees, may be one way in which a foundation can increase diversity of ideas and perspectives.

Another radical strategy for encouraging creativity is to cultivate critics. 'Active critics are a great asset. Without the slightest expenditure of time or effort, we have our weakness and error made apparent and alternatives proposed. We need only listen carefully, dismiss that which arises from ignorance, ignore that which arises from envy or malice and embrace that which has merit' (Hock 2002).

Building and Maintaining Commitment

One key quality of board members in a foundation adopting a creative approach is an awareness of the complexities and uncertainties of social and policy change. Staying focused on the role and tasks of the creative approach requires constant attention. As some interviewees commented, there is sometimes a distinction between board (and staff) nominally agreeing to these changes, and evidence that they have really taken them on as their own. The importance of this distinction is underlined by the fact that the outcomes the foundation seeks to achieve usually require long-term commitment, and in the short term there may be few obviously visible results. Board members and staff need to remain confident and committed. Several of the foundations studied suggested that board members more easily cope with the 'slow-burn' marathon of the creative approach if the foundation also has some more immediately satisfying shorter-term projects or grants. Another strategy to ease the 'ache' of the slow burn may be to ensure some early results by knocking at already half-open policy doors.

Achieving the often long 'drip drip' of social change is especially frustrating in a culture that likes to be constantly keeping score and moving on. However, the process of change in organizations and in society is 'more like a soccer match; you have to appreciate the seemingly endless positioning that precedes the sporadic scoring'; 'the progress resulting from discontinuous change is actually the sum of dozens, even hundreds, of difficult and unheralded events that together keep the battleship turning in the right direction' (Lawrence 1998: p. 307). Selecting milestones and trumpeting the small successes along the way are important comforts on the journey.

Risk and Communication

Other suggestions for 'keeping the board on board' included ensuring genuine involvement, regular and informative (as distinct from cursory) progress evaluations on current work, and advance warning of any looming controversies. Carson identifies board leadership as one of three key elements that enabled the Minneapolis Community Foundation to adopt a creative approach, and notes that this involves building shared values, open communication about risks beforehand, and continued communication and feedback throughout (Carson 2003).

Staff: Changing Mind-Sets

The manager of a foundation adopting a creative approach also has to build new perceptions of the foundation's role among staff. Staff may be more resistant to change than the board. In more than one of the case studies, staff attachment to old cultures and practices was an obstacle to adoption of a creative approach. Changing the mind-sets of staff may require considerable time and investment of effort in winning hearts and minds. Achieving change is a campaign, not an event. As Lawrence has remarked, managers should not expect people easily to embrace the need for change; the manager's job is to create a readiness to change by encouraging dissatisfaction with current achievements and ways of doing things (Lawrence 1998). As several of our case studies demonstrate, readiness comes from dissatisfaction, education and guiding people to their own conclusion that change is necessary.

Adopting a creative approach involves both gaining acceptance of the value of that approach, and helping staff (and board) to be creative, to approach old problems from new angles, to redefine problems, to put together new combinations, and so on. One strategy is to bring in facilitators and consultants who combine expertise in techniques of creativity with a lack of knowledge of, or detachment from, the specific problem. Training in creativity reinforces the message that the foundation takes it seriously, as well as providing experience and understanding of techniques for stimulating creativity.

Some businesses use lunch-time creativity groups in which one person brings a problem to the group who use two or three techniques to explore the problem and generate new ideas, More controversially, at one stage British Airways appointed a 'corporate jester', an experienced manager prepared to take risks and comment constructively on any aspect of the business (Clegg 1999). Table 8.1 summarizes the dos and don'ts of developing a culture of creativity in organizations.

Other techniques for encouraging new approaches to what the foundation does and how it approaches specific issues include:

- Enhancing variance – accepting that new ideas can come from what appears to be varied sorts of anomalies, exceptions and 'junk'.

- Seeing old things in new ways – for example, Sutton tells the story of Abraham Wald's discovery of the best places to strengthen US warplanes. Wald marked the places of bullet holes in planes returning from battle and then suggested putting more armour in places with the least holes (because the planes Wald was looking at were those that had survived, so it was the holes he was not seeing that needed extra protection).

- Break from the past – but remember that the tried and true often wins out (Sutton 2002).

Hiring for a Creative Approach

One strategy for increasing creativity is to hire creative people, including people unfamiliar with the way in which foundations conventionally do things. But hiring for creativity obviously requires some care, depending on the nature and the level of the post.

In addition to looking for different qualities for existing posts, given the range of tasks involved in adopting a creative approach, new and different staff will often be needed, for instance, staff with skills in communications, evaluation and so on. While conventional foundations tend largely to comprise programme officers with a broadly shared set of skills and cultures, the manager of a creative approach will have to manage the competing norms, values, demands and expectations of a variety of different professions and disciplines. Communications staff may see things very differently from programme staff, and both may see things differently from evaluation staff.

Leadership not Management

It may be misleading to talk about managing a foundation adopting a creative approach. As we have emphasized above, a creative approach requires the flexibility to adapt and

Table 8.1 Developing and Implementing a Culture of Creativity

When Developing a Culture of Creativity

Do:	Don't:
• propagate the benefits of creativity to stakeholders	• Force creativity as yet another formal process
• Develop and tutor staff in creative philanthropy	• Present creativity as yet another 'philanthropic fad'
• Instill principles of creativi ty in board, staff and grantees	• Command to become creative
• Encourage communication internally as well as with external stakeholders	• Control creativity
• 'Throw away' the organization chart and consider reorganization even 'disOrganization'	• Restrict communication, particularly lateral and bottom-up
• Lead by example and display creativity	• Rely overly on established job descriptions
	• Try tinkering with processes bound by the same faults
	• Say one thing and do another

When Exploring the Problem Area

Do:	Don't:
• Obtain a broad understanding by listening to different stakeholders	• Try to obtain every bit of information in depth
• Ask 'why' and 'why should we care?' of everything	• Make assumptions about the problem, the solution and the desired outcome without questioning them
• Look at different ways of phrasing the problem, and let yourself be challenged	• Take the problem and your intervention as given
• Consider doing nothing and ask 'so what?' often	• Mistake philanthropic action for a solution
• Examine the obstacles to success, and what successful philanthropy would imply	• Focus only on the desired outcome without considering alternatives
• Make sure you have a clear problem statement before considering solutions	• Assume everyone knows what has to be done

Continued on next page

Table 8.1 (cont.)

When solving problems and generating ideas

Do:

- Use different creativity techniques
- Let ideas flow freely
- Move away from the problem
- Generate many possible answers
- Build on other people's ideas
- Be bold and unconventional
- Explore a variety of philanthropic approaches and tools
- Respect the obvious
- Pass useful ideas on to other foundations, organizations, grantees and individuals

Don't:

- Wait for inspiration
- Evaluate ideas as they emerge and before collecting and putting them in a context
- Always keep the problem at the centre of attention
- Look for the right answer or the single and central solution
- Criticize other people's ideas without being constructive
- Be restricted by practicality and short-term feasibility
- Get in a rut with techniques
- Look for new solutions when obvious ones are available
- Worry about the ideas which are not used

When evaluating and refining ideas

Do:

- Pick ideas with appeal
- Use intuition
- Look at the positive aspects and how to make them even better
- Look at the negative aspects and how to fix them
- Consider the basic requirements to implement
- Be prepared to go back and choose again

Don't:

- Pick ideas on immediate practicality
- Use logic alone
- Mix positive and negative
- Simply state the negative
- Put together a detailed implementation plan
- Consider decisions to be cast in concrete

(Continued on next page)

Table 8.1 (cont.)

When implementing and evaluating	
Do:	**Don't:**
• Use prototyping and time boxing • Monitor key milestones • Consider risk • Celebrate success and failure • Learn from failure • Feed lessons back into the process • Use a mix of evaluation techniques • Evaluate process and outcome • Take a long-term perspective • Consider unintended consequences • Engage grantees in evaluation • Develop and adopt exit strategy • Be flexible and let the problem define action rather than internal procedures	• Use overly detailed project plans • Monitor every possible variable • Focus too much on what can be quantified • Let risk control everything • Be too busy to celebrate anything • Castigate failure and neglect small, interim successes • Cover up failures • Impose exit strategies • See grant action and outcomes in isolation

Source: Based on Clegg 1999

react to changing environments. Whereas traditional management is about setting and monitoring specific objectives, a creative approach requires flexibility and thus trust – it requires leadership. This is one reason why Kao describes the manager of a creative organization as an impresario – someone with plenty of personal drive who can pick the right people, and rely on respect rather than authority (Kao 1996). Similarly, Heifetz *et al.* talk about adaptive leadership to deal with the complexity of achieving social change through encouraging new ways of thinking and new relationships, focusing attention and mediating conflict (Heifetz *et al.* 2004).

Balancing Creative Practice and Process

Foundations adopting a creative approach have to be 'ambidextrous organizations', mastering the art of 'not only but also' (Tushmann *et al.* 1998). A creative approach requires flexibility and opportunism; planning is always a work in progress. But, at the same time, the foundation needs structure and process to get things done. Creativity without process becomes unmanageable, but process without creativity becomes meaningless routine. The manager's task is to balance the two forces in 'creative abrasion' (Brown and Dugiud 2002).

Board and Staff

Both staff and board members need to gain satisfaction from their involvement, but in the foundation adopting a creative approach these will not be the obvious ones of dispensing money to grateful recipients.

Again, both board and staff need to be encouraged to take a long view, accepting that sustainable change is a long, slow process. Along the way, staff and board will need the encouragement of celebrating 'small wins'. The time required to achieve the tasks of a creative approach obviously has a variety of other implications for board and staff continuity and change, and for spending patterns and costs. These are discussed further below.

Finally, both board and senior staff need to be able to balance the variety of tasks and stages involved in running the marathon of a creative approach.

Resources

The management and board of a foundation adopting a creative approach need to inculcate a different approach to the foundation's resources. Whereas conventional foundations focus on their assets and income and see their key resource as money, foundations adopting a creative approach are conscious of their lack of financial resources relative to problems and see their key resources as knowledge, networks, and an independent voice. Conventional foundations focus on building, and giving away, financial resources; foundations adopting a creative approach focus on building, using and sharing knowledge, networks and an independent voice.

Defining knowledge as one of the foundation's key resources has a number of implications for management. Some foundations already have a considerable body of knowledge in their fields of interest, although this may not be codified. In many foundations there are vast quantities of knowledge, but this is left 'lying around' on desks and in filing cabinets, as well as in people's heads. If the foundation does not already have a body of knowledge in its chosen field, then it will have to build one. Building a coherent, sound body of knowledge is neither quick nor easy, and will require time and money.

Auditing and Managing Knowledge

Foundations adopting a creative approach need to audit the knowledge they have, or need, and consider ways in which this knowledge can best be managed. Such foundations increasingly devote time and resources to knowledge management, and some employ specialist staff to set up systems and manage the foundation's knowledge. Knowledge management involves both gathering and organizing the foundation's knowledge into easily accessible, user-friendly systems; the latter task is obviously complex, but the former may also be difficult. Staff have to be convinced that it is worth the time and effort involved in supplying knowledge; there may be resistance to sharing knowledge either because it gives competitive advantage or because staff are not confident that this particular information really counts as 'knowledge'.

Building a Reputation for Knowledge

Having a sound, organized body of knowledge is not sufficient in itself. The creative approach needs knowledge for its own sake in identifying problems and solutions; but it also needs a knowledge-base to gain legitimacy and credibility for its contributions to policy and practice debates. The foundation has to build its reputation as a knowledgeable player. Traditionally, endowed foundations have paid relatively little attention to managing their reputations – except perhaps in times of crisis. Insofar as reputation has been an issue it has largely been seen as a matter of due diligence in managing money and 'good grant-making'. Foundations adopting a creative approach consciously build reputation in a substantive field and then manage it carefully.

Controlling the Quality of Knowledge

Building and managing a reputation for knowledge involves consideration of, among other things, quality control. How does the foundation ensure that the knowledge it produces is sound? Controlling the quality of knowledge issued by or associated with the foundation may involve difficult decisions in relationships with academics and other experts. For example, in some cases the foundation may not wish to be associated with a research report or other publication it has funded; the foundation will need policies and processes in place to avoid a situation in which the foundation has to publicly dissociate itself from a publication.

Maintaining an Independent Voice

As noted above, foundations adopting a creative approach see having an independent voice as one of their most important resources. Maintaining, protecting and managing the foundation's independent voice is closely related to building and managing a reputation for sound knowledge, and throws up many of the same issues and dilemmas. In addition, the foundations we have studied attached considerable significance to maintaining a non-partisan position, and taking care to use ideologically neutral language. These were seen as important devices not only in maintaining the foundation's reputation as an independent voice but also in effective communication. This non-partisan approach is one difference between our foundations and the conservative foundations adopting many similar methods.

Managing Networks

Networks are a third element in the key resources of the foundation adopting a creative approach. Wide and rich networks provide the foundation with knowledge, credibility, and routes of two-way communication. Managing network creation and maintenance again requires different skills and tasks from those required in conventional foundations. Building rich and wide networks involves considerable time being out of the office, making contacts. Staff may spend more time away from their desks than at them and may be geographically dispersed at demonstration sites. This has obvious implications for managing at a distance, for organizational integration and communication, and for performance measurement. Going to meetings and events, talking to people and so on — seen by many foundation managers as 'extras', even time-wasting — become as, or more, important than doing things inside the organization. As one foundation manager remarked, 'how many relationships have you had today becomes an important question'. Network building and maintenance is a slow and potentially expensive process with few easily attributable results, and the board may need some convincing that this is a useful way for staff to spend time and money.

When a foundation sees money as its key resource, life is deceptively simple. Money is invested by investment managers and it does or does not grow in value in clearly measurable ways; grants are made and then tracked in more or less satisfactory ways. Money comes in and money goes out and there is a relatively clear trail of activity. In the foundation that sees knowledge, independent voice and networks as among its key resources, life is far more complicated. Knowledge, independence and networks are less tangible than money, and cannot be measured and tracked so easily. In addition, as discussed below, building and managing knowledge, independence and network creation are costly, long-term activities that add to overheads.

Starting With an Outcome

In order to make a grant decision, conventional foundations typically start with a set of policies and processes, receive grant applications for projects, and assess the applicant organization, project viability, budget, and so on. Foundations adopting a creative approach start with a desired outcome and assess what would have to happen, and be done, to achieve it.

This has fundamental implications for the way in which the foundation works. The foundation adopting a creative approach first has to identify a desired outcome. This is easier said than done, and will often require considerable thought, discussion, time and constant reiteration to get it right. These foundations accept that some outcomes are too big, too difficult, or in other ways inappropriate, for pursuit by this, or perhaps any, foundation. The foundation's resources, knowledge, and networks play a part in assessing the choice of outcomes to be pursued, but so too does the nature of the issue, the structure and culture of the field in which it is situated, and the likelihood of change.

Knocking on Locked Doors?

While some foundations are willing to highlight unrecognized issues and actively create conversation, several of the foundations studied suggested that in choosing an outcome it is important to choose emerging issues where there is likely to be interest in new approaches and debate. Policy windows have to be open, or be about to open. As one person put it, 'there's no point in knocking on tight-shut doors'. In these foundations, chosen priorities are related to analysis of needs *and* analysis of likely points of influence or leverage for change. Foundations adopting this approach need to have a sound understanding of the policy environment as well as an instinct for likely change and openings.

Thus, starting with an outcome requires different management tasks and skills from those required in the conventional approach. Starting with an outcome also requires a fundamentally different approach to policies and practices of grant-making.

Policies and Practices of Grant-making

In the conventional foundation the purpose or type of funding, and the size of grant to be awarded, is usually determined by rules and formula decided by the foundation in advance, applied to all, and related in large part to the foundation's own perceived organizational needs. Starting with an outcome means that the purpose, amount and duration of funding is determined by what is necessary to achieve the desired outcome. This clearly makes the task of managing grants more individually focused, more demanding and more time-consuming. Tailoring grants to what is necessary to achieve outcomes also creates an element of uncertainty in duration and size of grant, and thus in the foundation's budgetary commitments. These foundation managers do not have the same safety blanket of foundation rules and regulations. As discussed below, this means, among other things, that exiting from a grant or a programme becomes a much more difficult issue than it is for the conventional foundation, where exit criteria are built into the initial grant.

Starting with an outcome has other consequences, including the tendency to fund for longer periods than the conventional foundation approach. Again, this places considerable onus on foundation staff to 'get it right' from the beginning. Longer-term funding also reduces flexibility for new initiatives, and raises the spectre of a foundation 'silting up' as fresh activity gradually ceases. Ensuring that staff and board members remain fully committed to the foundation's agreed strategy may require considerable management skill and time.

Starting with an outcome requires a different mind-set in relation to almost everything the foundation does. The conventional foundation tends to see programmes as a largely administrative series of headings or boxes (under which applications are considered and grants accounted for), encompassing a collection of loosely related grants seen as individual transactions; the creative foundation sees grants as pieces of a whole programme, working from different angles and at different levels. Whereas the conventional foundation tends to see grant-making as the foundation's main activity and usually the end of the process, the creative approach sees grant-making as only the start of a longer and wider process involving a range of very different activities undertaken by people, with different professional skills, inside and outside the foundation. Managers in these foundations are responsible, not merely for grant-making but also for planning, co-ordination, execution and integration of these different activities.

Theory of Change[1]

Managing in a foundation adopting a creative approach involves developing a theory of how change happens. All foundations work with some assumptions about how change happens – they give this grant rather than that on the assumption that this one will make more of a (sustainable) difference than another. But in the conventional foundation these assumptions are implicit and rarely articulated, let alone examined. In foundations adopting a creative approach the theory of how change happens is explicit, and usually contested. Managers need to help the board and staff to identify and critically examine their assumptions about what would be necessary to achieve the foundation's chosen outcome.

Articulating and examining assumptions about the foundation's potential role in change involves asking and answering the following sorts of questions:

- What is the problem that stops the outcome being achieved?

- What are seen as the causes of the problem?

- What would a solution to the problem look like?

- Who or what needs to change (e.g. individuals, families, the education system, welfare services, the health-care system, legislation at regional or national level, and so on)?

- How could the foundation reach, influence, or change the groups and structures above?

In answering these questions the foundation will need to think about the geographical and political level at which it would need to work, and the legal and other constraints under which the foundation operates.

What tools or processes would the foundation need to change or influence the above groups or structures? For example:

- Enabling direct action by citizens.

- Providing ideas, research and knowledge.

- Supporting maverick individuals.

- Supporting community or personal self-help.

- Funding nonprofit organizations.

- Encouraging government intervention, perhaps for legislative or procedural change.

- Providing incentives to change.

- Imposing sanctions against lack of change.

The foundation will also need to consider what obstacles there might be.

- What financial and knowledge resources, skills and time would the foundation need to employ effectively to reach the target groups identified?

- Which resources does the foundation already have?

- What skills, knowledge and other resources does the foundation need to develop?

- Which skills and resources could the foundation 'borrow' from others?

- Who else is working in this field or issue? Is the foundation prepared to work in partnership with others?

At the end of this process, the foundation will have an outline of:

- The problem it wants to address.

- Its definition or theoretical understanding of the problem.

- The desired outcome.

- A plan of intervention, including target groups, tools, time-scale, and required resources.

Although the exercise above is an important tool in identifying issues in which the foundation considers it appropriate to be involved, and in developing strategies for addressing the issue, it should not be taken as a plan to be slavishly followed. As we have stressed repeatedly above, social change is a discontinuous, serendipitous process; a creative approach requires open-mindedness, constant attention and flexibility to respond to ever-changing circumstances and opportunities.

Relationships with Others

While a creative approach recognizes the importance of their independence, and independent voice, it also recognizes that foundations are relatively powerless alone; they need to work on and with others if they are to have an impact beyond the narrow confines of their direct grant recipients and achieve the sustainable outcomes they seek.

Conventional foundations tend to be predominantly inward looking, building limited relationships with a narrow range of others. Foundations adopting a creative approach pay close attention to the wider environment, and build rich, wide networks. They value these networks for two major reasons. First, to aid creativity in developing new solutions to often old problems, they need diverse perspectives and ideas. Second, to ensure widespread debate about proposed solutions, they need 'messengers' and champions at diverse levels and in a variety of institutions. Foundations adopting a creative approach do not set pre-determined limits on the groups they will relate to; they will work wherever and with whomever is necessary to achieve the desired outcome.

We have already discussed some of the management implications of the value that foundations adopting a creative approach attach to rich and wide networks. Another implication is that managers must be skilled in networking at all levels, moving, perhaps, from a meeting with high-level politicians in the morning to one with local activists in the afternoon. It also means that managers must make space for the time involved in creating, developing and maintaining networks, and make the difficult decisions about which networks are worth persevering with and which have limited value.

Approach to Planning

'Strategic' planning has become one of the conventional foundation mantras. For the foundation adopting a creative approach planning is necessary to provide the focus and concerted effort to build knowledge, reputation and relevant networks. Focus is crucial for foundations adopting a creative approach, not least because it is impossible to be expert in very many areas. Planning is also necessary to identify desired outcomes and the strategies necessary to achieve them.

Space for Opportunism and Flexibility

Although boards and managers in foundations adopting a creative approach do not reject planning, they see it as providing a framework rather than a blueprint. Opportunism plays an important role in a creative approach.

Foundations adopting a creative approach also recognize the need for flexibility, to be open to new ideas, to respond to changing environmental conditions, and to exploit opening policy windows and opportunities. For this reason managers and staff in these foundations spend time scanning the environment, doing their homework, and staying one step ahead in developing knowledge.

Managers in such foundations acknowledge the need to be flexible in, for example, choosing the right moment and the right place to release research results or launch a report. One director described this as 'waiting for the wave' of political and public interest. While planning is necessary to provide focus and discipline, flexibility is also important to allow space for creative ideas and strategies. Managers and boards of these foundations have the difficult job of balancing the tightrope between focus for sound knowledge and concerted strategies, with the flexibility to take advantage of new opportunities, ideas, and approaches. Planning for the foundation adopting a creative approach is always a work in progress – with all the uncertainty that that entails for board, managers, staff and budgets.

Implementation

Although conventional foundations frequently talk about 'demonstration' projects and 'innovation', they rarely follow through to implementation on any scale. 'Going to scale' has become a new element in the foundation lexicon in recent years but this is usually treated as another goal or end-state. For foundations adopting a creative agenda, implementation on a larger scale is part of a more complex process, just one part of the marathon of a creative approach.

Learning from Doing

Implementation on a larger scale is another step in the learning process. Working in other areas provides new opportunities for testing the validity and viability of the approach, for understanding and overcoming obstacles, and refining plans and methods. Demonstration is part of the creative strategy in building not only learning but also credibility and support. Demonstration in a variety of sites is part of the foundation's research, knowledge-building, learning and communication strategy, and, in many cases, demonstrations may speak louder than a thousand words. First-hand experience and involvement may be hugely powerful in overcoming political and professional scepticism and indifference, as well as being another small piece in the jigsaw of widespread adoption/change.

Challenges of Implementation

Implementation clearly presents additional and new challenges for foundation managers. Managing project or site implementation presents a host of new demands, skills and tensions. In addition to the time and costs involved, managers need to be able to manage the process of service implementation (or to supervise those who do), as well as the complex and contentious process of building access and support for implementation in new places or on a larger scale. In an important sense, building access and support for implementation of demonstrations turns the conventional grant-making relationship on its head. The foundation becomes something closer to supplicant rather than patron. Achieving access and support in new areas may require creation and management of systems of incentives, such as matching funding, as well as high-level political involvement.

Evaluation and Performance Measurement

Although foundations adopting a creative approach value flexibility, this does not mean that 'anything goes'. A creative approach is guided by evaluation and performance measurement. However, as discussed above, their approach to evaluation and performance measurement is somewhat different from that of the conventional foundation.

In the conventional foundation, if evaluation and performance measurement are considered at all, the focus is predominantly on outputs, and far less frequently on outcomes. Grants and programmes tend to be judged in terms of whether or not they achieved the agreed objectives. Evaluation is about 'success' and 'failure', and it is implicitly assumed that the grant, or grant recipient, is responsible for both. As discussed above, the conventional foundation's approach is largely rationalist and managerialist. Furthermore, evaluation is seen as the last stage in the process of grant-making.

Foundations adopting a creative approach take a different position. First, evaluation is seen as being about learning rather than success or failure. Evaluation is fed back into the organization as part of a constant learning loop. In an important sense, creative grants and programmes can only 'fail' if learning does not occur. But if constant learning is to happen, managers have the difficult task of creating a culture in which the foundation has a different – more open and honest – relationship with grantees, as well as staff willingness to share 'mistakes' as well as 'successes', thoughts and observations. In addition, managers need to create structures and processes that normalize such discussions, and, crucially, ensure that knowledge and learning are fully incorporated back into the organization via effective knowledge management.

Because foundations adopting a creative approach recognize that desired outcomes are rarely achieved in much less than 10 years, 'final' evaluation and performance measurement is a similarly long-term process. But that does not mean that these foundations wait 10 years to assess the value of their strategies and grants. Not least because they have a culture of self-criticism and enquiry – and because planning is always a work in progress – foundations adopting a creative approach identify interim measures and indicators of progress in advance.

Finally, because foundations adopting a creative approach accept that change is an uncertain process, affected by a variety of both foreseeable and unforeseeable, known and unknown actors and factors, they accept that the foundation's role in achieving any given outcome is always uncertain, and often unknowable with any precision. For this reason, foundations adopting a creative approach accept the value of soft performance measures.

They also accept, and have to live with, uncertainty over their precise role in achieving desired outcomes. Adopting a creative approach requires courage and humility.

All of this is easier to say than to do, not least because it goes against the grain of conventional management wisdom. Adopting a creative approach, building innovation and learning, requires from both staff and grantees that they:

- De-emphasize individual accountability, and focus on goals rather than assign blame and responsibility.

- Avoid undue quantification of goals and over-rigid budgets; asking people to be innovative without departing from standardized plans, budgets and operating procedures does not work.

- Not punish mistakes. Failing early and failing often is better than failing once at the end of a programme. 'Enlightened trial and error outperforms the planning of flawless intellects' (D. Kelley quoted in Pfeffer 2002: p. 102).

- Discourage internal competition and short-term 'deliverables'.

Communication

For the conventional foundation, communication and dissemination (if considered at all) are usually left to the grantee, or are of relatively minor importance. Communication is often in written form to a standard list of contacts, or is a matter of putting something on the foundation's website or in a newsletter. Dissemination is usually a one-off, time-limited process at the start or the end of the grant.

For the foundation adopting a creative approach, communication is an essential and major part of the marathon of achieving the outcome they seek. These foundations accept that changing the way that people, at a variety of levels, think about social issues is a crucial ingredient in achieving sustainable change. Failure to communicate actively and strategically is the cost of a wasted opportunity.

Communications strategy is built in from the very beginning. Each strategy is individually planned in the light of an analysis of target audiences and the best ways to reach them, and is adapted in the light of experience; communication is an on-going long-term learning process.

Foundations adopting a creative approach usually employ communications specialists who have a detailed understanding of modern communications theory and practice (see Bales and Gilliam 2004). They understand that getting the means, the format, and the language right for the designated target audience is critical. Foundations adopting a creative approach are creative in their communications strategies, sometimes using radio and television to stimulate knowledge, awareness and debate about the nature of issues and potential solutions. These foundations know that change involves changing hearts as well as minds, and recognize the power of the media in agenda-setting, framing and persuasion. Use of non-partisan language and jargon (politically correct or otherwise) is one step in re-framing the way in which people think about an issue.

But foundations adopting a creative approach do not have any simple one-size strategy – they relate the communications strategy to the nature of the problem and the key target audiences, that is, the people who need to listen and hear if change is to happen. Unlike some foundations, those adopting a creative approach tend to take a wide view of their target audiences, and work at a variety of levels. For example, rather than focusing solely on politicians, some foundations will seek to communicate with journalists or the wider public, not least because politicians sometimes need to be helped to find the political will to reconsider issues. Foundations adopting a creative approach frequently work in the corridors of indifference, as well as power.

Active, carefully planned communications strategies clearly require new skills from managers. They also entail costs that require both support and management.

The demands and schedules of communications strategies have to be balanced with other foundation activities.

Active communications strategies also raise more fundamental and more difficult issues to do with both branding and ownership. To whom do the results of a project belong, the foundation or the grantee? Who is responsible for quality control of publications? Can, or should, the foundation put its name, and logo, to anything it has funded? Can, or should, it refuse to put its name to something it has funded but with which it does not wish, for a variety of reasons, to be associated? Is all communication good, or is some likely to damage the foundation and its mission? Does the real power of foundations lie in working behind the scenes, or is that an excuse for sitting on the fence and a recipe for ineffectiveness? Foundations have traditionally tended to keep a low profile; active communications strategies raise important and contentious issues about branding, or as several respondents described it, 'flying above the radar'.

Tensions and Open Questions

We are, of course, only at the beginning of a fuller understanding and a more developed set of tools for the management of creative philanthropy. This is particularly the case for managing tensions and critical issues that are likely to arise as foundations begin to adopt and implement a creative approach. We will briefly touch upon a number of such tensions and issues.

One recurring theme in the case studies presented in Chapter 5, and operating in the background of some of the discussion above, is around spending issues. We suggest that foundations adopting a creative approach use a different approach to spending altogether. Because creative foundations start with an outcome they want to achieve, spending is, within the limits of their resources, driven by what it takes to achieve it. By contrast, conventional foundations too easily fall into a pattern that sets aside a fixed sum over a fixed number of years, and asks: what can we achieve with these resources at hand?

Yet there is more to spending policies than the difference between outcome-oriented funding and fixed-budget funding. We suggest that creative foundations move away from the distinction between project funding and core funding. Whereas conventional foundations generally believe that the lower the overhead costs of donor (for instance, grant administration) and grantee organizations (such as common operating expenditure or core costs) the better, the foundation adopting a creative approach sees overhead costs in terms of what is necessary for foundation as well as grantee effectiveness. Overhead, core or common costs are simply a necessary part of the support that foundations can give to grantees, and they are regarded as neither 'problematic' budget items nor something outside of what should or could be funded.

Indeed, creative foundations may well decide to move away from cost-based thinking and adopt an investment approach instead. By investment approach we mean that foundations begin to think of their grant disbursements as social investments for solving problems. They invest in grantees, which then use these funds to cover common or core costs as well as operating expenditures. Such an approach would also imply that budgets become investment budgets, organized around outcomes rather than projections of expenditure alone.

Another recurring theme is the need for time, patience and stamina in building knowledge, reputation, and networks, as well as keeping up with issues and changes in the environment. Stamina and the belief that the outcome can be reached are necessary to keep the foundation going through the lengthy process – the marathon – of achieving sustainable, wide-impact change.

The case studies revealed a number of tensions and issues with which managers were particularly concerned. Interestingly, many of the tensions and dilemmas faced by creative foundations are similar to those identified by Kao (1991) when discussing managing creativity in business:

- Can there be creativity on demand?

- How to balance the need for freedom with the need for structure.

- How to balance desire for unlimited development time with desire for deadlines.

- How to balance participation and informal communication with the need for hierarchy and structured authority.

- How to design useful systems for planning, resource allocation, and information flow.

- How to manage conflicts between the creative and the managerial.

- How to identify the potential value in such conflicts.

Some of the tensions included a concern about the management of networks and relationships. How could foundations ensure diversity in their sources of information and knowledge? How could they stay in touch with a rapidly changing environment and opening policy windows? Others addressed issues around knowledge and learning: How could foundations make space for creativity? How could they ensure constant learning, change and added value? How could they manage knowledge effectively and efficiently? How could they foster team building and develop trust for honest evaluation, learning and constant questioning? How could they build in constant reality checks? And how could they manage the costs of building and sharing knowledge?

Aspects of ownership and branding also came up: How could foundations best manage multiple perspectives and pressures? How could they negotiate the line between interference and encouragement of change? How could they manage leverage and leadership? How could they earn and keep a reputation? How could they negotiate the complex issues around branding? How could they manage exit from grants and programmes?

Likewise, board matters and accountability issues figured prominently. How could foundations generate and maintain board motivation for change, not charity, and acknowledge both the creative and the conservative? How could they satisfy board heads as well as hearts? How could they balance the benefits of new and different perspectives on the board with the benefits of stability? How could they manage the tension between keeping board members fully involved and informed with the risks of over-burdening them?

In terms of accountability, the issue of legitimacy and the often-delicate line between politics and philanthropy emerged as a critical issue. How could foundations maintain legitimacy? How could they balance openness with the foundation's needs to conserve time and resources, and in some circumstances, discretion? How could they manage the fine line between creativity and idiosyncrasy? How could they ensure appropriate performance measurement? How could they combine co-operation with staying independent? How could they maintain focus and commitment while avoiding arrogance? How could they manage criticism that the foundation is doing too little, is too narrow in its focus, is too 'political', is too partisan, or is not sufficiently partisan?

Finally, there are issues around communication and outreach. How could foundations identify target audiences and communicate with them most effectively? How could they manage the costs and tensions involved in being in 'show business'? How could they avoid the demands of communications strategies taking over their timetables and resources? Obviously, we can only list these open questions and issues of managing a creative foundation, and hope that we can develop answers and approaches as we gain experience from across different fields, organizations and settings.

9   The way forward

Current discussions of the need for a new philanthropy tend to focus on ways and means to capture more private money for the public good, and on using such funds more efficiently. The problem with focusing on capturing and spending more philanthropic money is that it does not speak to the rising crescendo of challenges to the roles and practices of foundations. Such a focus fails to provide any new, robust rationale for the existence of foundations in a democracy, and does not address the question of the effectiveness of existing, and potential new, foundations. Rather than simply asking for more philanthropic money, the need is to find ways of making new and existing resources work more effectively.

There is an urgent need for new philanthropic approaches that are better adapted to the needs and realities of the modern environment. Such a new approach should exploit the distinctive characteristics and advantages of foundations, overcome the limitations of existing practices, provide a robust rationale for the existence of foundations in a democracy, meet current challenges and criticisms of foundations, and provide ways of extending the impact of foundations beyond the necessarily limited scope of immediate grantees. A new approach needs to engage all of the resources of foundations (knowledge, networks and so on) rather than focusing solely on their money.

As part of the renewal of philanthropy, the underlying model of the philanthropist's role is itself shifting its social and cultural locus. Whereas the charity model of philanthropy that we discussed in Chapter 2 was closely linked to the philanthropist as patrician, the scientific model to that of the social planner and reformer, and the new-scientific philanthropy model to that of the investor and entrepreneur, the notion of creative philanthropy takes its inspiration from the roles of conductor and enabler.

To some extent, the role of philanthropists has come full circle, returning to its civil-society origins of the 19th century. Yet rather than being charitable and appeasing in the context of a society stressed by rising social inequalities and poverty, the creative philanthropists of today seek to encourage debate, social inclusion and change. The new approach to philanthropy seeks to link the distinctive characteristics of foundations to what are seen as the urgent current problems of modern society, including the decline of civic engagement (Putnam 2000), the crisis in democracy (Putnam and Pharr 2002), and a crisis in values (Baker 2005). Both the service or charitable and scientific approaches may have a place in a creative approach, but they are insufficient in themselves to exploit the distinctive potential of foundations fully.

Civic leadership becomes a critical resource in this respect, and we argue that foundations are well placed to assume a vanguard role in helping modern societies address deep-seated social, cultural and political problems. Indeed, Heifetz *et al.* (2004) put it well when they see the need and realization of adaptive leadership in philanthropy as perhaps the biggest shift in foundation thinking and practices: 'if foundations are to become effective institutions . . . they must understand the value of employing their expertise, political access, media skills, and bold strategies' (2004: p. 31). Heifetz *et al.* encourage foundations to 'reject the artificial dichotomy between proactive and passive grantmaking, and firmly lead social change without imposing the answer' (*ibid.*).

Creative foundations exist in complex and constantly changing social, political, economic, legal and organizational environments that impinge on, constrain, subvert, and support courses of action. Knowledge, authority, compliance, resources and so on are often limited and, for that reason as well as others, linkages and networks are often crucial in getting things done. Stimulating creative, constructive conversation and debate is often the first step in the process of change. Organizations and structures may give the comfort of the mappable, but people – individuals – may matter more than structures, not least in their capacity to constantly adapt to new demands and obstacles and to make relationships (Hogwood and Gunn 1984; Leat 1999).

In the long run, foundations will make their most valuable contribution to the public good by improving civil discourse about important issues using evidence, not ideology. In an important sense, creative foundations act as the 21st-century equivalent of the 18th- and 19th-century European salons and coffee shops, generating new ideas and conversation about social and policy issues. In another sense, creative foundations are akin to the patrons of Renaissance thinkers, inventors and artists. Creative foundations act as both entrepreneurs and underwriters of new conversation, debate and change.

Creative foundations take a less rationalist, perhaps more realistic view than conventional foundations typically do. They assume that lack of money is not the only resource missing in the resolution of social issues; new, constructive ideas, approaches and knowledge are often also lacking. Certainty is in short supply, and workable social plans are usually those that provide a basis for departure rather than a blueprint for action. Creative foundations are both strategic and opportunistic. They employ a variety of resources – financial and other – and not one but a battery of tools for change – authority, ideas and incentives – in varying degrees of combination and at different levels. As we have argued here, creative foundations are post-managerialist organizations. They are about passion and reason at the same time.

In conclusion, we will briefly address issues for future work and further reflection. For one, and while we emphasized philanthropy as organization throughout this book, there are a variety of new vehicles for individual philanthropists other than establishing a foundation. We suggest that they may be worth exploring in relation to creative philanthropy. For example, donor-advised funds offer philanthropists an attractive alternative to creating and operating their own foundations. Such funds, which are typically held at investment banks or community foundations, are increasingly popular because they allow individuals to direct their own giving, and bring a growing number of individuals of moderate wealth into philanthropy. How could such funds be used more creatively?

Likewise, e-philanthropy relates primarily to the tool of fund-raising and fund-distribution via the internet. Potential donors either search applicant websites or solicit proposals. Upon evaluating and selecting grantees, the e-philanthropist would then make a contribution to causes in line with the fund's objectives. What is the creative potential of e-philanthropy relative to more conventional organizational forms?

Throughout this book, we emphasized the use of philanthropic resources, and paid no attention to their origins or management. Yet one could make the argument that a close relationship could exist between creative input and the output of philanthropy. At the very least, philanthropic resources should be in line with principles of ethical investment practices. Yet there may well be creative ways of linking the generation of philanthropic funds to their application, which to us seems the true potential focus of the blended value proposition (Emerson 2004), which seeks to combine economic and social objectives.

The notion of philanthropy as investment, introduced in Chapter 8, could offer a useful avenue to explore a tighter fit between the creative generation and use of philanthropic funds. Programme-related investment strategies are one example already in use, as are credit guarantees and other ways of leveraging assets. Clearly, a closer relationship between business and philanthropy will most likely require legal and fiscal changes, and ways must be found to ensure that these approaches have impact beyond the scope of their immediate grantees, changing the way in which we think of financial and other instruments.

Yet creative foundations challenge not only the philanthropic–economic border. Perhaps most critically, it is the political boundary and the notion of philanthropic citizenship that presents a challenge relative to the more apolitical role of foundations. Indeed, we need to re-examine the relationship between foundations, democracy, and civil society, and ask: are creative foundations necessary for modern democratic societies to function?

For philanthropists, creative foundations offer a way to provide 'voice' and political space for those who would otherwise be excluded or less heard in the political process. For governments, foundations open up new political options and can search for answers and approaches outside the limits of party politics; they add independent voices to the policy process. In terms of their civil-society implications, foundations are independent bastions against the hegemony and controlling attitudes of government and the corporate world; they provide, as Prewitt (1999) and others have argued, the pluralism needed and support the dynamic political forces of today: think tanks and nonprofit organizations.

Yet, one could also posit counterclaims and argue that foundations are the province of self-righteous, self-appointed groups of do-gooders, and ultimately represent the voice of the elite and upper-middle class. Foundations interfere with the democratic process; they represent special interests, and rarely the public good, and should be treated as such. Foundations have no political legitimacy, nor are they democratically controlled. Ultimately, foundations are undemocratic, quasi-aristocratic bastions in a modern, formally egalitarian society. For a dynamic, inclusive civil society, their elitist, fossilizing, and bureaucratic characteristics make foundations more part of the problem than part of the solution. But, as our case studies demonstrate, foundations may also use their independence to stimulate democratic debate.

Working out these claims and counterclaims about the political role and impact of foundations seems to us the most critical policy issue for creative philanthropy. We see little in terms of implications for tax law, as the current tax law in most countries, and certainly in the United States, Canada, Australia and the European Union, offers sufficient 'political space' for creative philanthropy. Of course, the tax treatment of foundations could be improved, but it may not be as critical an issue as the more fundamental claims and counter-claims about political legitimacy.

This brings us to transparency. To us, this issue is more at the centre of potential debates about improving the policy environment for foundations. If foundations are to become the creative actors we propose in this book, then cultural changes may be needed more than legal changes. Foundations have to become more open about their visions, missions, and the outcomes they seek to achieve, and they have to offer accounts of how, and to what effect, they are using tax-privileged resources.

Achieving greater transparency is key to the wider acceptance of creative philanthropy, in particular given the proximity to policy debates that many foundations would seek. However, in many countries, greater transparency could well require some sort of 'cultural revolution' on foundation boards. Nonetheless, we suggest that publishing an annual report and maintaining a website may simply not be enough for creating and maintaining the political capital needed for the long-term legitimacy of foundations. A proactive strategy is called for – a reason why we stress the need for foundations to improve marketing and public relations.

In this book, we have tried to offer a vision for the future of philanthropy. Of course, many aspects of this vision remain to be developed in practice, and many policy and management implications are still to be worked out. Nonetheless, we see the broader conceptualization for the future of foundations presented here as a necessary step towards the renewal of philanthropy that many commentators demand and seek. We are eager to engage the philanthropic community in building on the platform this book has put in place, and we invite others to join us in the effort.

Notes

1 The debate about philanthropy

1 Chapter 2 will provide a fuller analysis of each approach.
2 For general reference on current issues including Senate Finance Committee recommendations, and comments by the Council on Foundations and by Independent Sector, see www.cof.org and www.independentsector.org, the Panel on the Nonprofit Sector 2005, and the National Committee for Responsive Philanthropy 2004.

2 Models of philanthropy in context

1 On the rise of science-oriented philanthropic foundations see, for example, Bulmer (1995); Karl and Katz (1981); Sealander (2003); Smith (1999); and the special issue of *Voluntas* (1996) 6 (3) on foundations.
2 It should be noted that the pluralism argument, which finds its clearest expression in the writings of Prewitt, has a long history in policy debates about the role of foundations, most prominently in the US Senate Report on Finance (1965) in the run-up to the 1968–69 reforms: 'private philanthropic organizations can be uniquely qualified to initiate thought and action, experiment with new and untried ventures, dissent from prevailing attitudes, and act quickly and flexibly . . . Equally important, because their funds are frequently free of commitment to specific operating programs, they can shift the focus of their interest and their financial support from one charitable area to another. They can, hence, constitute a powerful instrument for evolution, growth, and improvement' Ridings (1999).

3 Creative philanthropy

1 See Burt (2005) for a fuller discussion of homophily and heterophily, and applications of this theorem to various kinds of organizations and social settings.

4 Vignettes of creative philanthropy

1 www.ms.foundation.org
2 New York Foundation 2002 Annual Report; www.nyf.org

3 For further discussion of the case and issues, see *Foundation News and Commentary*, May/June 2002, pp. 23–24.

4 *Sharing Knowledge*, the Fannie Mae Foundation 2000 Annual Report; *Building Community Through Collaboration*, the Fannie Mae Foundation 2001 Annual Report; www.fanniemae.com

5 www.comminit.com; www.fex.org

6 See The Tides Foundation, *Annual Report 2001, 1976–2001: 25 Years of Bringing People Together for Positive Social Change*; and *Global Community Global Justice Annual Report (2001/2002)*; www.tides.org.

7 Ford Foundation, *2001 Annual Report*; Ford Foundation *2002 Annual Report*; www.ford-found.org.

8 The Minneapolis Foundation Annual Report 2000–2001: *Making Connections Large and Small*, 2002; www.minneapolisfoundation.org; see also Carson (2003a).

9 McKnight Foundation Annual Report 2002; www.mcknight.org

10 www.bbc.co.uk/worldservice/trust

11 www.bridgehousegrants.org.uk

12 www.theworkcontinues.org; Diana Princess of Wales Memorial Fund, Annual Review 2001

13 Esmée Fairbairn Foundation Annual Report 2002; www.esmeefairbairn.org.uk

14 The Myer Foundation Annual Report 2001–02; The Myer Foundation Annual Report 2002–03; www.myerfoundation.org.au

15 Millfield House Foundation, *Funding Policy Change for a Better Society in the North East of England, A Report on Grant-making 1996–2004*, undated; www.mhfdn.org.uk; see also: Funding Policy Change, *Trust and Foundation News*, Summer 2004.

5 Case studies of creative philanthropy

1 Unless otherwise indicated, quotations and information in all the case studies in this chapter are from interviews with the staff and board members of the relevant foundation.

6 What makes for creative philanthropy?

1 On the importance of communications strategies more generally see Bales and Gilliam (2004).

7 Managing creative philanthropy

1 On tools for exploring and examining theories of change for foundations see the web-based interactive approach developed by the International Network on Strategic Philanthropy at www.insp.efc.be.

Bibliography

Abramson, A. and Spann, J. (1998) *Foundations: Exploring their Unique Roles and Impacts in Society*, Washington, DC: Aspen Institute.

Alchon, G. (1985) *The Invisible Hand of Planning: Capitalism, Social Science and the State in the 1920s*, Princeton, NJ: Princeton University Press.

Allen, M.P. (1987) *The Founding Fortunes: A New Anatomy of the Super-Rich Families in America*, New York: E.P. Dutton.

Andrews, F.E. (1956) *Philanthropic Foundations*, New York: Russell Sage Foundation.

—— (1974) *Philanthropy in the United States: History and Structure*, New York: Foundation Center.

Anheier, H.K. (2001) 'Foundations in Europe: A Comparative Perspective', in A. Schlüter, V. Then and P. Walkenhorst (eds) *Foundations in Europe: Society, Management and Law*, London: Directory of Social Change.

—— (2003) 'Das Stiftungswesen in Deutschland: Eine Bestandsaufnahme in Zahlen', in Bertelsmann Stiftung (ed.) *Handbuch Stiftungen*, Wiesbaden: Gabler.

Anheier, H.K. and Daly, S. (2006) *Foundations in Europe: Roles and Visions*, London: Routledge.

Anheier, H.K. and Kendall, J. (eds) (2001) *Third Sector Policy at the Crossroads: An International Nonprofit Analysis*, London: Routledge.

Anheier, H.K. and Leat, D. (2002) *From Charity to Creativity: Philanthropic Foundations in the 21st Century—Perspectives from Britain and Beyond*, Bournes Green: Comedia.

Anheier, H.K. and Salamon, L.M. (2006) 'The Nonprofit Sector in Comparative Perspective' in W.W. Powell and R.S. Steinberg (eds), *The Nonprofit Sector: A Research Handbook*, second edition, New Haven and London: Yale University Press.

Anheier, H.K. and Toepler, S. (1999) 'Philanthropic Foundations: An International Perspective', in H.K. Anheier and S. Toepler (eds) *Private Funds, Public Purpose: Philanthropic Foundations in International Perspective*, New York: Kluwer Academic/Plenum.

Annie E. Casey Foundation (Fall 2002) *Casey Connects*, Baltimore, MD: Casey Foundation.

—— (2003a) 'Building a Support Called CMAR: Community Mobilization for Action and Results in Making Connections', *Summary of the Annie E. Casey Foundation Consultative Session (July 21–23, 2003), Ellicott City, Maryland*, Baltimore, MD: Casey Foundation.

—— (2003b) 'Measuring Performance and Managing for Results: A Making Connections Peer Technical Assistance Match Between Philadelphia, Pennsylvania and Montgomery County, Maryland', *Part of a Series from the Technical Assistance Resource Center of the Annie E. Casey Foun-*

dation and the *Center for the Study of Social Policy*, Baltimore, MD: Casey Foundation (see also www.aecf.org/initiatives/mc/tarc/peermatch/reports/pm_philly.pdf)

—— (2004) 'Ralph R. Smith Interview', *McKinsey Quarterly* 1.

Arnove, R.F. (1980) *Philanthropy and Cultural Imperialism: The Foundations at Home and Abroad*, Bloomington: Indiana University Press.

Aspen Institute (2004) *Philanthropy Letter Report*, Washington: Aspen Nonprofit and Philanthropy Research Fund.

Backer, T.E. and Smith, R.B. (2003) 'Who Comes to the Table? Stakeholder Interactions in Philanthropy', *INSP Working Paper*, Gütersloh: International Network for Strategic Philanthropy.

Baker, W. (2005) *America's Crisis of Values: Reality and Perception*, Princeton, NJ: Princeton University Press.

Bales, S.N. and Gilliam Jr., F.D. (2004) 'Communications for Social Good', *Practice Matters* paper no. 8, *Improving Philanthropy Project*, New York: Foundation Center (see also http://fdncenter.org/for_grantmakers/practice_matters/practicematters_08_paper.pdf)

Boris, E.T. (1999) 'The Nonprofit Sector in the 1990s', in C.T. Coltfelter and T. Ehrlich (eds) *Philanthropy and the Nonprofit Sector in a Changing America*, Bloomington: Indiana University Press.

Bothwell, R.O. (2001) 'Trends in Self-Regulation and Transparency of Nonprofits in the US', *International Journal of Not-for-Profit Law*, vol. 4, Issue 1 (see also www.icnl.org/journal/vol4iss1/bothwell1.htm).

—— (2002), 'The Decline of Progressive Policy and the New Philanthropy: Progressive Foundations and Other Alternatives to Mainstream Foundations Are Created and Become Substantial, But Fail to Reverse the Policy Decline', http://comm-org.wisc.edu/papers2003/bothwell/bothwell.htm

—— (2003), 'Liberal Billion Dollar Plus Funding Foundations, Stuck in Objectivity Trap, Are Left Behind by Right Wingers who Go For the Jugular', www.opednews.com/bothwell_foundations2.htm

Breiteneicher, C.K. and Marble, M.G. (2001) 'Strategic Programme Management', in A. Schlüter, V. Then and P. Walkenhorst (eds) *Foundations in Europe: Society, Management and Law*, London: Directory of Social Change.

Bridge House Trust (2001) *Annual Review*, London: Bridge House Trust.

—— (2004) *Annual Review*, London: Bridge House Trust (see also www.bridgehousegrants.org.uk/docs/annualreview04.pdf)

Brilliant, E. (2000) *Private Charity and Public Inquiry: A History of the Filer and Peterson Commissions*, Bloomington: Indiana University Press.

Brousseau, R.T. (2004) 'Experienced Grantmakers at Work, When Creativity Comes into Play', in P. Patrizi, K. Sherwood, and A. Spector (eds), *Improving Philanthropy Project*, New York: Foundation Center.

Brown, J.S. and Duguid, P. (2002) 'Creativity Versus Structure: A Useful Tension', in E.B. Roberts (ed) *Innovation: Driving Product, Process and Market Change*, San Francisco: Jossey-Bass.

Bulmer, M. (1995) 'Some Observations on the History of Large Philanthropic Foundations in Britain and the United States', *Voluntas* 6 (3): pp. 275–91.

—— (1999) 'The History of Foundations in the United Kingdom and the United States: Philanthropic Foundations in Industrial Society', in H.K. Anheier and S. Toepler (eds)

Private Funds, Public Purpose: Philanthropic Foundations in International Perspectives, New York: Kluwer Academic/Plenum.

Burkeman, S. (1999) 'An Unsatisfactory Company?', *1999 Allen Lane Lecture*, London: Allen Lane Foundation.

Burt, R. (2005) *Brokerage and Closure: An Introduction to Social Capital*, Oxford: Clarendon Press, and New York: Oxford University Press.

Carnegie United Kingdom Trust (2001) *88th Annual Report*, Dunfermline, Fife: Carnegie United Kingdom Trust.

— (2002) *89th Annual Report*, Dunfermline, Fife: Carnegie United Kingdom Trust.

— (2003) *90th Annual Report*, Dunfermline, Fife: Carnegie United Kingdom Trust.

— (2004a) *Annual Report*, Dunfermline, Fife: Carnegie United Kingdom Trust.

— (2004b) press release, 1 December, Dunfermline, Fife: Carnegie United Kingdom Trust.

— (2004c) *Preparing for the Next Five Years: 2005–2010*, Dunfermline, Fife: Carnegie United Kingdom Trust.

— (n.d.) *A Decade of Progress and Change*, Dunfermline, Fife: Carnegie United Kingdom Trust.

Carrington, D. (2002) *The Investor Approach: A Way Forward for the Community Fund?*, London: Community Fund.

Carson, E. (2003a) 'A Foundation's Journey into Public Policy Engagement', in F. Ellsworth and J. Lumarda (eds) *From Grantmaker to Leader: Emerging Strategies for 21st Century Foundations*, Hoboken, NJ: John Wiley.

— (2003b) 'A Worst Case Scenario or the Perfect Storm? Current Challenges to Foundation Board Governance', *Responsive Philanthropy* (Summer): pp. 1, 19.

Clegg, B. (1999) *Creativity and Innovation for Managers*, Oxford and Boston: Butterworth-Heinemann.

Cohen, R. (2003) 'Time for a New Commission on Philanthropy', *Responsive Philanthropy* (Summer).

Coleman, J.S., Menzel, H. and Katz, E. (1957) 'Diffusion of an Innovation Among Physicians', *Sociometry* 20: pp. 253–70.

Covington, S. (1997) 'Moving a Public Policy Agenda: The Strategic Philanthropy of Conservative Foundations', Washington, DC: National Committee for Responsive Philanthropy.

Crimm, N. (2002) 'Shortcomings in America's Federal Tax Regulatory Regime of Private Foundations: Insights for Australia', *Australian Tax Review* 31 (2): pp. 90–118.

Davies, J. (2004) 'The Foundation as a Political Actor: The Case of the Joseph Rowntree Charitable Trust', *Political Quarterly* 75 (3): pp. 275–84.

De Bono, E. (1996) *Serious Creativity: Using the Power of Lateral Thinking to Create New Ideas*, London: HarperCollins.

Diana Princess of Wales Memorial Fund (2001) *Annual Review*, London: Diana Princess of Wales Memorial Fund (see also www.theworkcontinues.org/pdfs/review2001.pdf)

Douglas, J. and Wildavsky, A. (1980–81) 'Big Government and the Private Foundations', *Policy Studies Journal* 9 (8): pp. 1175–90.

Dowie, M. (2001) *American Foundations: An Investigative History*, Cambridge, MA: MIT Press.

Drabble, L. and Abrenilla, M. (2000) *A Democratic Landscape: Funding Social Change in California,* Washington, D.C.: National Committee for Responsive Philanthropy.

Duncan, R. (1979) 'What is the Right Organizational Structure?' *Organizational Dynamics* (Winter): pp. 59–80.

Eisenberg, P. (2002) 'Philanthropy at the Crossroads', in R. Cohen (ed.) *State of Philanthropy 2002,* Washington, DC: National Committee for Responsive Philanthropy.

Emerson, J. (2004) *The Blended Value Proposition: Tracking the Intersects and Opportunities of Economic, Social and Environmental Value Creation,* www.blendedvalue.org.

Esmée Fairbairn Foundation (2002) *Annual Review,* London: Esmée Fairbairn Foundation (see also www.esmeefairbairn.org.uk/pdf/2002_ann_review.pdf)

Fischer, D. (1983) 'The Role of Philanthropic Foundations in the Reproduction and Production of Hegemony: Rockefeller Foundation and the Social Sciences', *Sociology* 17: pp. 206–33.

Fleishman, J. L. (1999) 'Public Trust in Not-for-Profit Organizations and the Need for Regulatory Reform', in C.T. Clotfelter and T. Ehrlich (eds) *Philanthropy and the Nonprofit Sector in a Changing America,* Bloomington: Indiana University Press.

—— (2005) 'Current Policy Debates and Philanthropy in the United States', presentation at the International Foundation Management Symposium, Berlin: Bertelsmann Foundation.

Flynn, P. and Hodgkinson, V. (eds) (2002) *Measuring the Impact of the Nonprofit Sector,* New York: Kluwer Academic/Plenum.

Ford Foundation (2002) *Annual Report,* New York: Ford Foundation.

Foundation Center (2002) *Foundation News and Commentary,* May/June.

—— (2004) *Foundation Giving Trends 2003,* New York: Foundation Center.

—— (2005) *Foundation Giving Trends 2004,* New York: Foundation Center.

Fowler, A. (1995) 'Assessing NGO Performance: Difficulties, Dilemmas and Way Ahead', in M. Edwards and D. Hulme (eds) *Non-Governmental Organisations Performance and Accountability: Beyond the Magic Bullet,* London: Earthscan.

Frumkin, P. (1998) 'The Long Recoil From Regulation: Private Philanthropic Foundations and the Tax Reform Act of 1969', *American Review of Public Administration* 28 (3): pp. 266–86.

Gardner, H. (1993) *Creating Minds,* New York: Basic Books.

Gaul, G.M. and Borowski, N.A. (1993) *Free Ride: The Tax-Exempt Economy,* Kansas City: Andrews and McMeel; first published as 'Warehouses of Wealth: the Tax-Free Economy', *Philadelphia Enquirer,* April 18–23, 1993

Gomez, P. and Zimmermann, T. (1993) *Unternehmensorganisation: Profile, Dynamik, Methodik.* Frankfurt: Campus.

Gronbjerg, K.A. (1998) 'Markets, Politics and Charity: Nonprofits in the Political Economy', in W.W. Powell and E.S. Clemens (eds) *Private Action and the Public Good,* New Haven, CT: Yale University Press.

Hammack, D. (1999) 'Foundations in the American Polity, 1900–1950', in E.C. Lagemann (ed) *Philanthropic Foundations: New Scholarship, New Possibilities,* Bloomington: Indiana University Press.

Harrison, Shelby M., and Andrews, F. Emerson (1946) *American Foundations for Social Welfare,* New York: Russell Sage Foundation.

Heifetz, R.A., Kania, J.V. and Kramer, M.R. (2004) 'Leading Boldly', *Stanford Social Innovation Review*: pp. 21–32.

Hock, D. (2002) 'The Art of Chaordic Leadership', in F.R. Hesselbein and R. Johnston (eds) *On Mission and Leadership*, San Francisco: Jossey-Bass.

Hogwood, B.W. and Gunn, L. (1984) *Policy Analysis for the Real World*, Oxford: Oxford University Press.

Holcombe, R.G. (2000) *Writing Off Ideas: Taxation, Foundations, and Philanthropy in America*, New Brunswick, NJ: Transaction.

Hood, C. (1983) *The Tools of Government*, London: Macmillan.

Hopkins, E.M. (2005) *Collaborative Philanthropies*. Lanham, MD: Lexington.

Ilchman, W.F. and Burlingame, D.F. (1999) 'Accountability in a Changing Philanthropic Environment: Trustees and Self-government at the End of the Century', in C.T. Clotfelter and T. Ehrlich (eds), *Philanthropy and the Nonprofit Sector in a Changing America*, Bloomington: Indiana University Press.

Joseph Rowntree Charitable Trust (2000–02) *Triennial Report*, York: Joseph Rowntree Charitable Trust.

Kanter, R.M. (1983) *The Change Masters*, New York: Simon and Schuster.

Kao, J. (1991) *Managing Creativity*, Englewood Cliffs, NJ: Prentice Hall.

— (1996) *Jamming: The Art and Discipline of Business Creativity*, London: HarperCollins, and New York: HarperBusiness.

Karl, B.D. (1997) 'The Troublesome History of Foundations', *Reviews in American History* 25 (4): pp. 612–18.

Karl, B.D. and Karl, A.W. (1999) 'Foundations and the Government: A Tale of Conflict and Consensus', in C.T. Coltfelter and T. Ehrlich (eds) *Philanthropy and the Nonprofit Sector in a Changing America*, Bloomington: Indiana University Press.

Karl, B.D. and Katz, S.N. (1981) 'The American Private Philanthropic Foundations and the Public Sphere, 1890–1930', *Minerva* 19: pp. 236–70.

— (1985) 'Grantmaking and Research in the US, 1933–83', *Proceedings of the American Philosophical Society* 129 (1): pp. 1–19.

— (1987) 'Foundations and Ruling Class Elites', *Daedalus* 116 (1): pp. 1–40.

Katz, S.N. with Karl, B.D. (1977) 'Donors, Trustees, Staffs: An Historical View, 1890–1930' in *The Art of Giving: Four Views on American Philanthropy* (Proceedings of the Third Rockefeller Archive Center Conference, October 14, 1977), Pocantico Hills, New York: Rockefeller Archives Center.

Knight Foundation (2001) *Annual Report*, Miami: John S. and James L. Knight Foundation.

— (2002) *Annual Report*, Miami: John S. and James L. Knight Foundation.

— (2003) *Annual Report*, Miami: John S. and James L. Knight Foundation.

Knight Foundation, American Institutes for Research, and Princeton Survey Research Associates International (2004) 'Listening and Learning: Community Indicator Profiles of Knight Foundation Communities and the Nation', Miami: John S. and James L. Knight Foundation. (see also www.knightfdn.org/publications/listeningandlearning 04/ListeningAndLearning2004.pdf)

Koestler, A. (1989) *The Act of Creation*, London: Penguin.

Kramer, R. (1990) 'Change and Continuity in British Voluntary Organizations, 1976 to 1988', *Voluntas* 1 (2): pp. 33–60.

Lagemann, E.C. (ed.) (1999) *Philanthropic Foundations: New Scholarship, New Possibilities*, Bloomington: Indiana University Press.

Landry, C. (2000) *The Creative City: A Toolkit for Urban Innovators*, London: Comedia, Earthscan

Lawrence, D.M. (1998) 'Leading Discontinuous Change: Ten Lessons from the Battlefront', in D. Hambrick, D. Nadler and M. Tushman (eds) *How CEOs, Top Teams and Boards Steer Transformation*, Boston, MA: Harvard Business School Press.

Leat, D. (2005) 'Britain' in Anheier, H.K. and Daly, S. (eds) *Foundations in Europe: Roles and Visions*, London: Routledge.

— (1999) 'British Foundations: The Organization and Management of Grantmaking', in H.K. Anheier and S. Toepler (eds) *Private Funds, Public Purpose*, New York: Kluwer Academic/Plenum.

Letts, C., Ryan, W. and Grossman, A. (1997) 'Virtuous Capital: What Foundations Can Learn from Venture Capitalists', *Harvard Business Review*: pp. 36–44.

Magretta, J. (2002) *What Management Is: How it Works and Why it's Everyone's Business*, New York: Free Press.

McIlnay, D.P. (1998) *How Foundations Work*, San Francisco: Jossey-Bass.

Meffert, H. (2005) 'Strategic Marketing: Creating a Philanthropic Brand Identity', presentation at the International Foundation Management Symposium, Berlin: Bertelsmann Foundation.

Minneapolis Foundation (2002) *Annual Report*, Minneapolis, MT: Minneapolis Foundation.

Myer Foundation (2001–02) *Annual Report*, Melbourne: Myer Foundation (see also www.myerfoundation.org.au/groundcontrol/sitecontent/userfiles/0000000111.pdf)

— (2002–03) *Annual Report*, Melbourne: Myer Foundation (see also www.myerfoundation.org.au/groundcontrol/sitecontent/userfiles/0000000240.pdf)

National Committee for Responsive Philanthropy (1997) 'Moving a Public Policy Agenda: The Strategic Philanthropy of Conservative Foundations', Washington, DC: National Committee for Responsive Philanthropy.

— (2004a) 'Recommendations for Reform of the United States Philanthropic Sector: A Statement to the United States Senate Committee on Finance', Washington, DC: National Committee for Responsive Philanthropy

— (2004b) 'Axis of Ideology: Conservative Foundations and Public Policy', Washington, DC: National Committee for Responsive Philanthropy.

Nelson, D. (1999) Speech at Johns Hopkins Community Conversation Breakfast Series, Baltimore, MD.

Nicholls, A. (2005) 'The Philanthropic Entrepreneur: Entrepreneurial Strategies in Foundations', presentation at the International Foundation Management Symposium, Berlin: Bertelsmann Foundation.

Nielsen, W.A. (1972) *The Big Foundations*, New York: Columbia University Press.

— (1979) *The Endangered Sector*, New York: Columbia University Press

— (1985) *The Golden Donors: A New Anatomy of the Great Foundations*, New York: Truman Talley Books, E.P. Dutton.

— (1996) *Inside American Philanthropy: The Dramas of Donorship*, Norman: University of Oklahoma Press.

Odendahl, T. (1990) *Charity Begins at Home*, New York: Basic Books.

Orosz J. (2000) *The Insider's Guide to Grantmaking*, San Francisco: Jossey-Bass.

Oster, S. (1995) *Strategic Management of Nonprofits*, Oxford: Oxford University Press.

Ostrander, S.A. (1993) 'Diversity and Democracy in Philanthropic Organizations: The Case of the Haymarket People's Fund', in D.R. Young *et al.* (eds), *Governing, Leading and Managing Nonprofit Organizations*. San Francisco: Jossey-Bass.

Paget, K. (1998) 'Lessons of Right-Wing Philanthropy', *The American Prospect* 9 (40): pp. 89–96.

Panel on the Nonprofit Sector (2005) *Interim Report presented to the Senate Finance Committee, March 21*, convened by Independent Sector, Washington, DC: Independent Sector.

Pauly, E. (2005) 'The Role of Evaluation in the 21st Century Foundation', Gütersloh: International Network for Strategic Philanthropy (see also www.insp.efc.be/frameset.php?display = show.php&d = 74)

Perrow, C. (2001) 'The Rise of Nonprofits and the Decline of Civil Society', in H.K. Anheier (ed.) *Organisational Theory and the nonprofit Form*, London: Center for Civil Society, Report 2, London School of Economics.

Pew Charitable Trusts (2001a) 'Returning Results, Planning and Evaluation at the Pew Charitable Trusts', Philadelphia: Pew Charitable Trusts (see also www.pewtrusts.com/pdf/returning_results.pdf)

— (2001b) 'Sustaining the Legacy: A History of the Pew Charitable Trusts', Philadelphia: The Pew Charitable Trusts (see also www.pewtrusts.com/pdf/history.pdf)

— (2004) 'Pew Charitable Trusts Establishes New Nonprofit Research Organization to Help Better Inform Public & Policymakers on Issues & Trends. New Center to be "Fact Tank" for Independent Research', press release, 27 April, Washington, DC: Pew Charitable Trusts.

Pfeffer, J. (2002) 'To Build a Culture of Innovation, Avoid Conventional Management Wisdom', in F. Hesselbein, M. Goldsmith and I. Somerville (eds) *Leading for Innovation and Organizing for Results*, San Francisco: Jossey-Bass.

Pifer, A. (1984) 'Speaking Out: Reflections on Thirty Years of Foundation Work', Washington, DC: Council on Foundations.

Porter, M.E. and Kramer, M.R. (1999) 'Philanthropy's New Agenda: Creating Value', *Harvard Business Review*: pp. 121–30

Prager, D.J. (1999) *Raising the Value of Philanthropy: A Synthesis of Informal Interviews with Foundation Executives and Observers of Philanthropy*, Washington, DC: Grantmakers in Health (see p. 10).

— (2003) *Organizing Foundations for Maximum Impact: A Guide to Effective Philanthropy*. Washington, DC: Aspen Institute Nonprofit Sector and Philanthropy Program.

Prewitt, K. (1999) 'The Importance of Foundations in an Open Society', in Bertelsmann Foundation (ed.) *The Future of Foundations in an Open Society*, Gütersloh: Bertelsmann Foundation.

Princeton Survey Research Associates (2002) *Newsroom Training: Where's the Investment?*, Miami: John S. and James L. Knight Foundation.

Prochaska, F.K. (1990) 'Philanthropy', in F.M.L. Thompson (ed.) *The Cambridge Social History of Britain 1750–1950*, vol. 3, Cambridge: Cambridge University Press.

Putnam, R.D. (2000) *Bowling Alone: The Collapse and Revival of American Community*, New York: Simon and Schuster.

Putnam, R.D. and Pharr, S. (eds) (2002) *Democracy in Flux*, Oxford: Oxford University Press.

Reeves, T.C. (1969) *Freedom and the Foundation: The Fund for the Republic in the Era of McCarthyism*, New York: Knopf.

Reis, T. and Clohesy, S.J. (2001) 'Unleashing New Resources and Entrepreneurship for the Common Good: A Philanthropic Renaissance', in A. Schlüter, V. Then and P. Walkenhorst (eds) *Foundations in Europe: Society, Management, and Law*, London: Directory of Social Change.

Renz, L. (2004) *Foundation Giving: Yearbook of Facts and Figures on Private, Corporate and Community Foundations*, New York: Foundation Center.

Rethinking Schools (2001) 'War, Terrorism, and our Classrooms: Teaching in the Aftermath of the September 11th Tragedy', Milwaukee, WI: Ford Foundation (see also www.rethinkingschools.org/special_reports/sept11/pdf/911insrt.pdf)

Ridings, D. (1999) 'The Legitimization of Foundation Work', in Bertelsmann Foundation (ed.) *The Future of Foundations in an Open Society*, Gütersloh: Bertelsmann Foundation.

Roelofs, J. (1984/85) 'Foundations and the Supreme Court', *Telos* 62: pp. 59–87.

— (2003) *Foundations and Public Policy: The Mask of Pluralism*, Albany: State University of New York Press.

Rogers, E.M. (2003) *Diffusion of Innovations*, fifth edition, New York: Free Press.

Russell, J. (2005) *Funding the Culture Wars*, Washington, DC: National Committee for Responsive Philanthropy.

Salamon, L.M. and Anheier, H.K. (1997) *Defining the Nonprofit Sector: A Cross-National Analysis*, Manchester: Manchester University Press.

Schambra, W. and Shaffer, K. (2004) 'Grassroots Rising: A Conservative Call for Philanthropic Renewal', *Nonprofit Quarterly* 33 (3).

Schlüter, A., Then, V. and Walkenhorst, P. (eds) (2001) *Foundations in Europe: Society, Management and Law*, London: Directory of Social Change.

Schumann, M. (1998) 'Why do Progressive Foundations Give too Little to too Many?', *Nation* 12 (19).

Sealander, J. (1997) *Private Wealth and Public Life: Foundation Philanthropy and the Reshaping of American Social Policy from the Progressive Era to the New Deal*, Baltimore: Johns Hopkins University Press.

— (2003) 'Curing Evils at Their Source: The Arrival of Scientific Giving', in L. Friedman and M. McGarvie (eds) *Charity, Philanthropy and Civility in American History*, Cambridge: Cambridge University Press.

Sievers, B. (1997) 'If Pigs had Wings', *Foundations News and Commentary* (November/December).

Silverman, L. (2004) 'Building Better Foundations: A Senior Executive of the Annie E. Casey Foundation Discusses the Contentious Issues Facing 21st-century Philanthropy', *McKinsey Quarterly* 1: p. 98.

Simon, J. G. (1987) 'The Tax Treatment of Nonprofit Organizations: A Review of Federal and State Policies', in W.W. Powell (ed.) *The Nonprofit Sector: A Research Handbook*, New Haven, CT: Yale University Press.

Siska, D.M. and Lamb, K. (2003) 'Leaders, Risk-Takers and Advocates', *Foundation News and Commentary* 44 (3): pp. 20–21.

Skloot, E. (2001) 'Slot Machines, Boat Building and the Future of Philanthropy' *Waldemar Nielsen Lectures on Philanthropy*, Washington, D.C.: Georgetown University, Surdna Foundation.

Smith, J. and Borgmann, K. (2001) 'Foundations in Europe: The Historical Context', in A. Schlüter, V. Then and P. Walkenhorst (eds) *Foundations in Europe: Society, Management and Law*, London: Directory of Social Change.

Smith, J.A. (1989) 'The Evolving Role of Foundations', in V.A. Hodgkinson and R.W. Lyman (eds) *The Future of the Nonprofit Sector*, San Francisco: Jossey-Bass.

—— (1999) 'The Evolving Role of American Foundations', in C. Clotfelter and T. Ehrlich (eds) *Philanthropy and the Nonprofit Sector in a Changing America*, Bloomington: Indiana University Press.

—— (2002) 'Foundations and Public Policy Making: A Historical Perspective', www.usc.edu/philanthropy

Stefancic, J. and Delgado, R. (1996) *No Mercy: How Conservative Think Tanks and Foundations Changed America's Social Agenda*, Philadelphia: Temple University Press.

Sutton, R.I. (2002) 'Weird Ideas that Spark Innovation', in E.B. Roberts (ed) *Innovation: Driving Product, Process and Market Change*, San Francisco: Jossey-Bass.

Timmins, N. (1995) *The Five Giants: A Biography of the Welfare State*, London: HarperCollins.

Toepler, S. (1999) 'Operating in a Grantmaking World: Reassessing the Role of Operating Foundations', in H.K. Anheier and S. Toepler (eds) *Private Funds, Public Purpose: Philanthropic Foundations in International Perspective*, New York: Kluwer Academic/Plenum.

Tomei, A. (1998) 'Foundations: Active or Reactive?' paper delivered at The Hague Club Meeting, The Hague.

Tushmann, M.L., Anherson, P. and O'Reilly, C. (1998) 'Levers for Organization Renewal, Innovation Streams, Ambidextrous Organizations and Strategic Change', in D. Hambrick, D. Nadler and M. Tushman (eds).

Van der Ploeg, T.J. (1999) 'A Comparative Legal Analysis of Foundations: Aspects of Supervision and Transparency', in H.K. Anheier and S. Toepler (eds) *Private Funds, Public Purpose: Philanthropic Foundations in International Perspective*, New York: Kluwer Academic/Plenum.

Victorian Women's Trust (2000) *Purple Sage Report*, Australia: Victorian Women's Trust.

—— (2001) *Annual Report*, Australia: Victorian Women's Trust.

Vincent, J. and Pharoah, C. (2000) *Dimensions 2000*, vol. 3: *Patterns of Independent Grantmaking*, West Malling, Kent: Charities Aid Foundation.

Voluntas (1996) Special Issue 6 (3).

Wallace Foundation (2002) *Annual Report*, New York: Wallace Foundation (see also www.wallacefoundation.org/nr/rdonlyres/3e53d703-2fe2-4c0b-9145-4a3e17f46d52/0/wallaceannualreport2002.pdf)

—— (2003) *Annual Report*, New York: Wallace Foundation see also www.wallacefoundation.org/NR/rdonlyres/3E53D703-2FE2-4C0B-9145-4A3E17F46D52/0/WallaceAnnualReport2002.pdf

—— (2003–04) *Annual Report*, New York: Wallace Foundation.

Weiss, J. (2000) 'From Research to Social Improvement: Understanding Theories of Intervention', *nonprofit and Voluntary Sector Quarterly* 29 (1): 81–110.

Whitaker, B. (1974) *The Philanthropoids*, New York: William Morrow.

— (1979) *The Foundations: An Anatomy of Philanthropic Societies*, New York: Pelican.

Williams, R. (1998) 'Know Thy Critics', *Foundation News & Commentary*: pp. 25–29.

Wilson, K. (n.d.), *Public Policy and Private Action: Strategic Grantmaking*, San Francisco: Rosenberg Foundation

Yin, R.K. (1989) *Case Study Research: Design and Methods*, London: Sage Publications.

Index